ernational Legal
lish

ominant language of international business relations, and a good
dge of the language is essential for today's legal or business

vides a highly practical approach to the use of English in
contexts, and covers crucial law terminology and legal
with the needs of both students and practitioners in mind, this
suitable for readers whose first language is not English but
on a regular basis in legal contexts.
both written and verbal legal communication in typical
raightforward manner. In addition to chapters on the
tion utilised in legal writing, the book features sections on
he language used in negotiations, meetings and telephone
es a companion website which contains exercises
the topics covered in the book's chapters.
y revises and expands the content of the companion
lated examples, more detailed explanations of
expanded section on writing law essays.

rom Cambridge University in English in 1992 and
gland in 1997. He holds an LL.M. in Public International
and an MA in European Union Law from King's
ved in training legal professionals from 2002 until
lance lawyer-linguist. For more information see
com.

204 To

Preface

HOW TO USE THIS BOOK

The book and its website are not intended to be read straight through from beginning to end, although masochists may do so if they wish. They have been carefully modularised and integrated by topic, and the best way to use them is to dip into them on a topic-by-topic basis.

The book, together with its online component, has three aims:

- To clarify and explain, through reference to numerous examples, various tricky areas of legal English usage.

- To act as a reference resource, particularly regarding terminology usage, contract clauses and drafting issues.

- To offer an interactive self-study and teaching resource that students can access in order to test and improve their skills in relation to various different areas of legal English usage, and which teachers can access in order to obtain materials that may be of use in the classroom.

The first two of these aims are covered in the book, while the third is also covered in the online component. The online and paper elements of the book are integrated, so that having read one chapter of the book dealing with a certain topic, the reader can go to the website to find exercises on that topic and check his or her knowledge of it – and vice versa.

BRITISH AND AMERICAN ENGLISH

This book is written in British English but makes reference to American English standards where these depart significantly from British English. Chapter 9 contains a survey of the key differences between British and American English.

FEEDBACK

Feedback from students, practitioners and other readers of the book is one of the main methods by which it has been updated through its various editions and is always gratefully received. Comments and queries about the book may be emailed to the author at rupert@legalediting.com.

Part 1

WRITTEN ENGLISH

Introduction to legal English

THE DEVELOPMENT OF MODERN ENGLISH

The English language contains elements from many different European languages and has also borrowed words from a wide variety of other languages. It is impossible to grasp how these influences affect the language without knowing a little about the history of the British Isles.

Prior to the Roman invasion of 55 BC, the inhabitants of Britain spoke a Celtic dialect. Latin made little impression until St Augustine arrived in AD 597 to spread Christianity. Latin words are now regularly used in English, particularly in professional language. In the legal profession, Latin phrases like **inter alia** (among others) and **per se** (in itself) remain in current use.

Subsequently, the Angles, Saxons and Jutes invaded the British Isles from mainland northern Europe. The language they brought with them forms the basis of what is known as Old English. This gives us the most commonly used words in the English language (words like **god**, **man**, **land**, **bread**, **fish**, **beer**). A simple comparison with their modern German equivalents (**gott**, **mann**, **land**, **brot**, **fisch**, **bier**) indicates their common origin.

The Vikings began to raid the north-east of England from Scandinavia from the 8th century onwards. At a later date, a significant number of Vikings settled in this area and made their own linguistic contribution (which can be seen, for example, in the numerous place names in the north-east of England [and Scotland] ending in -**by**, -**thorpe**, -**wick**, -**ham** and in words such as **egg**, **husband**, **law**, **take**, **knife**).

In 1066 the Normans invaded from northern France and conquered England. Words such as **court**, **parliament**, **justice**, **sovereign** and **marriage** come from this period.

Later, the English helped themselves to further words from French, such as **chauffeur**, **bourgeois** and **elite**. As the British Empire expanded, further opportunities to borrow words arose – words such as **taboo** and **pukka** came into the English language from that period.

The result of this multiplicity of linguistic influences is a rich and diverse language with a complex grammar and many synonyms. For example, a coming together of two or more people could be a **meeting** or **gathering** (Old English), **assignation** or **encounter** (Old French), a **rendezvous**, **rally** or **reunion** (French), a **caucus** (Algonquin), a **pow-wow** (Narragansett) or a **tryst** (Old French).

Matters are complicated further still by the fact that from the 17th century onwards, the process of colonisation began in earnest. Starting with Ireland and then moving outside the British Isles to North America, Australia, the West Indies, India and numerous other territories, colonial influence – and with it the English language – began to spread around the globe.

Colonial rule largely collapsed after World War II, but English in different forms and dialects persists as the national language or an important second or third language in many countries. The English spoken in one country may be quite different from that spoken in another. Because of this, it is perhaps possible to speak of 'Englishes' rather than 'English'. Differences between the written English used in one country and another are less marked than those that exist between the types of spoken English used, but there are significant variations, in particular between British and American English (see Chapter 9).

1.2   SOURCES OF LEGAL ENGLISH

Legal English reflects the mixture of languages that has produced the English language generally. However, modern legal English owes a particular debt to French and Latin. Following the Norman invasion of England in 1066, French became the official language of England, although most ordinary people still spoke English. For a period of nearly 300 years, French was the language of legal proceedings, with the result that many words in current legal use have their roots in this period. These include **property**, **estate**, **chattel**, **lease**, **executor** and **tenant**.

During this period, Latin remained the language of formal records and statutes. However, since only the educated were fluent in Latin, it never became the language of legal pleading or debate.

Therefore, for several centuries following the Norman invasion, three languages were used in England. English remained the spoken language of the majority of the population, but almost all writing was done in French or Latin. English was not used in legal matters.

In 1356, the Statute of Pleading was enacted (in French). It stated that all legal proceedings should be conducted in English but recorded in Latin. Nonetheless, the use of French in legal pleadings continued into the 17th century in some areas of the law. In this later period, new branches of, in particular, commercial law began to develop entirely in English and remain relatively free of French-based terminology.

As the printed word became more commonplace, some writers made a deliberate effort to adopt words derived from Latin, with the aim of making their text appear more sophisticated. Some legal words taken from Latin in this way are **adjacent**, **frustrate**, **inferior**, **legal**, **quiet** and **subscribe**. Some writers also started to use a Latin word order. This led to an ornate style, deliberately used to impress rather than inform. Even today, Latin grammar is responsible for some of the ornateness and unusual word order of legal documents. It also lies behind the frequent use of **shall** constructions in legal documents.

English was adopted for different kinds of legal documents at different times. Wills began to be written in English in about 1400. Statutes were written in Latin until about 1300, in French until 1485, in English and French for a few years and in English alone from 1489.

WHAT MAKES ENGLISH DIFFICULT?

1.3

It is said of chess that the game takes a day to learn, and a lifetime to master. In similar vein, English is reputed to be an easy beginner's language but it is nevertheless very hard to achieve native-level fluency. Why is this?

There are probably four main factors that make English difficult to master:

1   Lack of clear rules of grammar. We have seen that English is a product of various different linguistic traditions. One of the most exasperating results of this is a confusing system of grammar, which is due to the rules of one linguistic tradition being forced to compromise with those of another. English does of course have grammatical rules, but they are complex and sometimes inconsistent. Furthermore, a great deal of English phrasal construction is purely idiomatic and therefore difficult to explain by reference to grammatical rules (see point three below). The way in which prepositions are used is an obvious but baffling example of this problem.

2   Extensive vocabulary. There are many different ways of saying the same thing in English. Again, this is because English draws upon different linguistic traditions. For example, if you wanted to say that something was legally permissible, you could use the Old Norse (Scandinavian)-derived word, **lawful**. Alternatively, you could use the Latin-derived word, **legitimate**. Or, if you wanted a more emotive word, you could use the Old English word, **right**. To take another example, when talking about employment do you say **calling**, **career**, **profession**, **employment**, **job**, **work**, **occupation** or **vocation**?

3   The use of phrasal verbs in English (and legal English). For example, you **put down** a deposit, and you **enter into** a contract. These combinations must be learned individually because they involve using a verb with a preposition or adverb or both; and, as noted in point one above, prepositions do not always follow clear grammatical rules. Some of the phrasal verbs most commonly used in legal English are set out in a glossary at the back of the book.

4 The use of idioms. Idioms are groups of words whose combined meaning is different from the meanings of the individual words. For example, the expression **over the moon** means 'happy'. Idioms are frequent in ordinary English – they are a distinctive element of the way native English speakers use the language. They are found less often in legal English, but exist in some legal jargon. For example, the expression **on all fours** is used to refer to a case in which the legal issues correspond exactly to the legal issues present in a previous case.

1.4 WHAT MAKES LEGAL LANGUAGE DIFFICULT?

One of the main reasons why legal language is sometimes difficult to understand is that it is often very different from ordinary English. This arises partly from the purposes for which it is used and partly from certain habits of writing that derive from its historical linguistic roots.

1.4.1 The purpose of legal language

The main purpose of legal language is not so much to communicate as to regulate. This is very clearly the case where legislation is concerned, but is also true of private arrangements between parties that are intended to have legal effect.

A contract, for instance, is essentially a system of rules agreed between the parties designed to regulate their commercial relationship, or certain aspects of it. It lays down the conditions on which the contract or certain parts of the contract come into effect, states the obligations to which each party is subject, makes clear what each party may or may not do in performing the contract and contains provisions dealing with what will happen in the event of a breach of contract.

In the chapters that follow, we will see how the considerations sketched above affect the language used in practice.

1.4.2 Odd habits of legal writing

The general trend of modern legal writing reflects a greater effort to resemble ordinary modern business writing. However, traditional legal writing (which stubbornly persists in certain countries and certain types of law) is characterised by a number of odd features.

Here are some of them.

- Sentences often have apparently peculiar structures and wording. For instance, 'due performance by the Employer of the Contract in the manner hereinafter appearing' means that the employer must carry out the terms of the contract in the way the contract specifies in the provisions lower down in the document than this one.

- Punctuation is used insufficiently. This is particularly the case in documents relating to land, such as deeds and conveyances.

- Foreign phrases are sometimes used instead of English phrases (e.g. **inter alia** instead of **among others**, **void ab initio** instead of **invalid from the start**).

- Unusual pronouns are used (**the same**, **the aforesaid** etc.).

- Unusual set phrases are used (**null and void**, **all and sundry**).

- Semi-archaic **here-**, **there-** and **where-** formulations such as **hereof**, **hereinafter**, **whereas**, **therein** and **hereby** remain in fairly frequent use in contracts and other legal documents.

Difficult and unfamiliar words and phrases   1.4.3

In addition, a large number of difficult and unfamiliar words and phrases are used in legal English. These fall into four categories, brief details of which are given below.

Legal terms of art   1.4.3.1

Legal terms of art are technical words and phrases that have precise and fixed legal meanings, and which cannot usually be replaced by other words. Some of these will be familiar to the layperson (e.g. **patent**, **share**, **royalty**). Others are generally only known to lawyers (e.g. **bailment**, **abatement**).

A number of frequently encountered terms of art are defined in the glossary of legal terminology at the back of this book.

Legal jargon   1.4.3.2

Terms of art should be differentiated from legal jargon. Legal jargon comprises words used by lawyers that are difficult for non-lawyers to understand. Jargon words range from near-slang to almost technically precise words. Well-known examples of jargon include **boilerplate clause** (a standard clause included in a contract that helps define the relationship between the parties but has no direct relevance to the subject-matter of the contract) and **corporate veil** (the concept that a company has a legal personality separate from that of its shareholders that protects them from personal liability for the company's actions).

Legal jargon includes a number of archaic words no longer used in ordinary English. These include words like **annul** (to declare that something, such as a contract or marriage, is no longer legally valid) and **bequest** (to hand down as an inheritance property other than land).

It also includes certain obscure words that have highly specialised meanings and are therefore not often encountered except in legal documents. Examples include **emoluments** (a person's earnings, including salaries, fees, wages, profits and benefits in kind) and **provenance** (the origin or early history of something).

Jargon words should be replaced by plain-language equivalents wherever possible.

1.4.3.3   Legal meaning may differ from the general meaning

There is also a small group of words that have one meaning as a legal term of art and another meaning in ordinary English. One example is the word **distress**, which as a legal term of art refers to the seizure of goods as security for the performance of an obligation. In ordinary English it means anxiety, pain or exhaustion.

Here are some additional examples.

For further details on the meanings of these and other words and phrases, refer to the glossaries dealing with obscure words and phrases at the back of the book.

Word and its legal English meaning	Word and its ordinary English meaning
Consideration in legal English means an act, forbearance or promise by one party to a contract that constitutes the price for which the promise of the other party is bought. Consideration is essential to the validity of any contract other than one made by deed. For example, 'The rights were transferred to Laxby Ltd in exchange for a consideration of £5 million'.	**Consideration** in ordinary English means (1) careful thought, (2) a fact taken into account when making a decision, (3) thoughtfulness towards others.
Construction in legal English means interpretation. For example, 'A strict construction was placed upon the exemption clause in the contract'. 'To construe' is the infinitive verb form of the term.	**Construction** in ordinary English means (1) the action of constructing (e.g. a building), (2) a building or other structure, (3) the industry of erecting buildings.
Contemplation in legal English is often used to mean a non-binding intention to do something. For example, 'it is contemplated that Party X may buy further quantities of the Product'.	**Contemplation** in ordinary English means thinking deeply about something.

Express in legal English means specific, definite and clear. For example, 'the contract contains express terms dealing with pay and working hours'. It is often contrasted with **implied**, which means inferred from the facts or from the law. For example, 'the duty of mutual trust is an implied term in the contract'.	**Express** in ordinary English usually means fast ('an express train'), but can also be used in the sense indicated opposite.
Find in legal English is generally used to refer to a judge's final decision in court or to a ruling on evidence. For example, 'the judge found for the defendant' and 'the judge found that the evidence submitted did not support the claimant's argument'.	**Find** in ordinary English is a synonym for 'discover'.
Furnish in legal English is often used to mean to provide or send documents or information. For example, 'please furnish us with the title deeds'.	**Furnish** in ordinary English generally refers to the furnishing of a room and is associated with the noun 'furniture'.
Hold in legal English generally refers to a decision on the evidence, issues or law in question reached by a judge in court proceedings. For example, 'the judge held that the evidence obtained in the search of the premises could not be used against the defendant'.	**Hold** in ordinary English means (1) to grasp something ('he held a stick'), (2) to have a certain position ('she held the position of human resources manager'), (3) to arrange an event ('they held a party'), (4) to keep or detain ('he was held by the police').
Prefer in legal English refers to the formal bringing of charges by the prosecutor in a criminal case. For example, 'the Prosecutor preferred charges against the company'.	**Prefer** in ordinary English means to like one thing better than another.
Redemption in legal English means the return or repossession of property offered as security on payment of a mortgage debt or charge. For example, 'the mortgagor has the right to redeem the mortgage at any time after 31 December 2024'.	**Redemption** in ordinary English means either Christian salvation or, in a more general sense, an act of atonement for a mistake or fault.
Tender in legal English means an offer to supply goods or services. Normally a tender must be accepted to create a contract. For example, 'the tender, together with all supporting documents, must be submitted through our online portal no later than 31 May 2021'.	**Tender** in ordinary English means (1) gentle and kind, (2) (of food) easy to cut or chew, (3) (of a part of the body) painful to the touch, (4) young and vulnerable, (5) easily damaged.

1.5 THE IMPORTANCE OF LEGAL ENGLISH

1.5.1 Overview

Legal English is important because law is important; it provides the means by which law, when written in English, is articulated, applied and enforced.

Law can be divided into two types – national and international. National law provides the means by which countries govern the relationships between the state and its subjects (criminal law) and between the subjects themselves (civil law). International law provides the means by which international relations between countries (public international law) and between individuals and organisations based in different countries (private international law) are regulated.

1.5.2 Countries in which English and the common law system are relevant

National law of course reflects the languages used in each individual country. In this regard, it may be noted that English is the principal language in a number of countries, including the USA, UK, Australia, New Zealand and Canada.

English is also an important second language in a number of other countries formerly under British colonial influence, such as India and Pakistan. In such countries, the common law system is also relevant to some degree, although in most the legal system used draws upon a mixture of different legal traditions, of which common law is only one.

Here is a list of the countries in which the English language and English common law are relevant.

- American Samoa
- Antigua and Barbuda
- Australia
- Bangladesh
- Barbados
- Belize
- Botswana
- Cameroon
- Canada
- Cook Islands
- Cyprus
- Dominica
- Federated States of Micronesia
- Fiji Islands

- Ghana
- Grenada
- Guyana
- Hong Kong
- India
- Ireland
- Israel
- Jamaica
- Kenya
- Kiribati
- Lesotho
- Malawi
- Malaysia
- Maldives
- Malta
- Marshall Islands
- Mauritius
- Mozambique
- Namibia
- Nauru
- New Zealand
- Nigeria
- Niue
- Pakistan
- Papua New Guinea
- Samoa
- Seychelles
- Sierra Leone
- Singapore
- Solomon Islands
- South Africa
- Sri Lanka
- Swaziland
- Tanzania
- Thailand
- Tokelau
- Tonga
- Trinidad and Tobago
- Tristan da Cunha
- Turks and Caicos
- Tuvalu
- Uganda
- UK

- USA
- Vanuatu
- Western Samoa
- Zambia
- Zimbabwe

1.5.3   English in international law

Furthermore, the practice of both branches of international law (public and private) is heavily dominated by the English language. In this regard, the importance of English as a common global language has been strongly boosted by the increase in global trade over the past decades. This has had a knock-on effect on the importance of legal English as a specialist branch of international English usage.

Particularly given the economic power and influence of the US over the past century, it is no surprise that many common law concepts relating to contract law inform the way in which the international business community approaches the composition of business contracts.

As we have seen above, legal English differs from ordinary English in a number of key respects. As with other forms of professional language (e.g. medical English), it has its own writing conventions, punctuation standards, terms of art and set phrases, which, at times, differ markedly from ordinary English usage. To some extent these oddities are the product of centuries of usage, and this is particularly the case where certain archaic constructions such as the **here-**, **where-** and **there-** words still found in legal drafting are concerned.

Grammar for legal writing

The aim of this chapter is not to provide comprehensive coverage of all aspects of grammar, but to offer guidance on various issues that may cause difficulty in the context of legal writing.

ARTICLES

Articles in English include **the**, **a** and **an**.

A few simple rules clarify the way in which these articles should be used.

A and **an** are indefinite articles. **A** is used when mentioning something for the first time ('a client walked into the office'). **An** is used in the same circumstances but only where the following word begins with a vowel ('an attorney walked into the office').

The is the definite article. It is used when referring to something already mentioned before ('the client then sat down'), when referring to something that is the only one of its kind ('the sun') or when referring to something in a general rather than specific way ('the internet was an important development').

In some circumstances, articles should be omitted. For example, when a sentence links two parallel adjectival phrases, the article should be omitted from the second phrase. Here is an example:

The judge ruled that Cloakus Ltd was a validly registered and ~~an~~ existing company.

In addition, when using certain abstract nouns in a general, conceptual sense, it is not necessary to use an article to precede the noun. For example:

In the event of conflict between the definitions given in Appendix 1 and the definitions given in the contract, the contract shall prevail.

There is no need here to precede **conflict** with **a**, since **conflict** is used in a general conceptual sense. However, when referring to a specific conflict, articles should be used. For example:

The efforts of negotiators to end the conflict between the two warring nations have so far been unsuccessful.

In this example, 'the' is needed before 'conflict' to indicate that a specific conflict is being referred to.

| 2.2 | **PREPOSITIONS** |

2.2.1   Overview

Prepositions are single words (*at*, *on*, *by*, *to* etc.) or a combination of two words (*as of*, *as regards* etc.) or three words (*in relation to*, *in accordance with* etc.). They are used as connectors showing the relationship between a noun or pronoun and some other word in the sentence. For instance, in the phrase 'the judge was in court' the preposition *in* shows the relationship between the judge and the court.

While preposition usage is a complicated feature of English usage, there is a glimmer of hope in the fact that the following nine prepositions make up about 90% of preposition usage:

- with
- at
- by
- to
- in
- for
- from
- of
- on

2.2.1.1   Place, position, time and method (and quantity, purpose and condition)

Prepositions are primarily used to show the place, position, time or method in relation to a noun or pronoun in the context of the sentence in which it appears. They are also used to show quantity, purpose and condition.

Opposite is an illustrative chart showing these seven functions at work in a contractual context.

The point the chart seeks to make is that because prepositions provide the means of these functions, they are an essential part of legal writing. Their correct use is one of the key means of expressing detailed obligations in a precise manner. Conversely, their incorrect use can cause interpretative difficulties – see section 2.2.1.2 below.

Function	Preposition
Quantity	Five units **of** the Product shall be delivered.
Condition	Five units of the Product shall be delivered **in** good condition.
Method	Five units of the Product shall be delivered **in** good condition **by** air.
Place	Five units of the Product shall be delivered in good condition by air **to** the Buyer's premises.
Position	Five units of the Product shall be delivered in good condition by air to the Buyer's premises **at** 1 Warkley Road, Nottingham.
Time	Five units of the Product shall be delivered in good condition by air to the Buyer's premises at 1 Warkley Road, Nottingham **no later than** 18 May 2021.
Purpose	Five units of the Product shall be delivered in good condition by air to the Buyer's premises at 1 Warkley Road, Nottingham **no later than** 18 May 2021 **for** use by the Buyer in its factory.

Prepositions and meaning
2.2.1.2

In certain circumstances, it may be possible to use more than one preposition to fulfil the same function without there being any particular difference in meaning between them. For example:

I am writing to you with regard to/with respect to/in relation to/about the delivery of the goods on 18 May 2021.

However, there are small but important differences in meaning between certain prepositions in certain circumstances. For example, the sentence:

The goods shall be moved to the warehouse

is subtly different from

The goods shall be moved into the warehouse.

The use of *into* in the second sentence makes it clear that the goods must be put inside the warehouse, while *to* could also be interpreted as meaning that it is sufficient for the goods simply to be put outside the warehouse but close to it.

In other words, this minor difference in drafting could have serious practical consequences. Imagine if the goods in question were highly perishable foodstuffs (fish, milk etc.), the warehouse was refrigerated, the delivery was made late on Friday afternoon after most of the warehouse staff had gone home and it was the middle of summer. You get the picture…

Here is another example:

The goods shall be delivered in seven days

is subtly different from

The goods shall be delivered within seven days.

In the first sentence, the use of **in** gives the impression that the goods will be delivered no earlier than the seventh day. The use of **within** in the second sentence makes it clear that the goods can be delivered at any time during the seven-day period, but not after it.

Here is one more example:

The fee shall be paid by each company within the group of companies.

is subtly different from

The fee shall be paid in respect of each company within the group of companies.

The use of **by** in the first sentence makes it clear that each company in the group is directly responsible for paying the fee. However, the use of **in respect of** in the second sentence creates a looser connection between the company and the fee. It makes it clear that the fee **attributable** to each company shall be paid, but does not specify who must pay the fee.

There are also situations in which the use of different prepositions offers variations in meaning that may be significant in certain contexts but unimportant in others. For example, while the distinction between 'on the market' and 'in the market' can be important in certain situations,[1] 'traded on the market' and 'traded in the market' are both permissible.

2.2.1.3   Difficulties with prepositions

Prepositions are a difficult area of English usage for non-native speakers because while they are sometimes used logically, this is not always the case. It is possible to identify several categories of prepositions.

- Prepositions used logically. This can be seen in simple sentences that express concrete facts. For example, **the tort textbook is on the table** or **our head office is in Sydney**.

- Prepositions used in metaphorical expressions. For example, **when Tatiana got a job at a top law firm in Moscow, she certainly**

Note

1 See this interesting thread for a discussion of these differences: https://english.stac kexchange.com/questions/110507/in-the-market-or-on-the-market

went up in the world. Here, the phrase 'went up in the world' is used metaphorically. Tatiana did not literally ascend, but she made big progress in her career. The preposition 'up' is still used logically, but it expresses a metaphorical rather than concrete idea.

●   Pronouns used in phrasal verbs found in idiomatic expressions. For example, ***I cannot put up with this***, ***you deal with that client***, ***let's wrap up this meeting at 5pm***. These expressions all employ a phrasal verb to create an idiomatic expression whose meaning is either unclear from the context or may differ markedly from the literal meaning. For instance, one can wrap up a present in wrapping paper (literal meaning), but to wrap up a meeting means bringing it to a conclusion (metaphorical meaning).

Phrasal verbs come with their own fixed preposition, adverb or both, as discussed in section 2.10. There is also a glossary of phrasal verbs, together with examples of typical usage, at the back of the book.

Between   2.2.1.4

The preposition ***between*** should be followed by an object pronoun like ***me***, ***him*** or ***us*** instead of a subject pronoun such as ***I***, ***she*** and ***we***. It is therefore correct to say 'this matter is between you and me' and incorrect to say 'this matter is between you and I'.

List of prepositions with examples of usage   2.2.2

Here is a non-exhaustive list of prepositions in common usage in legal English, together with examples of usage. Note that prepositions are sometimes used in twos (***pursuant to***, ***owing to***, ***due to*** etc.) and even threes (***as far as***, ***by means of***, ***in accordance with*** etc.), and examples of prepositions strung together in this way are also included below.

One word   2.2.2.1

about – The lawyer was ***about*** to go into court when the telephone rang.

above – Please refer to the paragraph ***above***, which deals with the insurance arrangements.

across – She went ***across*** to the court to issue the proceedings.

after – The contract was signed ***after*** the parties had agreed the prices to be paid for the goods.

against – The company began trademark infringement proceedings ***against*** one of its competitors.

along – The client did not go *along* with the advice given by the lawyer.

among (or *amongst*) – A copy of the plan of the property was found *among* the papers in the file.

around – We expect the purchase price to be *around* EUR 500,000.

at – The contract stipulates that the goods must arrive *at* the depot *at* 10.00 on 13 July.

before – The lawyer appeared *before* the judge in court and argued her client's case.

behind – It seemed likely that a criminal gang was *behind* the thefts from the local garage.

below – The company was not prepared to consider offers *below* a threshold of three million dollars.

beneath – The Emperor of Ruritania considered it *beneath* his dignity to open a supermarket in Inverness.

between – An agreement was reached *between* Haxter Ltd and Tollby Ltd on 14 September 2017.

beyond – It is important not to go *beyond* what was agreed without discussing the matter with the client first.

by – The invoice must be paid *by* the client *by* 3 May.

concerning – We have received further information *concerning* the warranties to be included in the share purchase agreement.

despite – We have instructions to proceed with the case *despite* the points raised in the defence.

down – The lawyer advised her client to turn *down* the offer made by the defendant.

during – A great deal of new evidence emerged *during* the course of the testimony given by the witness.

except – This restriction applies to all applications *except* those already received by the company.

excluding – The contract contains a provision *excluding* liability in certain cases of default.

following – The *following* items must be supplied no later than 25 January.

for – Payment *for* the goods shall be made on delivery.

from – We have now received the necessary undertakings **from** the defendant's lawyer.

in – The price list is set out **in** Schedule 1.

including – We seek delivery of all the missing parts, **including** those currently stored in the defendant's warehouse.

into – The clerk asked the parties to go back **into** court following the adjournment.

near – The court is **near** the cathedral.

next – The client agreed to bring the documents to the **next** meeting.

of – The attorney was a member **of** various professional organisations.

off – Certain discussions took place between the lawyers **off** the record.

on – The new law **on** employment contracts comes into force tomorrow.

opposite – The court is located **opposite** the cathedral in the central square.

out – The lawyers worked **out** the terms of a compromise agreement.

over – A dispute arose between the landowners **over** the positioning of the boundary.

per – A travel allowance of EUR 60 **per** day was paid to the employee.

plus – The invoice came to EUR 4000 **plus** VAT.

regarding – Negotiations took place **regarding** usage of the storage facilities owned by the company.

since – There have been a number of significant developments in the case **since** the previous court hearing.

than – The amount of damages awarded by the court was more **than** the lawyer had anticipated.

through – The lawyer read **through** the papers in the file.

to – Delivery shall be made to an address notified by the purchaser **to** the vendor.

towards – A great deal of progress has been made **towards** settlement of the case, but a little more time is required in order to reach final agreement between the parties.

under – The witness gave evidence **under** oath.

until – It is unlikely that the case will be settled **until** the morning of the hearing.

up – He brought **up** the question of our fees again.

upon – The proceedings were served **upon** the defendant yesterday.

via – All contact with the claimant was conducted **via** her lawyer.

with – He was charged **with** murder.

within – The goods must be delivered **within** 14 days of signature of the contract.

without – The total amount of the invoice is EUR 30,450 **without** VAT.

2.2.2.2 **Two words**

according to – **According to** the contract, rent must be paid on the third day of each month.

ahead of – We should schedule a further meeting **ahead of** the next court hearing.

apart from – There are no further matters to be resolved **apart from** the copyright issue.

as of – The new law on employment comes into force **as of** midnight tonight.

as regards – **As regards** payment of our fee, we can offer an instalment option.

aside from – There are one or two issues we need to address **aside from** the question of trademarks.

because of – This litigation arose **because of** the unreasonable position taken by the defendant.

close to – The case is now **close to** settlement but there are several issues still to be resolved.

due to – The office is closed tomorrow **due to** a public holiday.

far from – The contract is **far from** ready to be signed since a number of amendments need to be made to it.

instead of – Overtime worked by the employee shall be compensated by extra holiday **instead of** payment.

out of – Payment was made **out of** the company's account.

owing to – The advice given to the client was amended **owing to** a recent decision of the Court of Appeal.

prior to – The consent of the bank must be obtained **prior to** the share transfer being made.

pursuant to – The company changed its name ***pursuant to*** the new legislation on company names.

regardless of – Our client wishes to seek an injunction against his neighbour ***regardless of*** whether the building work is suspended or not.

subsequent to – The court's decision was handed down ***subsequent to*** the new law coming into force.

thanks to – A satisfactory outcome was achieved in the case, ***thanks to*** the meticulous work undertaken by the claimant's lawyers.

that of – One issue still remains to be resolved – ***that of*** the payment method to be used.

Three words

as far as – The summons has not yet been served ***as far as*** I know.

as well as – The vendor must deliver the software ***as well as*** the hardware no later than 10 December.

by means of – Payment shall be made ***by means of*** direct bank transfer.

in accordance with – The sum of $45,000 must be paid on 5 October ***in accordance with*** the court order.

in addition to – Certain legal documents require the signature of witnesses ***in addition to*** the parties in order to be valid.

in case of – ***In case of*** fire the lifts should not be used.

in lieu of – The employee shall receive time off ***in lieu of*** payment.

in spite of – The assignment was completed by the agreed deadline ***in spite of*** several unforeseen difficulties that arose along the way.

on account of – We have had to terminate Mr Taylor's employment contract ***on account of*** his unsatisfactory performance at work.

on behalf of – The lawyer appeared ***on behalf of*** her client at the pre-trial review.

on top of – The employee received a bonus of EUR 10,000 ***on top of*** his regular salary at the end of the year.

with regard to/with respect to – ***With regard to/with respect to*** the question of costs, we consider that the sum of EUR 35,000 should be adequate.

2.3   PRONOUNS

A pronoun is a word used instead of a noun to indicate someone or something already mentioned or known. For example, *I*, *you*, *this*, *that*.

Pronouns are used to avoid repeated use of a noun. They are usually used to refer back to the last used noun.

Legal drafters have traditionally avoided using personal pronouns such as *he*, *she*, *we* and *they*, instead replacing them with formulations such as *the said*, *the aforesaid* or *the same*. The reason for this is a fear of ambiguity in cases where it is unclear to which noun the pronoun might refer if a number of parties are mentioned in the document.

Here is an example of a sentence made ambiguous by unclear use of personal pronouns:

James attended the meeting with John, and he then drafted the relevant documents.

The problem here is that since both James and John are male, 'he' could refer to either of them, so we don't know for sure which of them drafted the documents.

The modern trend, however, is to use pronouns where possible, as their use makes documentation less formal and intimidating. For example, 'you must pay the sum of £1,500 per month to me' is easier for a layperson to understand than 'the Tenant must pay the sum of £1,500 per month to the Landlord'.

However, their use is inappropriate where the aim of the drafter is to impress the reader with the seriousness of the obligations being undertaken, as pronouns often lead to a chattier and lighter style than is found in traditional legal documentation.

One aspect of pronoun use that is highly relevant lies in the desire to avoid sexist language in legal and business English. This subject is discussed further in section 8.2.

2.4   ADJECTIVES

An adjective is a word used to describe a noun or make its meaning clearer (e.g. *excellent*, as in 'an excellent law student'). Some words in the English language have the ability to change parts of speech. For example, the word *principal*, often used in legal English, can be used as an adjective ('the principal sum') or as a noun ('the principal instructs the agent').

Common adjective endings

Adjectives often take the following endings:

-able/*-ible* – e.g. manageable, legible

-al – e.g. legal, internal

-ful – e.g. harmful, careful

-ic – e.g. terrific, manic

-ive – e.g. persuasive, decisive

-less – e.g. careless, groundless

-ous – e.g. dangerous, disastrous

However, many common adjectives do not fall into the categories above. Examples include *bad*, *cold*, *common*, *dark*, *difficult*, *good*, *honest*, *real*, *silent* and a number of other words.

Uncomparable adjectives

Some adjectives are described as uncomparable adjectives, meaning that they describe something that can only be absolute. Such adjectives cannot be qualified by words like *most*, *more*, *less*, *very*, *quite* or *largely*. For example, if a provision in a contract is void it cannot be 'largely void' or 'more void' – it is simply void.

A short list of uncomparable adjectives is set out below:

- absolute
- certain
- complete
- definite
- devoid
- entire
- essential
- false
- final
- first
- impossible
- inevitable
- irrevocable
- manifest
- only
- perfect

- principal
- stationary
- true
- uniform
- unique
- void
- whole

One way of shortening a sentence without loss of meaning is to check whether it contains an uncomparable adjective with a qualifying word, and then cut the qualifying word. For instance:

- *I am **absolutely** certain* – cut *absolutely*.
- *This sentence is **entirely** devoid of meaning* – cut *entirely*.
- *That is **totally** impossible* – cut *totally*.
- *It is **quite** unique* – cut *quite*.

That said, these types of phrases are common in spoken English because they offer a way of adding informal emphasis to the speaker's message. For instance: **I'm absolutely, totally, one hundred percent certain that I sent the contract to the client on Friday**.

See 7.4.2 for further discussion of the use of adjectives in legal contexts.

2.5 ADVERBS

An adverb is a word that modifies or qualifies a verb (e.g. **walk slowly**), an adjective (e.g. **really small**) or another adverb (e.g. **very quietly**).

Most adverbs consist of an adjective plus the ending **-ly**. A number of words act both as adjectives and as adverbs and do not take the suffix **-ly**. These include:

- alone
- enough
- far
- fast
- further
- little
- long
- low
- much
- still
- straight

COLLECTIVE NOUNS

A collective noun (sometimes called a mass noun) is one that refers to a group of people or things (***jury***, ***government***, ***committee***). Such nouns can be used with either a singular verb ('the jury was made up of people from many different backgrounds') or a plural verb ('the jury are all in the court now').

It should be remembered that if the verb is singular any following pronouns (words such as ***he***, ***she*** or ***they***) must also be singular, e.g. 'the firm is prepared to act, but not until it knows the outcome of the negotiations' (not '…until they know the outcome').

In general, it is better to use the singular when referring to collective nouns. The exception to this is where the plural is used to indicate that one is referring not primarily to the group but to all the individual members of the group (e.g. 'the staff were unhappy with the changes that had been proposed').

Here is a short list of collective nouns used in legal and business English:

- audience
- board (e.g. of directors)
- class
- club
- committee
- company
- crew
- government
- group
- jury
- majority
- nation
- panel (of experts)
- parliament
- party (i.e. a body of persons)
- staff
- team
- union
- the Cabinet
- the public

2.7 UNCOUNTABLE NOUNS

2.7.1 Overview

Some nouns in English are uncountable. In other words, they are not used with the indefinite article *a* or *an* and do not have plural forms. For example, the word *information*, as in the phrase *I need some information*, cannot be expressed in the singular as 'an information' or in the plural as 'some informations'.

Therefore, when faced with an uncountable noun, you have three choices.

1 Use it in its usual form. For example, *I have received some information*.

2 If it is important to specify a particular amount of an uncountable noun, join the noun to a word that is itself countable. For example, the word *piece* could be used with *information* to create a plural: *I have received five pieces of information*.

3 Use a countable synonym instead. For example, if the information has come in the form of reports (which are countable), you could write, *I have received five reports*.

Uncountable nouns are often abstract in nature – as in words like *advice*, *remuneration*, *equipment* and *knowledge*. However, this is not always the case, as a number of very commonplace and concrete words such as *butter*, *rice*, *sugar* and *milk* are also uncountable.

2.7.2 Table of uncountable nouns

Here are a few examples of uncountable nouns sometimes found in legal and business writing, together with suggestions on how to make them countable.

Uncountable noun	A particular number
accommodation	an apartment/house
advice	a piece of advice
	a briefing
baggage	a bag
	an item of baggage
coffee	a cup/mug of coffee
employment	a period of employment
	a position/post
equipment	a piece of equipment

evidence	a piece of evidence
hardware	a piece of hardware
information	a piece of information
	a report
	a fact
insurance	an insurance policy
knowledge	a fact
litigation	a litigation matter
	a case
	a claim
	a lawsuit
luggage	a piece/item of luggage
	a suitcase
	a bag
machinery	a piece of machinery
	a machine
pollution	an instance/example of pollution
	a pollution event
	an emission
publicity	an instance/example of publicity
	a report
	an article
	an advertisement
	an announcement
	a media campaign
punctuation	a punctuation mark
	a comma/semi-colon/colon (etc.)
remuneration	a salary
	a wage
	a payment

shopping	an item of shopping
	a purchase
software	a piece of software
	an application
	a program
traffic	a lot of traffic
training	a lecture/a lesson/a training course/a training
	programme/a seminar/a workshop
transportation	a mode/method of transportation

2.7.3   **Nouns that are both countable and uncountable**

English contains a number of nouns that are countable when used in one sense but uncountable when used in another. Several of these appear commonly in legal usage, and include the following words.

Compensation is countable when used in a non-financial sense. For example, *My job is not well paid but has certain compensations, such as the opportunity to travel*. However, it is uncountable when used in a purely financial or legal sense. For example, *The company was obliged to pay compensation to a number of former clients*.

Justice is countable when used to mean an English magistrate. For example, *The defendant appeared before the Justices*. It is uncountable when used in a general conceptual sense. For example, *Everyone hopes to see justice prevail in court today*.

Liability is countable when used in the sense of financial liabilities. For example, *The liabilities listed on the balance sheet include accounts payable, deferred tax and promissory notes*. In this financial sense, it is often used to mean the opposite of *assets*. However, it is uncountable when used to refer to legal responsibility in civil law. For example, *The company admits liability for the breach, but disputes the amount claimed*.

Paper is countable when used in the sense of a research paper or thesis. For example, *Professor Virtanen has published over 30 papers in his field of specialisation*. However, it is uncountable when used to refer to the paper itself as opposed to the content of what is written on it. For example, *We ordered some more paper for the printers today*.

A word of caution...

The question of whether a certain noun is or is not uncountable is a matter of surprisingly fierce debate, not only between users of British, American and other types of English but within different cultures too. There is clear global consensus over a number of basic words like **information** and **knowledge**, but debate over words like **litigation**, with some holding that 'litigations' is correct usage in certain circumstances and others arguing that it is not.

The point is that this is an area of English usage that is clearly undergoing change, meaning it is wise to keep up with current trends.

PAST TENSES

2.8

One of the main difficulties experienced by non-native speakers in using tenses concerns which form of past tense to use in different situations. The subject is more complex than the guidance given below might indicate, but these notes cover the most common areas of difficulty.

Past-perfect tense

2.8.1

This tense is sometimes called the pluperfect and refers to a past action that was completed before a more recent time in the past. It is formed using **had**. For example:

The judge granted an injunction on 28 May. On 27 May the witnesses had given evidence in court.

Simple past

2.8.2

This tense refers to completed actions that occurred in the past. For example:

The judge granted an order.

Past continuous

2.8.3

This tense refers to an action that occurred in the past and is not described as having been completed. For example:

The witness was giving evidence at the trial yesterday.

A common mistake made by non-native speakers is to use the past continuous when the simple past or past-perfect tense should be used. In legal contexts this can easily lead to ambiguity. For example, to say, 'In 2018, I was working as a commercial lawyer' leaves it unclear as to whether you still work as a commercial lawyer.

2.8.4 Example of different tenses in practice

Here is an example of different tenses in practice. The tenses are noted in brackets.

Summary of the facts of _Donoghue v Stevenson_ (1932)
On 9 April 1929 Mrs Mary M'Alister or Donoghue **brought (simple past)** an action against David Stevenson, an aerated water manufacturer from Paisley, in which she **claimed (simple past)** £500 as damages for injuries **sustained (simple past)** by her through **drinking (past continuous)** ginger beer that **had been manufactured (past-perfect)** by the defendant.

2.9 VERB FORMS

2.9.1 The conditional form

This form is used to express a condition; or to put it another way, to express that something is dependent on something else.

Would is the conditional form of **will** and expresses a conditional intention. Thus, **I would go if I felt better** means I would, in fact, go if I felt better.

Could is the conditional form of **can** and expresses a conditional possibility. Thus, **I could go if I felt better** means I would be able to go if I felt better.

Should is the conditional form of **shall** and expresses a conditional obligation. Thus, **I should go if I felt better** means I should be obliged to go if I felt better.

Should also goes with **I** and **we**, and **would** goes with **you**, **he**, **she**, **it** and **they** in the same sense as **would** in such (ultra-polite) sentences as:

We should be much obliged if you would forward the documents to us.

However, this rule is often disregarded even by well-educated English native speakers. Consequently, using the wrong word is not a very serious error.

2.9.2 The subjunctive form

2.9.2.1 Overview

The subjunctive is a rather difficult and, in some respects, rarefied form. However, it persists in a number of set phrases which you may be familiar with.

For instance, if your closest friend suggested having a go at sky-diving from an aeroplane without bothering with any prior training, you might well say:

I wouldn't do that if I were you.

And in his play *Twelfth Night*, Shakespeare wrote:

If music be the food of love, play on.

The common factor between these two very different phrases is that both express a hypothesis. In the first phrase, the speaker ('I') is not the person being addressed ('you') but is imagining for a moment that he or she is that person. In the second phrase, Shakespeare is painting a metaphor – music is not literally the food of love.

These hypotheses are made grammatically possible by the 'were' in the first sentence and the 'be' in the second, which make it clear that the ideas expressed in the sentences are expressed on a hypothetical basis.

Construction

2.9.2.2

The subjunctive is used in the following circumstances:

- To express what is imagined ('Let's imagine that he **were** here today').

- To express what is wished ('I wish that he **were** here today').

- To express what is possible ('if only that **were** possible!').

It is usually the same as the ordinary form of the verb except in the following circumstances:

1 In the third-person singular (**he**, **she**, **it**) the normal -s ending is omitted. For example, you should say **face** rather than **faces** in the sentence 'the report recommends that he face the tribunal'.

2 When using the verb **to be** in the present tense the subjunctive form is **be**, whereas the ordinary present tense is **am**, **are** or **is**. For example, 'the report recommends that he be dismissed'.

3 When using the past subjunctive form of **to be**, you should use **were** instead of **was**. For example, 'I wouldn't try it if I were you'.

Here are some examples of sentences that use the subjunctive:

1 If I **were** to suggest to my client that she **take** those steps, it is unlikely that it would be accepted (past subjunctive of 'to be' and subjunctive form of 'to take').

2 The panel proposes that he **face** an enquiry (third-person singular omits -s ending).

3 We think it best that the claim **be** prepared by a lawyer who specialises in this area of law (present subjunctive of 'to be').

4 In view of the extreme complexity of the matter, the firm would be happier if you **were** to accept a 20% uplift on our usual fee (past subjunctive of 'to be').

5 If we **were** to reduce payment of our usual fee without uplift, we would expect you to accept a penalty for late payment (past subjunctive of 'to be').

2.9.2.3 Usefulness

It is easy to think of the subjunctive as being an obscure grammatical construction that has no practical use nowadays. It is true that it is seldom absolutely essential, and that given its difficulty it may be best avoided where possible.

However, as the sentences set out above demonstrate, it does provide an excellent means of presenting proposals in a hypothetical form. In this way, the writer can put forward ideas without actually committing himself or herself to them. This is particularly clear in the last sentence, which offers a workable structure for making a counterproposal without formally rejecting the initial proposal.

2.9.2.4 A word of warning...

The subjunctive can be ambiguous in circumstances, where it is not completely clear whether what is being expressed is a factual situation that already exists or a hope that such a situation might be brought into existence. Take this sentence for example:

The most important thing for this firm is that they accept our offer.

While this is grammatically correct, it leaves doubt in the reader's mind as to whether it means that 'they' do accept the firm's offer and that this is important, or that the firm hopes that 'they' will accept its offer, and that this is important. In order to clarify which meaning is intended, the sentence could be rewritten in one of two ways.

1 'They' do accept the offer:

The most important thing for this firm is that they have accepted our offer.

2 'They' have not yet accepted the offer, but the firm hopes 'they' will do so:

The most important thing for this firm is that they should accept our offer.

And a typical mistake

A mistake often made by non-native speakers is to use the conditional instead of the subjunctive in a sentence in which both forms should be used. Consequently, the sentence, 'I wouldn't try it if I were you' is often incorrectly expressed as 'I wouldn't try it if I would be you'.

PHRASAL VERBS

Overview

Phrasal verbs are phrases that consist of a verb used together with an adverb (e.g. **break down**) or a preposition (e.g. **call for**) or both (e.g. **put up with**). They range from extremely informal phrases only really used in spoken English (**do with**, **rake in**, **scrape by**) to phrases that are for practical purposes legal terms of art (e.g. **enter into**, **serve upon**, **put down**).

Phrasal verbs can cause particular problems for non-native speakers of English where the verbs used have ordinary meanings when used without an adverb or preposition, but form an idiom when used with an adverb or preposition. In such cases, the literal meaning of the words differs from the real meaning. For example, the phrasal verb **to brush up on** means to practise or study something in order to get back the skill or knowledge you had in the past but have not used for some time. For example, 'I must brush up on my French before visiting Paris'.

Most prepositions and adverbs can only be paired with a limited number of verbs to create a workable phrasal verb. For instance, **aback** can only be paired with the verb **taken** to create the phrasal verb **taken aback**, meaning to be surprised by something.

On the other hand, some verbs can be given a range of very different meanings by adding different adverbs or prepositions to them. For instance, using the verb **deal**, the following phrasal verbs can be made: **deal in**, **deal on**, **deal with** and **deal out** – each of which has entirely separate meanings. To find out what they are, please refer to the glossary of phrasal verbs at the back of the book. The glossary sets out the most common phrasal verbs in legal usage together with explanations of their meanings and examples showing how they are used.

Example

Here is an example of a short paragraph that employs a number of phrasal verbs. In each case, while the phrasal verbs used are the most natural way of conveying the meaning of the sentences, an alternative one-word replacement for the phrasal verb used is given in brackets. Note that no alternative is given for **served upon** since this is a term of art.

*My client told me that his firm **carried out** (performed)* building assignments *for major developers. The firm **entered into** (concluded)* a contract with a new *supplier. However, when this new supplier **handed over** (delivered)* the first *batch of supplies, they were found to be of extremely poor quality. Therefore, my client **served** notice of termination **upon** (formally delivered)* the supplier. *Unfortunately, this was not done in the manner stipulated in the contract, which I **pointed out** (indicated)* to the client.

It is worth noting that sometimes the parts of a phrasal verb become slightly separated, as in the phrase 'served notice of termination upon'. This is a natural feature of phrasal verb usage but (as with knees when skiing) it is dangerous to let them get too far apart. The dangers of doing so are outlined in section 8.1.

2.11   NEGATIVES

Negatives are formed in English by using prefixes. The most common of these are **un-**, **in-**, **il-**, **im-**, **ir-**, **non-** and **anti-**.

Here are some common negative forms often used in legal English:

- unlawful
- unfamiliar
- impractical
- illegal
- unfair
- invalid
- independence
- injustice
- impartiality
- inequitable
- unwritten
- impracticable
- unconstitutional
- illicit

2.11.1   Dis-

The Latin prefix **dis-** (literally 'apart', 'asunder', 'away', 'utterly') is used in a slightly different way to the prefixes listed above. It does not necessarily denote a direct negative but is used in the sense of having a negative or reversing force. Here are some examples:

- disable
- disagree
- disbelieve
- disconnect
- discontent
- disembark
- disenfranchise
- dislike
- dissimilar
- distrust

Certain words can be prefaced with either **un-** or **dis-** to create different meanings. For instance, 'Contract law is quite **unlike** tort law, but I don't **dislike** either of them'.

Non- and un-   2.11.2

The prefixes **non-** and **un-** both mean 'not' but they tend to be used in slightly different ways. **Non-** is more neutral in meaning, while **un-** means an opposite and thus often suggests a particular bias or standpoint.

For example, **unnatural** means that something is not natural in a bad way, whereas **non-natural** simply means 'not natural'. As a consequence, where there is a genuine choice about which prefix to use, **non-** is preferred in legal writing.

However, in some cases, both the **non-** and **un-** forms are in use but have different meanings. For instance, **non-statutory** refers to something not found in a statute (for instance, a common law principle) while **unstatutory** refers to something that actively breaches a statute.

Note also that some words look like negatives but are in fact synonyms. For example, **flammable** and **inflammable** both mean easily set on fire.

RELATIVE PRONOUNS   2.12

As noted above, relative pronouns include **who**, **whom**, **whose**, **which** and **that**. Here are some brief notes about their use.

Who or whom?   2.12.1

The correct use of **who** and **whom** is a matter that many non-native and native speakers of English alike have difficulty with. The distinction between them is that **who** acts as the subject of a verb, while **whom** acts as the object of a verb or preposition. This distinction is not particularly important in informal speech but should be observed in legal writing.

For example, **whom** should be used in the sentence:

> *I advised Peter, John and Mary, all of whom are contemplating claims against RemCo Ltd.*

Who should be used in this sentence:

> *I saw Peter, who is contemplating a claim against RemCo Ltd.*

When **who** is used, it should directly follow the name it refers to. If it does not, the meaning of the sentence may become unclear. For example, 'I saw Peter, who was one of my clients, and James' instead of 'I saw Peter and James, who was one of my clients'.

2.12.2   Which or that?

The main difference between **which** or **that** is that **that** has a restrictive effect on the word or phrase it modifies, while **which** has a non-restrictive effect but is used to provide further information.

For instance, in the phrase 'the contract that was signed on 1 June 2020' the scope of 'contract' is narrowed down by the use of **that** to link it to a date. On the other hand, the effect of using **which** with commas is simply to provide further information about the word or phrase being modified: 'the contract, which was signed on 1 June 2020, covers the sale of car parts'.

In summary:

- When introducing clauses that define or narrow the scope of a word or phrase, use **that**. For example, 'a book that deals with current issues in international trade law'.

- Use **which**, but never **that**, to introduce a clause giving additional information about something. For example, 'the contract, which took several weeks to draft, runs to over 200 pages' and not 'the contract, that took several weeks to draft, runs to over 200 pages'.

2.12.3   Who, whom, which or that?

Who or **whom** should not be used when referring to things that are not human. **Which** or **that** should be used instead. For example, 'the company that sold its shares' is correct. 'The company, which sold the shares, is based in Ljubljana' is also correct. 'The company who sold the shares' is incorrect.

That should be used when referring to things that are not human and may be used when referring to a person. However, it is usually thought **that** is more impersonal than **who**/**whom** when used in this way. As a result, it is better to say 'the client who I saw yesterday' than 'the client that I saw yesterday'.

Punctuation for legal writing

GENERAL POINTS

One of the most unusual aspects of old-fashioned contract drafting was the belief among lawyers and judges that punctuation was unimportant. The prevailing view in common law jurisdictions was that the meaning of legal documents should be ascertained from the words of the document and their context, rather than from punctuation. Accordingly, old-fashioned legal drafting tends to involve little or no punctuation. This makes it extremely hard to read and potentially highly ambiguous.

For example, consider these unpunctuated sentences:

This contract said the judge is indecipherable.
Punctuation without it contracts would be difficult to read.

Now consider the same sentences with punctuation:

This contract, said the judge, is indecipherable.
Punctuation – without it, contracts would be difficult to read.

Fortunately, modern legal drafters have begun to use punctuation in the same way that ordinary writers use punctuation – to give guidance about meaning.

PUNCTUATION MARKS

Full stop/period (.)

Full stop is the British English term for this punctuation mark, and **period** is the American English term for it. Full stops/periods should be used in the following situations:

- At the end of all sentences that are not questions or exclamations. The next word should normally begin with a capital letter.

- After abbreviations of single words. For example, 'Sun. 10 June'.

- When a sentence ends with a quotation that itself ends with a full stop, question mark or exclamation mark, no further full stop is required. However, if the quotation is short, and the sentence introducing it is more important, the full stop is put outside the quotation marks. For example: on the door were written the words 'No entry'.

- A sequence of three full stops (known as an **ellipsis**) indicates an omission from the text. A fourth full stop should be added if this comes at the end of a sentence. For example, 'this handbook…is exceptionally useful…I refer to it every day'.

3.2.2 **Comma (,)**

Commas are used to show a short pause within a sentence. They should be used with care as a misplaced comma can alter the intended meaning of the sentence. For example:

The lawyer advised Ian and Edward, then hurried to court.
The lawyer advised Ian, and Edward then hurried to court.

At the same time, commas should be used where necessary to clarify meaning. Simply omitting the commas often leads to ambiguity or an unintended meaning. For example:

This lawyer, said the judge, is a fool.
This lawyer said the judge is a fool.

There are eight main situations in which commas should be used:

1 To separate items in a list of more than two items. For example, 'cars, trucks, vans, and tractors'. In this sentence, there is a comma after **vans** to show that the list contains four separate categories of items – cars, trucks, vans, tractors – and that **vans and tractors** do not make up a single category.

2 To separate coordinated main clauses. For example, 'Cars should park here, and trucks should continue straight on'. In this sentence, the comma after **here** marks the separation between the different clauses in the sentence.

3 To mark the beginning and end of a sub-clause in a sentence. For example, 'James, who is a corporate lawyer, led the seminar'.

   Here, the commas after **James** and **lawyer** allow the writer to indicate to the reader in passing that James is a corporate lawyer, while at the same time placing the main emphasis on the fact that James led the seminar.

4 After certain kinds of introductory clause. For example, 'Having finished my work, I left the office'.

5 After certain kinds of introductory words. When a sentence begins with a word that does not form part of the clause that follows it, a comma usually appears after this word. These are usually words – or combinations of two or three words – inserted by the author to indicate to the reader how the rest of the sentence should be understood and how it relates to the previous sentence. For example, **however**, **therefore**, **of course**, **nevertheless**.

6 To separate a phrase or sub-clause from the main clause in order to avoid misunderstanding. For example:

I did not go to Paris yesterday, because the meeting was cancelled.

Here, the comma after **yesterday** makes it clear that the writer did not go to Paris, and the reason he or she did not go to Paris was that the meeting was cancelled. If the comma were to be removed, the sentence would be ambiguous – it would give the impression that the writer **did** go to Paris but that the reason for going to Paris was not that the meeting was cancelled:

I did not go to Paris yesterday because the meeting was cancelled. I went because I had urgent shopping to do!

7 Following words that introduce direct speech (e.g. **said**). For example, 'He said, "my lawyer is a genius!"'

8 Between adjectives that each qualify a noun in the same way. For example, 'a small, dark room'. Here, a comma is placed after **small**.

However, where the adjectives qualify the noun in different ways, or when one adjective qualifies another, no comma is used. For example, 'a distinguished international lawyer'.

Commas are softer in effect than full stops and semi-colons, and are therefore unsuitable for long lists. They should not be used simply as an alternative to using short sentences or if there is any risk of ambiguity.

Colon (:)   3.2.3

The colon is usually used to point to information that follows it. It may also be used to link two clauses. Here are some examples of usage:

- To precede a list (e.g. 'The following items are included:').

- To introduce a step from an introduction to a main theme or from a general statement to a particular situation (e.g. 'The remedy is simple: introduce new rules.').

- To show cause and effect (e.g. 'An energetic new director has been appointed: this accounts for the rise in share prices.').

- To precede an explanation (e.g. 'The argument used by the defence was as follows:').

Colons should not be followed by a dash (–). The dash serves no useful purpose in this context.

3.2.4   **Semi-colon (;)**

The semi-colon is used to separate parts of a sentence when a more distinct break is needed than can be provided by a comma but the parts of the sentence are too closely connected for separate sentences to be used. For example:

The advocate argues the case before the court; the judge decides it.

It is also used to provide a higher-level division in a sentence that is already divided with commas. For example:

The lawyer had an interview with a new client, who wished to bring a claim against his former employer, and advised that the client's case was weak; but instead of accepting this advice, the client sought a second opinion.

In legal writing semi-colons are used to punctuate the end of any sub-clause or paragraph that forms part of a longer sentence. However, if the sub-clause or paragraph constitutes the last part of the sentence, a full stop may be more appropriate.

In a list of items beginning with an introductory sentence, you should begin with an introductory colon, begin each item with a lowercase letter or a numeral, put a semi-colon at the end of each item, and end the list with a full stop. Here is an example:

Prior to the annual stakeholder engagement meeting the organiser should:

(a) *draw up a draft agenda setting out the key issues arising from the stakeholder engagement survey;*

(b) *no later than 14 days prior to the meeting, distribute the draft agenda to the attendees requesting that they submit their comments within seven days;*

(c) *following expiration of the seven-day period specified in (b) finalise the agenda; and*

(d) *no later than three days prior to the meeting, circulate the agenda to the attendees.*

See also the discussion of 'faulty springboards' at 12.2.2.

3.2.5   **Parentheses ( )**

Parentheses are also known as brackets, and are used to enclose words, phrases or whole sentences. If a whole sentence is in parentheses, the end punctuation stays inside it. For example:

(Stanning plc is hereinafter referred to as 'the Company'.)

Where only the end part of the sentence is in parentheses, the end punctuation goes outside the parentheses. For example:

Stanning plc (hereinafter referred to as 'the Company').

The main circumstances in which parentheses are used are as follows:

- To enclose remarks made by the writer of the text himself or herself. For example, 'Mr X (as I shall call him) then stood up to speak'.

- To enclose mention of an authority, definition, explanation, reference or translation.

- In the report of a speech, to enclose interruptions by the audience.

- To enclose reference letters or figures. For example, '(1)(a)'.

Avoid parentheses within parentheses – use commas or dashes instead. Dashes are a useful way of separating concepts within sentences.

Square brackets [ ]

3.2.6

These enclose comments, corrections, explanations or notes not in the original text but added at a later stage by new authors or editors.

Square brackets are used in legal writing to adjust the format of quoted material. For example, they may be used to indicate that a letter now in lowercase was in capitals in the original text ('The court ruled that [e]xistence of the subject-matter of the contract precluded a finding of **force majeure**.').

Dashes (–)

3.2.7

Dashes (–) can be used in the following situations.

- To indicate an interruption, especially in transcribed speech. For example, '"Of course it's not da–" he said, and was promptly blown off the side of the cliff'.

- To connect a proposition to a conclusion in a slightly informal manner. For example, 'There was only one winner – Bill'.

- As a substitute for parentheses. For example, 'Jean-Pierre – an extreme sports enthusiast – gave an interesting presentation on personal injury litigation from the perspective of the claimant'.

- As a substitute for **to** when indicating routes and similar informal sequences. For example, 'the proposed route is Helsinki – London – New York – Helsinki'.

3.2.8 **Hyphen (-)**

The question of when to use a hyphen (i.e. a horizontal line connecting two words) often causes problems.

Hyphens (-) are used in the following situations.

● To create prefixes.

● To create a connection between different words. These functions are discussed further below.

3.2.8.1 **Prefixes**

Most writers are comfortable with the idea of using hyphens to connect certain prefixes to a word. For instance, terms beginning with **non-** are almost always hyphenated in British English (though not in American English), as are a number of terms beginning with **pre-**, **post-**, **co-** and various other prefixes.

Here is a table showing some commonly hyphenated prefixes:

Prefix	Hyphenated examples
anti	anti-American
	anti-inflationary
co	co-finance
	co-manage
	co-opt
counter	counter-cyclical
	counter-inflationary
inter	inter-company
	inter-enterprise
	inter-office
	inter-regional
intra	intra-Community
	intra-continental
	intra-regional

multi	multi-currency
	multi-million
	multi-purpose
	multi-year
non	non-bank
	non-durable
	non-party
	non-resident
	non-statutory
over	over-expansionary
	over-optimistic
post	post-depression
	post-tax income
	post-war
pre	pre-announced
	pre-select
	pre-specified
	pre-trial
re	re-establish
	re-examine
self	self-sufficiency
sub	sub-committee
	sub-manager
	sub-paragraph
	sub-section
	sub-set
super	super-boom
	super-liquidity
under	under-reporting
	under-utilisation

3.2.8.2   **Connected words**

Confusion often arises when it comes to connecting separate words together using hyphens.

In brief, the rule is that hyphens are used to connect words that are more closely connected to each other than the surrounding syntax. This is often the case when one word is a noun (e.g. *tax*) and the other is an adjective (e.g. *exempt*) or adverb (e.g. *neutrally*), and particularly where these words taken together have an adjectival function. For example, take the sentence:

The company made a tax-exempt transfer.

The words **tax-exempt** are clearly more closely connected than the surrounding words, and taken together they have the role of an adjective in relation to the word **transfer** – they describe the nature of the transfer. In other words, if you were to ask what kind of transfer was involved, you would get the answer – a tax-exempt transfer. And a hyphen would appear between **tax** and **exempt** to emphasise the unity of this term.

However, if both words involved are nouns, they are more likely to stand alone and not require hyphenation. So, while **tax-exempt** is hyphenated, **tax exemption** should not be hyphenated.

See the glossary of commonly hyphenated terms at the back of the book for further guidance.

3.2.9   **Apostrophe (')**

There are two uses for the apostrophe. First, it is used to show that a word has been shortened or that two words have been combined. For example:

I'll be there, so don't say that I won't.

This use of the apostrophe to shorten a word is not usually seen in legal writing as it is considered too informal for most situations.

Second, the apostrophe is used to express the genitive form (sometimes called the possessive form). For example:

The client's payment was late.

When more than one person or thing owns something, put the apostrophe after the s. For example:

The clients' payments were late.

You could put this another way by saying 'the payments of the clients were late'. However, this looks very clumsy and laborious by the standards of modern English.

Take care when using **its**. It only takes an apostrophe when it is short for **it is** or **it has**. For example:

It's a straightforward case.

When using **its** in a possessive sense, the apostrophe should be omitted. For example:

This agreement has its advantages.

Quotation marks (' ' and " ")   3.2.10

In British English, single quotation marks (' ') should be used for a first quotation. For example:

He wrote, 'that is the most important question'.

Double quotation marks should be used for any quotation within a quotation. For example:

He wrote, 'she said "that is the most important question"'.

Single quotation marks should be used again for any quotation inside a quotation inside a quotation. For example:

He wrote, 'she said "that is the most important question he asked during his 'Marlborough Hall' speech"'.

The closing quotation mark should come before all punctuation marks unless these form part of the quotation itself. For example:

Did the judge really say, 'that lawyer is a fool'?

but:

The judge asked, 'is that lawyer a fool?'

Question mark (?)   3.2.11

The circumstances in which question marks are used are as follows:

- To follow every question that requires a direct answer. For example, 'what does that mean?' However, note that a question mark is not required after indirect questions. For example, 'he asked me what that meant'.

- A question mark may also be placed before a word or phrase the accuracy of which is doubted. For example, 'Josie (?) Zaniuderghoshihaho'.

3.2.12 Exclamation mark (!)

The exclamation mark is used after an exclamatory word, phrase or sentence. It usually forms the concluding full stop but need not do so. It may also be used within square brackets after quoted text to indicate the writer's feelings of, for example, amusement, surprise or disagreement. For example, 'The court then heard the defendant mutter, "this judge is a fool"' [!].

3.2.13 Forward slash (/)

The main use for the forward slash in legal text is to express ratios or situations in which two words are being contrasted with one another. Here are some examples:

and/or

debt/equity swaps

price/earnings ratio

sterling/dollar rate

risk/return relationship

The forward slash is also sometimes seen in certain abbreviations, particularly in British English. Examples include c/o ('care of'), w/o ('without') and S/E ('single engined').

3.2.14 Capital letters

Legal texts are rather frequently littered with excessive capitalisation, which is (1) grammatically incorrect; and (2) distracting for the reader. Capital letters should only be used in the following situations:

- At the beginning of a sentence (e.g. 'Thank you for your letter').

- When writing proper names (e.g. London, Angela Merkel, Fleet Street).

- When writing names that derive from proper names (e.g. Christianity, Marxism).

- For certain abbreviations (e.g. USA, NATO, WTO).

- For a defined term in a legal document where the definition uses a capital letter (e.g. 'Roggins plc, hereinafter referred to as the "Company"').

The main difficulty that arises is that writers fail to distinguish clearly between (1) proper names and ordinary nouns; and (2) defined terms and ordinary nouns.

So next time you find yourself using capitals for such terms as 'a group of companies' or 'the sales contract', ask yourself whether the noun in question is either a proper name or a defined term. If the answer to both these questions is 'no', change to lowercase.

A particular problem arises where a certain word, such as 'company', appears as both a defined term and an ordinary noun in a document. In these cases, it is necessary to identify which is which. The use of the definite article 'the' before the defined term and of words such as 'a', 'any' or 'other' before the ordinary noun should be of assistance in this regard. For instance:

The Company has the same rights as any other company.

See Chapter 5 for guidance on the use of capitals in headings.

4 Sentence structure

ACTIVE AND PASSIVE VOICE

4.1.1 Overview

Sentences may take either the active or the passive voice or use a combination of the two.

The term 'voice' refers to the relationship between a clause's subject and its verb.

When using the active voice, the subject of the sentence acts upon the object through the verb in such a way as to make the relationship between subject and object clear. For example:

The lawyer represented the client.

In this sentence, **the lawyer** is the subject (or actor), **represented** is the verb and **client** is the object. The active voice makes it clear who represented the client – it is brisk and direct.

When using the passive voice, it is possible to create a grammatically complete sentence without mentioning the actor (the lawyer in this case). For example:

The client was represented.

It is also possible to lengthen this sentence by identifying the actor. For example:

The client was represented by the lawyer.

4.1.2 Pros and cons

Legal drafters have a tendency to use passive forms ('a meeting is to be called') rather than active forms ('John Smith will call a meeting') because this form creates an indirect and formal tone with which lawyers instinctively feel comfortable.

However, overuse of the passive can lead to lack of clarity. The example given above leaves it unclear as to who is going to call the meeting. It also leads to less effective and less forceful communication with the reader.

By contrast, sentences using the active voice tend to be shorter, brisker and more direct. In general, when writing in English for any purpose it is better to use the active voice.

However, there are two situations in which the passive voice is useful.

1 Where it is more important to focus attention on the thing being acted upon in the sentence. Consider this brief exchange:

Why is the jury not present in the courtroom?
The jury was dismissed.

Here, the emphasis is on the jury having been dismissed. The information about how and why this occurred can come later.

2 When the actor in the sentence is not important. This situation often arises in scientific writing. For example:

At the beginning of the experiment, exactly 20 ml of acid was added to the beaker, causing effervescence.

It would be possible to rephrase this using the active voice, to include the actor:

At the beginning of the experiment, Tiffany Bryan added exactly 20 ml of acid to the beaker, causing effervescence.

However, it was not Tiffany Bryan who caused the effervescence, but the addition of 20 ml of acid to the beaker. Consequently, mentioning Tiffany – a talented comedian whose routine about talking kangaroos once reduced a party of Russian government ministers to tears of mirth – distracts the reader from the main message of the sentence, as has occurred in the previous sentence.

BUILDING A SENTENCE

4.2

Assuming that we are using the active voice, the general rule in English is that a simple declarative sentence should be structured as subject – verb – object. For example:

The lawyer drafted the contract.

In this sentence, **the lawyer** is the subject, **drafted** is the verb and **contract** is the object.

Subject

4.2.1

The subject is the part of the sentence that usually comes first and on which the rest of the sentence is predicated. It is typically – but not always – a noun phrase. In traditional grammar it is said to be the 'doer' of the verbal action.

A subject is essential in English sentence structure – so much so that a dummy subject (usually 'it') must sometimes be introduced (e.g. **It is raining**). However, they are unnecessary in imperative sentences (e.g. **Listen!**) and in some informal contexts (e.g. **See you soon**).

4.2.2   Verb

Verbs are traditionally described as 'doing' words. They are usually essential to clause structure.

Verbs may be classified either as **main** or **auxiliary**. Auxiliary verbs are traditionally described as 'helping verbs', and include **be**, **do** and **have**. Compare:

I have perused the documents.
I have been perusing the documents.

4.2.3   Object

The object is usually a noun phrase. In a simple declarative sentence, it follows the verb. The object is usually said to be 'affected' by the verb.

Objects may be either **direct** or **indirect**. In the sentence **I owe you nothing**, **you** is the direct object and **nothing** the indirect object.

4.3   MORE COMPLEX SENTENCES

In more complex sentences, it may be necessary to introduce other parts of speech. These include:

4.3.1   Adjectives

An adjective is a word used to describe a noun or make its meaning clearer. For example:

A shabby courtroom.
A modern office.

Adjectives go before the nouns they qualify. For example:

The commercial lawyer drafted the sales contract.

4.3.2   Adverbs

Adverbs are words or phrases that add more information about place, time, manner or degree to an adjective, verb, other adverb or sentence (e.g. **greatly**, **very**, **fortunately**, **efficiently**).

Therefore, adverbs may be added to modify the meaning of our example:

The commercial lawyer efficiently drafted the sales contract.

LINKING CLAUSES

In order to build more complex sentences, it is necessary to find ways of linking clauses together.

One way of achieving this is by using prepositions (**in**, **at**, **on**, **to**, **from** etc.) or conjunctions (**and**, **or**, **but**, **since**, **when**, **because**, **although** etc.). For example:

The commercial lawyer efficiently drafted the sales contract for the company, but the client requested various amendments and additions.

Punctuation can be used to coordinate clauses in a sentence. For example:

The commercial lawyer efficiently drafted the sales contract, her assistant sent it to the client and the client approved the draft.

In addition, relative pronouns (e.g. **who**, **whom**, **whose**, **which**, **that**) provide a convenient means of linking sentences together. For example:

The commercial lawyer efficiently drafted the sales contract, which the client read and approved.

More information on relative pronouns is set out in section 2.12.

SUBJECT–VERB AGREEMENT

When relating the subject of a sentence with the main verb, the basic rule is that a singular subject takes a singular verb, while a plural subject takes a plural verb. The difficulty lies in knowing whether the subject and verb are singular or plural.

Here are some specific rules together with examples of usage. Note that this is not an exhaustive list.

1   When the subject of a sentence is composed of two or more nouns or pronouns connected by **and**, use a plural verb. For example:

The attorney and her assistant are in court today.

2   Two singular subjects connected by **or** or **nor** require a singular verb. For example:

My lawyer or my accountant is attending the meeting today.

3   Two singular subjects connected by **either/or** or **neither/nor** require a singular verb. For example:

Neither my lawyer nor my accountant is available.

4 When a singular subject is connected by **or** or **nor** to a plural subject, put the plural subject last and use a plural verb. For example:

Your signature, as well as those of the other parties, go at the bottom of the document.

5 In circumstances where the subject is separated from the verb by words such as **along with**, **as well as**, **besides** or **not**, disregard these expressions when deciding which verb form to use. For example:

My lawyer, along with my accountant and one of her colleagues, is expected to arrive later.

6 The pronouns **each**, **everyone**, **every one**, **everybody**, **anyone**, **anybody**, **someone** and **somebody** are singular and require singular verbs. For example:

Each of the candidates is capable of doing the job well.

7 The phrase **the number** should be followed by a singular verb, but the phrase **a number** should be followed by a plural verb. For example:

The number of different companies involved in this process is five.

But:

A number of different companies are involved in this process.

8 A singular verb should be used with sums of money or time periods. For example:

Five years is a long time to wait for a court hearing.

9 Nouns ending in 's' normally, but not always, require plural verbs. The words **news** and **mathematics**, among others, require singular verbs. For example:

The news is very bad – apparently the judge has given an indication that she believes that much of the evidence on which our client bases her claim is inadmissible.

See also 2.6 on the use of plural and singular verb forms with collective nouns.

WHEN IS A SENTENCE NOT A SENTENCE?

4.6

Here are some examples of failed sentences, with explanations of what is wrong with them.

1 *Regarding your letter dated 17 November about clause 5 of the contract.*

This sentence has no verb. It could work as the first clause of a sentence consisting of two clauses. For example:

Regarding your letter dated 17 November about clause 5 of the contract, we cannot accept your argument.

2 *Working long into the night to prepare for the upcoming tort exam.*

There is a verb here, but no subject–verb relationship. It could be corrected by introducing the subject at a later point. For example:

Working long into the night to prepare for the upcoming tort exam, Paula found herself drinking far too much coffee.

3 *Even though the barrister for the defence had the better arguments and was a more persuasive speaker.*

There is a subject here, as well as two verbs, but the sentence fails because the phrase **even though** acts as a conjunction but has nothing to connect to. We need to add something to it to complete the sentence. For example,

Even though the barrister for the defence had the better arguments and was a more persuasive speaker, she still lost the case.

Incidentally, in this sentence 'the' appears before 'better arguments' to concretise the superiority of the defence barrister's arguments in relation to those of her opponent.

4 *After six hours waiting to be called into court, the case was adjourned.*

This example is more problematic, because at first glance it appears grammatically correct. However, the construction of the sentence suggests that the case was waiting to be called into court, but, since 'case' is abstract, this is illogical. The sentence would make sense if it referred to participants in the case waiting to be called into court. For example:

After the jurors had spent six hours waiting to be called into court, the case was adjourned.

Legal writing standards
Dates, numbers, citations and headings

DATES

When using British English, dates should be written as follows:

- 21 February 2020 – not 21st February 2020 or February 21, 2020

- 7 October 2019 – not 07 October 2019

- 2019–20 – not 2019–2020 or 2019/20

However, dates are written differently in American English, since the month is placed before the day, and a comma is often placed after the day. For example, February 21st, 2020 or October 7th, 2019.

A hyphen can be used to replace 'to' in phrases such as 'during the period October-December 2019', but not in 'from…to' or 'between…and' expressions. For example, write:

…from October 2019 to July 2020

And:

…between October and December 2020 (not between October–December 2020)

NUMBERS

The general rule is that all numbers ten and below should be spelled out and numbers 11 and above should be put in numerals. However, there are certain exceptions to this:

- If numbers recur through the text or are being used for calculations, then numerals should be used.

- If the number is approximate (e.g. 'around six hundred years ago') it should be spelled out.

- Very large numbers should generally be expressed without using rows of zeros where possible (e.g. $3.5 million instead of $3,500,000). In contracts, the use of both words and numbers is common in order to increase certainty. For example, 'THREE THOUSAND FIVE HUNDRED EUROS (EUR 3,500)'.

- Percentages may be spelled out (twenty per cent) or written as numbers (20%).

- Numbers that begin sentences should be spelled out.

In English writing, the decimal point is represented by a dot (.) and commas are used to break up long numbers. Commas cannot be used to represent a decimal point.

Therefore, the number ten thousand five hundred and fifty-three and three-quarters is written like this in English:

10,553.75

while in most Continental European countries, it is written like this:

10.553,75

When referring to sums of money, the following rules apply:

- When writing numerical sums, the currency sign goes before the sum (e.g. $100). Note that there is no gap between the sign and the figure that follows it.

- When spelling out numbers, the name of the currency is put after the number (e.g. 'one hundred pounds sterling').

The percentage sign (%) appears after the number to which it relates, and there is usually no gap between the sign and the number (e.g. 95%).

CITATIONS **5.3**

References to statutes **5.3.1**

The title of every UK statute has a long form and a short form. For example, the long form of the title of the Enterprise Act 2002 is:

An Act to establish and provide for the functions of the Office of Fair Trading, the Competition Appeal Tribunal and the Competition Service; to make provision about mergers and market structures and conduct; to amend the constitution and functions of the Competition Commission; to create an offence for those entering into certain anti-competitive agreements; to provide for the disqualification of directors of companies engaging in certain anti-competitive practices; to make other provision about competition law; to amend the law relating to the protection of the collective interests of consumers; to make further provision about the disclosure of information obtained under competition and consumer legislation; to amend the Insolvency Act 1986 and make other provision about insolvency; and for connected purposes.

This is not especially snappy, so the short-form title is more frequently used for citation purposes.

When citing a statute, its name should be written without a comma between the name of the statute and the year it was enacted, and 'the' should not be capitalised unless you are starting the sentence with it. For example, 'I will now refer to the Enterprise Act 2002'.

When referring to a section of a statute write 'section' in full using a lowercase 's' (unless starting a sentence). For example, 'section 6 of the Sales of Goods Act 1979 deals with contracts in respect of goods that have perished'.

When referring to a particular subsection of a statute do not use the word 'subsection'. Use the word 'section' followed by the relevant number and letter. For example, 'under section 270(1) of the Companies Act 2006 a private company is not required to have a secretary'.

5.3.2   References to European Union legislation

European Union (EU) legal acts have a long title, a short title used for citation purposes and an informal title.

Consider, for instance, the Energy Efficiency Directive:

- Long form: Directive 2012/27/EU on energy efficiency, amending Directives 2009/125/EC and 2010/30/EU and repealing Directives 2004/8/EC and 2006/32/EC.

- Informal title: the Energy Efficiency Directive.

- Cite as: Directive 2012/27/EU.

Note that references to EU legal acts are dynamic, which means that any reference to an act currently in force is deemed to include all amendments made to it. There is no need, and it is incorrect, to list any such amendments separately.

The full texts of all EU legislation can be accessed, in 24 European languages, through the Eurlex portal at: http://eur-lex.europa.eu

References to cases

Case citations fulfil two functions. They name the case and also tell the reader where a report of the judgment can be found.

UK cases

In UK case citations, the name of the case itself appears in **italics**, with the word 'versus' replaced by '*v*'. The notation that appears after the name of the case indicates where the case report can be found.

For example, consider the citation **Donoghue v Stevenson** [1932] AC 562 (HL).

This tells us that the case involved a claimant with the surname of Donoghue and a defendant with the surname of Stevenson, can be found in the 1932 volume of the series of the Law Reports called the 'Appeals Cases' at page 562, and was decided by the UK House of Lords (HL).

US cases

There is a minor difference in the way in which case citations appear in the US and the UK in that in the US a dot (.) appears after the '*v*' for versus: '*v.*'.

In the US, case citations appear like this: **Roe v. Wade**, 410 U.S. 113 (1973).

Here, Roe was the surname of the claimant ('plaintiff' in the US) and Wade is the surname of the defendant; 410 is the volume number of the 'reporter' that reported the Court's written opinion; U.S. is the abbreviation of the reporter (it stands for United States Reports); 113 is the page number of the report; and 1973 is the year the court gave its decision.

EU cases

The method of citing EU cases has changed recently with the introduction of the European Case-Law Identifier (ECLI), which has been retrospectively applied to all EU cases heard since 1954 and to the Opinions and Views of the Advocates General. The ECLI comprises a four-part code that forms part of the case citation.

For example, the ECLI of the judgment of the Court of Justice of 12 July 2005, **Schempp** (C-403/03), is as follows: 'EU:C:2005:446'. In this ECLI:

- 'EU' tells us that the decision was delivered by a court of the EU itself (the code corresponding to the relevant Member State appears instead of 'EU' for decisions of national courts or tribunals).

- 'C' indicates that this decision was delivered by the Court of Justice (decisions delivered by the General Court would be indicated by the letter 'T' and those of the Civil Service Tribunal by 'F').

- '2005' indicates that the decision was delivered in 2005.

- '446' indicates that it is the 446th ECLI assigned in respect of the year in question.

When citing EU cases, the relevant information should appear in the following order: the part of the case report (judgment or opinion), the name of the case in italics, the case number, the ECLI number, the paragraph number of the judgment or opinion (if applicable). For example:

Judgment of 13 November 1990, ***Marleasing SA v La Comercial Internacional de Alimentacion SA***, C-106/89, ECLI:EU:C:1990:395, paragraph 11.

The case-law of the CJEU can be searched through the Curia portal at: http://curia.europa.eu and via Eurlex (see section 5.3.2 above).

5.3.4   Footnotes in academic texts

When writing an academic text, you should provide evidence for claims made in the text (e.g. 'by longstanding convention dating back to the execution of Anne Boleyn in 1536 all English barristers wear green underwear in court') by providing a footnote in which you cite your sources. In legal writing, these include primary sources such as cases, statutes etc., and secondary sources such as books, journal articles and websites.

Footnotes should be indicated with a superscript number placed after the punctuation in the text. The footnote marker should generally appear at the end of the sentence unless clarity dictates that it should go directly after the word or phrase to which it relates (for instance, if the sentence contains more than one footnote).

When citing articles in footnotes, the following rules apply:

- The names of authors are generally given first, followed by a comma (,). For example, T. B. Rutherford, R. C. Taylor and B. A. Footner.

- Then give the title of the article within single quotation marks. For example, 'The Future of Fossil Fuels'.

- After the title, give publication information in this order: (1) year of publication, in square brackets if it identifies the volume, or in round brackets if there is a separate volume number; (2) the volume number if relevant; (3) the name of the journal in full or abbreviated form; (4) the page number. For example, (2006) 35 Env L Rev. p. 67.

Using this approach produces the following reference: see footnote.[1]

Note

1 T. B. Rutherford, R. C. Taylor and B. A. Footner, 'The Future of Fossil Fuels' (2006) 35 Env L Rev. p. 67.

Standard bibliographical abbreviations

5.3.5

Here is a table listing the standard bibliographical abbreviations that can be used when citing works in footnotes.

Full name	Abbreviation
edition	edn.
editions	edns.
editor	ed.
editors	eds.
et alii, meaning 'and others' (used when referring to a publication to indicate that it has more authors than those named)	et al.
et sequens, meaning 'and the following things' (used to indicate that the cited part extends to the pages following the cited page)	et seq.
footnote	fn.
ibidem, meaning 'in the same place' (used to refer to something mentioned directly above)	ibid.
line	l.
lines	ll.
number	No.
page 35	p. 35
pages 35–43	pp. 35–43
paragraph	para.
paragraphs	paras.
revised/revision	rev.
supra, meaning 'over' or 'above' (used to refer to something mentioned earlier in the text)	supra
translator/translated	trans.
volume	Vol.

For further guidance on citing legal sources, please refer to the Oxford University Standard for Citation of Legal Authorities ('OSCOLA'), which can be found at www.law.ox.ac.uk/published/OSCOLA_4th_edn_Hart_2012.pdf.

5.4 HEADINGS

When capitalising the initial letters of words in headings or titles, the following rules should be followed:

- Capitalise the first letter of every important word in the heading, such as a noun, pronoun, verb, adjective and adverb.

- Capitalise the first letter of the first and last word regardless of what part of speech they are.

- Also capitalise the first letter of any word that follows a colon or dash.

- Put articles (***the***, ***a***, ***an***), conjunctions (e.g. ***and***, ***or***) and prepositions of four or fewer letters (e.g. ***of***, ***by***, ***with***) in lowercase – unless they are the first or last word of the heading or the first word following a colon or dash.

Using this system produces headings that look like this: ***The Treatment of Snake and Spider Bites: A Comprehensive and Practical Manual***.

Terminology and linguistic peculiarities

This chapter covers various types of terminology and linguistic peculiarities that are encountered from time to time when reading legal text. The purpose of covering them here is not to recommend their usage – except in the limited circumstances in which this might be appropriate – but to present them so that they may be recognised and interpreted by the reader.

TERMS OF ART

6.1

Legal English, in common with many other professional languages, employs a great deal of terminology that has a technical meaning and is not generally familiar to the layperson. These are sometimes referred to by lawyers as 'terms of art'.

Examples include **waiver**, **restraint of trade**, **restrictive covenant** and **promissory estoppel**. See the glossary of legal terminology for more information.

FOREIGN TERMINOLOGY

6.2

A number of Latin and French words and phrases (such as **inter alia**, **mutatis mutandis**, **ad hoc** and **force majeure**) are in regular use in legal English. While these should not be overused, a number of them are regarded as indispensable by lawyers because they express a legal idea much more succinctly than could be achieved in English. For example, the phrase **inter alia** is sometimes rendered in English as 'including but not limited to'.

See the glossary of foreign terms used in law at the back of the book for more information.

DOUBLETS AND TRIPLETS

6.3

There is an historical tendency in legal English to string together two or three words to convey what is usually a single legal concept. Examples of this include **null and void**, **fit and proper**, **perform and discharge**, **dispute, controversy or claim**, and **promise, agree and covenant**. These are often called 'doublets' or 'triplets'.

These should be treated with caution because sometimes, for practical purposes, the words used mean exactly the same thing (**null and void**); and sometimes they do not quite do so (**dispute, controversy or claim**).

Modern practice is to avoid such constructions where possible and use single-word equivalents instead. For example, the phrase ***give, devise and bequeath*** could be replaced by the single word ***give*** without serious loss of meaning.

However, the pace of change in legal usage is slow, and as a result it is still quite common to see some typical doublets and triplets in certain legal documents. Some of the most common of these are listed below (with suggested equivalents in brackets).

Able and willing	(= able)
Agree and covenant	(= agree)
All and sundry	(= all)
Authorise and direct	(= authorise OR direct)
Cancelled and set aside	(= cancelled)
Custom and usage	(= custom)
Deem and consider	(= deem)
Do and perform	(= perform)
Due and owing	(= owing)
Fit and proper	(= fit)
Full and complete	(= complete)
Goods and chattels	(= goods)
Keep and maintain	(= maintain)
Known and described as	(= known as)
Legal and valid	(= valid)
Null and void	(= void)
Object and purpose	(= object OR purpose)
Order and direct	(= order)
Over and above	(= exceeding)
Part and parcel	(= part)
Perform and discharge	(= perform OR discharge)
Repair and make good	(= repair)

Sole and exclusive	(= sole OR exclusive)
Terms and conditions	(= terms OR conditions)
Touch and concern	(= concern)
Uphold and support	(= uphold)
Cancel, annul and set aside	(= cancel)
Communicate, indicate or suggest	(= communicate)
Dispute, controversy or claim	(= dispute)
Give, devise and bequeath	(= give)
Hold, possess and enjoy	(= hold)
Pay, satisfy and discharge	(= pay)
Possession, custody and control	(= possession OR custody OR control)
Promise, agree and covenant	(= promise OR agree)
Repair, uphold and maintain	(= repair OR uphold OR maintain)
Way, shape or form	(= way)

HERE-, THERE- AND WHERE- WORDS

6.4

Overview

6.4.1

Words like **hereof**, **thereof** and **whereof** (and further derivatives ending in -**at**, -**in**, -**after**, -**before**, -**with**, -**by**, -**above**, -**on** and -**upon** etc.) are not often used in ordinary English. They are still sometimes used in legal English, primarily as a way of avoiding the repetition of names of things in the document – very often, the name of the document itself.

While it is sometimes thought that the use of such words is dying out even in legal English, a small group of them prove remarkably durable. A quick search using the 'search terms' facility of the Eurlex portal[1] on 3 July 2020 revealed 48,677 appearances of **hereto** in European legislation and case law, 48,403

Note

1 See http://eur-lex.europa.eu

appearances of **_hereinafter_**, 109,203 appearances of **_hereby_** and 258,120 appearances of **_whereas_**.

The large number of appearances of **_whereas_** in this Eurlex search can be explained by reference to convention: this word is typically used to introduce a recital in a contract or legal act (see 10.1.2). However, the popularity of the other words is partly due to slow-moving legal tradition but also partly because they have some practical use – as illustrated below.

6.4.2 Construction

Although at first sight these words may appear very strange indeed, there is a certain logic to their construction. Essentially, they are prepositions and pronouns rolled into one.

For example, take the following sentence:

This contract becomes valid on the date of signature of this contract.

Probably the most striking aspect of the sentence is that the repetition of 'this contract' makes it appear long-winded and rather absurd. This could be avoided with judicious use of **_hereof_**:

This contract becomes valid on the date of signature hereof.

This sentence is shorter and has a weightier feel. What is essentially happening is that the **_here-_** word used retains the preposition **_of_** and replaces **_this contract_** with **_here_**, thus creating economy and removing the need to repeat 'this contract'.

6.4.3 Examples

Here is a non-exhaustive list of some of these words, together with examples of usage.

Hereafter means 'from now on or at some time in the future'. For example, 'the contract is effective hereafter'.

Hereat means (1) 'at this place or point' or (2) 'on account of or after this'. For example, 'hereat the stream divided'.

Hereby means 'by this means; as a result of this'. For example, 'the parties hereby declare'.

Herefrom means 'from this place or point'. For example, 'the goods shall be collected herefrom'.

Herein means 'in this document or matter'. For example, 'the terms referred to herein'.

Hereinabove means 'previously in this document or matter'. For example, 'the products hereinabove described'.

Hereinafter means 'later referred to in this matter or document'. For example, 'hereinafter referred to as the Company'.

Hereinbefore means 'previously in this document or matter'. For example, 'the products hereinbefore described'.

Hereof means 'of this matter or document'. For example, 'the parties hereof'.

Hereto means 'to this place or to this matter or document'. For example, 'the parties hereto'.

Heretofore means 'before now'. For example, 'the parties have had no business dealings heretofore'.

Hereunder means 'later referred to in this matter or document'. For example, 'the exemptions referred to hereunder'.

Herewith means 'with this letter or document'. For example, 'I enclose herewith the plan'.

Thereafter means 'after that time'. For example, 'The products shall be transported to 1 Granger Road. Thereafter, they shall be stored in a warehouse'.

Thereat means (1) 'at that place' or (2) 'on account of or after that'. For example, 'thereat, payments shall cease'.

Thereby means 'by that means; as a result of that'. For example, 'the parties thereby agree'.

Therefor means 'for that'. For example, 'the equipment shall be delivered on 13 September 2020. The Company agrees to pay therefor the sum of $150,000'. Therefor should not be confused with 'therefore', which means 'for that reason'.

Therein means 'in that place, document or respect'. For example, 'The parties shall refer to the contract dated 4 May 2020. It is agreed therein that…'.

Thereinafter means 'later referred to in that matter or document'. For example, 'thereinafter, it is agreed that…'.

Thereof means 'of the thing just mentioned'. For example, 'Reference is made in paragraph 5 to the contract dated 4 May 2020. The parties thereof agreed that…'.

Thereon means 'on or following from the thing just mentioned'. For example, 'The machine rests on a wooden block. There is placed thereon a metal bracket…'.

Thereto means 'to that place or to that matter or document'. For example, 'the parties thereto'.

Thereupon means 'immediately or shortly after that'. For example, 'delivery shall take place on 13 September 2021. Thereupon the equipment shall be stored in the Company's warehouse'.

Whereabouts means 'the place where someone or something is'. For example, 'the Company shall be kept informed as to the whereabouts of the products'.

Whereat means 'at which'. 'The seller attempted to charge extra interest on late payment, whereat the buyer objected'.

Whereby means 'by which'. For example, 'the contract dated 4 May 2020, whereby the Company agreed to purchase the products'.

Wherefore means 'as a result of which'. For example, 'the buyer breached the contract, wherefore the seller suffered damage'.

Wherein means (1) 'in which' or (2) 'in which place or respect'. For example, 'the contract dated 4 May 2020, wherein it is stated that…'.

Whereof means 'of what or of which'. For example, 'the Company one of the directors whereof is a foreign national'.

Whereupon means 'immediately after which'. For example, 'The sum of $15,000 shall be paid by the buyer to the seller on 13 September 2020, whereupon the buyer's liability to the seller shall be discharged'.

6.5 WHATSOEVER, WHERESOEVER AND HOWSOEVER

In addition to the words listed above, you may also encounter the words **whatsoever**, **wheresoever** and **howsoever**. In writing, these have extremely limited practical meaning and exist as a result of legal tradition only. However, in speech they are sometimes used as a means of adding emphasis. For instance:

I asked Clive to help me with the case, but he's done no work on it whatsoever!

These words have the following meanings.

Whatsoever means 'whatever', i.e. 'no matter what' in contractual contexts.

Wheresoever means 'wherever', i.e. 'in or to whatever place' in contractual contexts.

Howsoever means 'however', i.e. 'in whatever way or to whatever extent'.

These words are occasionally used together; for example, in the following sentence:

This limitation shall apply in any situation whatsoever, wheresoever and howsoever arising.

The word **whosoever** may also be encountered. This simply means 'whoever'.

HENCE, WHENCE AND THENCE

The words **hence**, **whence** and **thence**, and the derivatives **henceforth** and **thenceforth**, are all archaic forms in ordinary English that are, however, still occasionally seen in legal English. Their meanings are briefly outlined below.

Hence means (1) for this reason and (2) from now on. **Henceforth** means from this or that time on.

Whence means (1) from what place or source; (2) from which or from where; (3) to the place from which; or (4) as a consequence of which.

Thence means (1) from a place or source previously mentioned and (2) as a consequence.

Thenceforth means from that time, place or point onwards.

-ER, -OR AND -EE NAMES

Legal English contains a large number of names and titles, such as **employer** and **employee**, in which the reciprocal and opposite nature of the relationship is indicated by the use of -**er**/-**or** and -**ee** endings. These endings derive from Latin.

In the example given here, the employer is the one who employs the employee. Hence, the employee is employed by the employer.

Here are some further examples that you may have encountered.

Assignor is a party who assigns (transfers) something to another party.

Assignee is the party to whom something is assigned.

Donor is a party who donates something to another party.

Donee is the party to whom something is donated.

Interviewer is a person who is interviewing someone.

Interviewee is a person who is being interviewed by the interviewer.

Lessor is a party who grants a lease over a property. He or she is therefore the landlord.

Lessee is the party to whom a lease over a property is granted. He or she is therefore the tenant.

Mortgagor is a lender who lends money to a property owner (the mortgagee) in return for the grant by the mortgagee of a mortgage over the property as security for the loan.

Mortgagee is the property owner to whom money is loaned by the mortgagor in return for the grant of a mortgage over the property.

Offeror is a party who makes a contractual offer to another party.

Offeree is the party to whom a contractual offer is made.

Payer is a party who makes a payment to another party.

Payee is the party to whom payment is made.

Promisor is a party who makes a promise to another party.

Promisee is the party to whom a promise is made.

Representor is a party who makes a contractual representation to another party.

Representee is the party to whom a contractual representation is made.

Transferor is a party who transfers something to another party.

Transferee is the party to whom something is transferred.

Note that these words are not always used in the way the examples given above might lead one to expect. For example, a **guarantor** is someone who provides a **guarantee**. However, the person to whom a guarantee is given is known technically as the **principal debtor**, not the guarantee. The guarantee is the document by which the secondary agreement that constitutes the guarantee is made.

6.8   UNFAMILIAR PRONOUNS

Unfamiliar pronouns represent an archaic usage in legal English, and include such formulations as **the same**, **the said**, **the aforementioned**, etc.

The use of such pronouns in legal texts is interesting since very frequently they do not replace the noun – which is the whole purpose of pronouns – but are used to supplement them. For example, **the said John Smith** means the John Smith previously mentioned in the document as opposed to a different John Smith.

6.9   DEEMING

The word **deem** is frequently used in legal English. It is sometimes referred to as denoting a 'legal fiction': it is used to treat a thing as being something that it is not, or as possessing certain characteristics that it does not in fact possess – or that it need not be conclusively demonstrated to possess.

For instance, although it would seem absurd to a layperson, from the point of view of common law drafting practices it would be perfectly acceptable to write in a contract:

In this agreement all references to 'dogs' shall be deemed to be references to cats.

The implication behind this is that the parties to the contract have agreed, for reasons unknown, that it is convenient to refer to cats using the word 'dogs'.

More typically, one might find **deemed** being used in this sort of clause:

Notice shall be deemed served: if sent by email, within 24 hours of dispatch.

The purpose of such a clause is to indicate that the parties to the contract agree that they will regard a notice as having been properly served under the contract if one party has sent it by email and 24 hours have gone by. The advantage of this is that the party who has sent the notice is not also required to prove that the other party has received it – which might be difficult because obtaining such proof would depend on the honesty and goodwill of the other party.

In ordinary language, **deem** is simply an old-fashioned term meaning to consider in a specified way. It is a synonym for think or judge.

ABBREVIATIONS

6.10

There are two kinds of abbreviations. The first kind is the acronym. An acronym is made from the initial letters or parts of a phrase or compound term. It is usually referred to as a single word. For example, **radar** = radio detection and ranging.

The second kind is an initialism, which is made from the initial letters or parts of a phrase or compound term. These are usually referred to letter by letter rather than as a single word, e.g. **USA** = United States of America.

In general, abbreviations that refer to an entity, such as **UK**, **USA**, **NATO**, should be capitalised without dots between the letters.

Abbreviations that are used as grammatical shorthand, such as **e.g.** and **i.e.**, are usually written in lowercase letters with dots between the letters.

Certain terms are referred to in speech as a single word but are capitalised in writing. For example, **NATO** = North Atlantic Treaty Organization.

A list of abbreviations can be found in the glossary of abbreviations at the back of the book.

7 Elements of good style
Clarity, consistency, effectiveness

7.1 GENERAL CONSIDERATIONS

Style in legal writing is, to some extent, a matter of personal preference or company policy. The only unbreakable rules of style in legal documents and letters are that your writing should be as easy to understand as possible and that it should avoid offensive terms.

In addition to drafting letters, emails and other communications, most lawyers also spend a considerable amount of time creating legal documents for a variety of purposes. These may be intended for use either in court proceedings or in non-contentious business such as sales of land, goods or services.

Typical documents prepared by lawyers for use in court include statements of claim, witness statements, divorce petitions, petitions for bankruptcy and affidavits.

Typical documents prepared by lawyers for non-contentious purposes include transfers of land, contracts for sale of goods, articles of association for companies, licences and options.

The style of writing used in legal documents differs from the style used in legal correspondence. This is because the purpose of legal documents is different from that of legal correspondence.

Most legal documents used in court proceedings either act as evidence in support or defence of a claim or make allegations and put forward arguments either in support or defence of a claim. Most legal documents used in non-contentious business generally record an agreement between parties. Such documents are intended primarily to regulate all aspects of the agreement reached between the parties. They lay down the obligations each party must carry out and specify the consequences of failure. They are intended to be legally effective in court. Consequently, the language used in legal documents displays certain typical features that often make them difficult to read. These include:

- Use of terms of art. These are words that have a precise and defined legal meaning. They may not be familiar to the layperson but cannot be replaced by other words.

- Use of defined terms. Many legal documents contain a definitions section in which the parties agree that certain words used repetitively throughout the document shall have an agreed meaning.

- Use of obscure legal phrasing. This can be confusing to the layperson, either simply because the language is unfamiliar, or because the words used have a different meaning in ordinary English.

- Repeated use of the words **shall** and **must** to express obligations, and **may** to express discretions (where the parties are entitled to do something but are not obliged to do it), as well as a number of other words and phrases of similar meaning.

These issues are dealt with in more detail in Chapter 10.

The writing used in legal correspondence usually has a different purpose. It is generally intended to provide information and advice, to put forward proposals and to provide instructions to third parties.

However, all legal writing should aim at achieving three goals – clarity, consistency and effectiveness. The notes set out below show how these goals can be achieved in practice.

CLARITY

7.2

Writing of all kinds should be as easy to understand as possible. The key elements of clarity are:

- Clear thinking. Clarity of writing usually follows clarity of thought.

- Saying what you want to say as simply as possible.

- Saying it in such a way that the people you are writing for will understand it – consider the needs of the reader.

- Keep it as short as possible.

- Write with a clear purpose.

Planning

7.2.1

Start by considering the overall purpose of your document or letter. Before starting to draft a document you need to be sure that you have a clear idea of what the document is supposed to achieve and whether there are any problems that need to be overcome to allow it to be achieved. Ask yourself the following questions:

- What do you want to achieve?

- Have you taken your client's full instructions?

- Do you have all the relevant background information?

- What is your client's main goal or concern?

- What are the main facts that provide the backbone of the document?

- What is the applicable law and how does it affect the drafting?

- Are there any good alternatives for the client? Would it be more effective or cheaper to approach the client's goal in a different way? For example, if it seems that drafting the necessary documentation in English will be too difficult, consider the following options:

  ○ Draft the document in your native language and have it translated and verified.

  ○ Engage the services of a native English-speaking lawyer as a consultant in respect of the case.

  ○ Draft the document as best as you can in English and have a legally qualified English native speaker check and correct the documents.

- Are there any useful **precedents** (generic legal documents on which specific legal documents can be based) that could be used for the draft?

More detailed notes on drafting documents are contained in Chapter 12.

More detailed notes on correspondence are contained in Chapter 13.

7.2.2   Words

Whether writing documents or correspondence, the following guidelines are relevant.

7.2.2.1   Use the words that convey your meaning

Use the words that convey your meaning, and nothing more. Never use words simply because they look impressive and you want to try them out. There is a tendency in legal writing to use unnecessarily obscure words rather than their ordinary equivalents, perhaps out of a feeling that the obscure words are somehow more authoritative. Here are some examples:

Obscure word or phrase	Ordinary equivalent
annex (i.e. a document to another document)	attach
append	attach
cease and desist	stop

conceal	hide
covenant and agree	agree
demise	death
detain	hold, delay
determine (as in **terminate**)	end OR decide (according to context)
donate	give
effectuate	carry out
employ (when not used in connection with labour relations)	use
endeavour	try
evince	show
expedite	hasten
expend	spend
expiration, expiry	end
extend	give
extinguish	end
forthwith	immediately, soon
forward	send
furnish	give, provide
hence	therefore
implement	carry out, fulfil
inaugurate	begin
indicate	state, show, say
initiate	begin
institute	begin
necessitate	require
occasion (as a verb)	cause

peruse	read
possess	have
present	give
prior	earlier
proceed	go (ahead)
quantum	amount
retain	keep
suborn	bribe (e.g. a juror or witness)
subsequently	then, after, later
terminate	end
utilise	use

Examples of obscure words and phrases used in business contracts can be found in the glossaries at the back of the book.

7.2.2.2   Use ordinary English words where possible

Do not use a foreign phrase or jargon if you can think of an ordinary English word that means the same thing. For example, do not write **modus operandi** when you can write **method**, or **de rigueur** when you can write **obligatory**.

In legal English, this is more difficult to achieve in practice than it is in ordinary English, because much of the terminology used (**inter alia**, **ab initio**, **force majeure**, **mutatis mutandis**) comes from French and Latin. As noted above, these often act as shorthand for a longer English phrase. Your choice of vocabulary – between English or French and Latin – will be influenced by who you are writing to or by nature of the document you are writing. A contract, for example, requires a different approach than an email.

7.2.2.3   Avoid negative structures

Avoid negative structures where possible. There is a tendency in much business and legal writing to try to soften the impact of what is being said by using **not un-** (or not **im-**, **il-**, **in-** etc.) formations such as:

- not unreasonable
- not impossible
- not unjustifiable
- not unthinkable
- not negligible
- not insignificant

Such structures make what you are saying less clear and definite. They become very hard to follow when more than one is used within a single sentence, e.g.:

It is not impossible that this matter will have a not inconsiderable bearing upon our decision.

Which, translated into ordinary English, reads:

It is possible that this matter will have a considerable bearing upon our decision.

Sentences

7.2.3

In addition to the notes on sentence structure set out in Chapter 4, bear in mind the following points.

Keep sentences short where possible

7.2.3.1

Use words economically to form your sentences. This does not necessarily mean that every sentence should be short (which might create a displeasing staccato effect) but that all unnecessary words should be removed: this will make your writing much more vigorous.

In particular, pay attention to phrases that introduce new pieces of information or argument. These can often be reduced to single words. Here are some examples:

Commonly used phrase	Single-word equivalent
at the present time	now
be a significant factor in	affect, influence
be in a position to	can, may
be inclined to the view that	think [that]
by dint of	because
give rise to	cause

have a detrimental effect upon	harm
have a tendency to	tend
have an effect upon	affect
have the effect of	(in most contexts) cause
having regard to	concerning
impact upon	affect
in spite of the fact that	despite, although
in the interests of (e.g. saving time)	to (e.g. save time)
in view of	because
it is arguable that	perhaps, maybe
make contact with	contact
meet with	meet
notwithstanding the fact that	despite, although
the fact that	delete phrase – replacement word usually unnecessary
turning now to the question of	concerning, regarding
with regard to the question of	concerning, regarding

7.2.3.2 Take care with *which*

Which is a useful word, but is frequently used unnecessarily, usually involving further unnecessary verbiage. For example, the sentence:

These situations are governed by agreements, which are made between different entities and which are complicated.

may be reduced to:

These situations are governed by complicated agreements between different entities.

Use pronouns where possible

The use of pronouns avoids repetition of nouns, which is useful particularly where lengthy noun phrases (such as the names of documents or laws) are involved. For instance, try to avoid writing sentences like this:

The 2020 Terms and Conditions for the Provision of Services within the Metalwork and Woodwork Sectors are now in force. The 2020 Terms and Conditions for the Provision of Services within the Metalwork and Woodwork Sectors replace the large number of different agreements previously used.

Write instead:

The 2020 Terms and Conditions for the Provision of Services within the Metalwork and Woodwork Sectors are now in force. They replace the large number of different agreements previously used.

Or, even better:

The 2020 Terms and Conditions for the Provision of Services within the Metalwork and Woodwork Sectors are now in force and replace the large number of different agreements previously used.

However, as discussed in Chapter 8, one of the most common reasons for ambiguity in a text is where a sentence contains two or more nouns along with one pronoun in such a way that it becomes unclear which noun the pronoun is intended to replace. For this reason, only use a pronoun when it is crystal clear to what it relates.

One main idea per sentence

Try to have only one main idea per sentence. Where you want to add more than one piece of additional information about a subject introduced in a sentence, consider starting a new sentence. Always start with the most important piece of information, then deal with lesser matters, qualifications or exceptions.

For example, the sentence:

Unless the order is for the goods described in Appendix 3, X shall deliver the goods to Y within 7 days.

would be better written as follows:

X shall deliver the goods to Y within 7 days of an order being received, unless the order is for the goods described in Appendix 3.

And this sentence:

The company, the headquarters of which are in Oxford, specialises in pharmaceutical products and made a record profit last year.

would be better split up as follows:

The company specialises in pharmaceutical products. Its headquarters are in Oxford, and it made a record profit last year.

7.2.3.5   Use positive phrases where possible

A positive phrase is usually better than a negative one. For example, 'Clause 2 shall apply only if…' is clearer than 'Clause 2 shall not apply unless…'.

However, restrictions are often difficult to express in the positive rather than the negative without either:

● Changing the meaning ('A shall not sell goods except those made by B' is a restriction whereas 'A shall sell goods made by B' is a positive obligation and therefore fundamentally different); or

● Using indirect language ('A may build anything except a house' is less direct than saying 'A may not build a house').

In these cases, therefore, the negative forms should be used. In other cases, they should be avoided.

7.2.3.6   Problematic long sentences

Here are three types of long sentence that are actually problematic, as opposed to merely undesirable, together with examples and solutions:

1 Sentences that introduce complex criteria. The problem here is usually that the nature of the criteria and the identities of the parties to which they apply are not made sufficiently clear.

Example:

Manufacturers involved in sector-specific activities involving the products listed in Annex II and distributors involved in the distribution of such products shall, where the Controlling Authority has classified such products as hazardous or in circumstances where advance notification to the Controlling Authority is impracticable or where secured vehicles are not available, refrain from transporting the products by road.

Here is one solution, which involves enumerating each individual criterion so that it completes the 'springboard' sentence:

Manufacturers involved in sector-specific activities involving the products listed in Annex II and distributors involved in their distribution may not transport such products by road if:

> *the Controlling Authority has classified such products as hazardous; or*
>
> *advance notification to the Controlling Authority is impracticable; or*
>
> *secured vehicles are not available.*

2 Sentences whose length and construction lead to an unclear relation between their subjects, verbs and objects.

Example:

Jane Tapley, a banking lawyer, attended a conference with three of her colleagues with four representatives of X Bank's Frankfurt branch in Frankfurt on 13 January 2020, the purpose of which was to discuss the composition of their audit committee.

The solution set out below involves using full stops to create separate sentences, thus clarifying the relationships between the subjects, verbs and objects in play:

Jane Tapley is a banking lawyer. On 13 January 2020 she attended a conference in Frankfurt with four representatives of X Bank's Frankfurt branch. The purpose of this conference, which was also attended by three of Ms Tapley's colleagues, was to discuss the composition of the bank's audit committee.

As a rule of thumb, it is often possible to split sentences at the point where a conjunction (e.g. *and*, *but*, *as well as*) or a relative pronoun (e.g. *who, which, whose*) appears.

3 Sentences that contain a proposition that is qualified by an exception, which is in turn qualified by a further exception. Even short sentences of this kind can be very hard to follow.

Example:

All transfers must be approved by the Ministry, except where they concern sums in an amount less than EUR 1 million save as to transfers to credit institutions located outside the jurisdiction of Ruritania.

Here is a solution that involves (1) recasting the nature of the proposition so that it encapsulates the first condition, and (2) use of a discourse marker (see section 7.2.7 for a discussion of discourse markers):

Transfers to credit institutions located within the jurisdiction of Ruritania must be approved by the Ministry unless each transfer involves sums in an amount of less than EUR 1 million. However, all transfers in any amount to credit institutions located outside the jurisdiction of Ruritania must be approved by the Ministry.

7.2.4   Paragraphs

Paragraphs should not be defined by length. They are best treated as units of thought. In other words, each paragraph should deal with a single thought or topic. Start a new paragraph when shifting to a new thought or topic.

Paragraphs should start with the main idea, and then deal with subordinate matters. The writing should move logically from one idea to the next. It should not dance about randomly between different ideas.

Single-sentence paragraphs should not be used too often but can be useful when drawing attention to a new issue or to make a pithy conclusion to a discussion.

Pay attention to the way the paragraphs look on the page. Text evenly divided into manageably sized paragraphs, with occasional shorter ones, looks inviting to the reader. Huge, unbroken sections of text are very off-putting to the reader and should be avoided, as should untidy sequences of very short paragraphs.

7.2.5   Vigour

As a general rule, as noted above, the fewer the words you can use to convey your meaning, the more vigorous your writing will be. Every time you write something, look back at it and think how many words you can cut out. Then do it. You will probably be surprised by the number of unnecessary words that creep into your writing.

For instance, consider this innocuous-looking sentence:

He successfully passed the test.

The word **successfully** can be cut, because it is impossible to pass a test unsuccessfully.

Certain other issues are relevant when trying to write vigorously. Here are some of them.

7.2.5.1   Use active verbs where possible

Use active verbs rather than nominalisations where possible. Nominalisations are produced when verbs are buried in longer nouns. They usually end with one of the following: *-tion*, *-sion*, *-ment*, *-ence*, *-ance* and *-ity*. Anglo-American lawyers are addicted to them. They should usually be avoided because they make writing longer and less dynamic.

Common examples include **give consideration to** instead of **consider**, **to be in opposition to** instead of **to oppose** and **to be in contravention of** instead of **to contravene**.

Here is an example of a sentence in which the verbs have become nouns:

It is important to effect a reduction of operating costs during the implementation of the agreement.

It's quite boring to read, isn't it?

However, by converting **reduction** and **implementation** into verbs, the sentence could be rewritten as follows:

It is important to reduce operating costs when implementing the agreement.

Which is an improvement.

However, there are certain occasions in legal writing when it is preferable to use nominalisations. For example, lawyers don't agree to **arbitrate** but to submit to **arbitration**: arbitration is a defined legal process and should be referred to in its nominalised form.

Here are some examples of commonly used nominalisations and their active verb equivalents.

Nominalisation	Active verb equivalent
agreement	agree
arbitration	arbitrate
arrangement	arrange
compulsion	compel
conformity	conform
contravention	contravene
enablement	enable
enforcement	enforce
identity	identify
implementation	implement
incorporation	incorporate
indemnification	indemnify

indication	indicate
knowledge	know
litigation	litigate
mediation	mediate
meeting	meet
negotiation	negotiate
obligation	obligate, oblige
opposition	oppose
ownership	own
perpetration	perpetrate
perpetuation	perpetuate
possession	possess
reduction	reduce
violation	violate

7.2.5.2   Use short words where possible

Try to avoid using a long word where a short one can be used. For example, avoid words like **notwithstanding** where simple words like **despite**, **still** or **even if** can be used instead.

Never use a phrase where you can use one short word. There is a creeping tendency to include unnecessary phrases like **with regard to**, **with respect to**, **in reference to** and so on (see table at section 7.2.3.1).

However, this rule is modified by the need to use (1) terms of art, and (2) defined terms properly – and these may be quite long or consist of a number of words strung together.

7.2.6   Precision

Use precise language and terminology. This means two things: choosing your words carefully and avoiding ambiguity. Refer to the guidance on the use of words above and the notes on avoiding ambiguity at 8.1 for further information on these topics.

Discourse markers

'Discourse markers' show how different ideas interrelate. They are basically signposts for the reader: they appear (usually) at the beginning of sentences and tell the reader how to view what follows. They provide an essential means of orientating the reader and assisting his or her comprehension of the text.

In practice, since there are only a limited number of language functions that are typically required in legal discourse, a small handful of words and phrases will cover most situations that a lawyer might expect to encounter in the course of daily working life.

Here are some examples:

1 ***In the event that*** *a trademark owner wishes to allow others to use the trademark, he or she must inform the Registrar.*

   Here, the opening phrase 'in the event that' indicates to the reader that what follows is a hypothesis. The word 'if' could also be used to the same effect.

2 *Where trademark infringement occurs, the owner of the trademark has the right to sue.* ***However****, a trademark may be lost if it is no longer distinctive.*

   Here, the opening word of the second sentence – **however** – indicates a qualification to the previous statement.

3 ***Of course****, if information is already in the public domain, it will no longer be regarded as confidential.*

   The opening phrase ***of course*** in this sentence indicates an assumption. The writer uses this technique to indicate to the reader that the idea conveyed in the rest of the sentence is generally accepted. Words such as ***naturally****,* ***clearly****,* ***obviously*** and ***undoubtedly*** may be used for the same purpose in this context.

   While the example given above shows correct usage of ***of course*** (the proposition stated is true), it is worth noting that lawyers sometimes use ***of course*** and its synonyms in a dubious manner to create the impression that what they are about to say is incontestably true when perhaps it is not. For example:

   Of course, your client's actions represent a clear violation of our client's rights under section 4.

By extension, whenever any discourse marker is used for any purpose one should ask oneself whether it genuinely fulfils that purpose in the wider context or whether the writer is simply trying to persuade the reader that it does.

4 ***Therefore***, *in such circumstances a confidentiality agreement covering such information will be ineffective.*

In this sentence, the opening word **therefore** indicates a logical step or deduction based on the information provided in the previous sentence.

The table below sets out some of the more common functions for which discourse markers are used (on the left) and some suggested words or phrases for those functions (on the right).

Function	Suggested word or phrase
Anticipating, acknowledging	We accept that, we do not contest that
Referring to the past	formerly, previously
Expanding on a point	besides, furthermore
Contrasting	on the other hand, conversely
Summarising	in short, in summary, by way of précis
Drawing a conclusion or inference	as a consequence, consequently, as a result
Drawing a parallel	likewise, similarly
Giving an example	for instance, for example
Emphasising	in particular, especially, it should be stressed that
Qualifying	however, it should also be borne in mind that, having said that
Making a logical step in the argument	therefore, thus, it follows that in particular
Beginning	firstly, to begin with
Making an assumption	of course, naturally, clearly, evidently
Referring to a new issue	turning to, with reference to, with respect to, with regard to, regarding
Hypothesising	in the event that, if
Bearing a factor in mind	given that, bearing in mind that, considering that
Stating an exemption	except, with the exception of, save for, save as to

Presentation

Pay attention to the layout of the document. It is a shame to write excellent English but present it badly on paper or on the screen. Here are some suggestions:

- Use a clearly legible font in an appropriate size (generally between 10 and 12 points, with 12 being standard).
- Use between 45 and 70 characters per line.
- Use plenty of white space – break up slabs of text, use wide margins around the text, and use appropriate line spacing (e.g. 1.5).
- Use headings to structure the text.
- Use italics rather than underlining to emphasise text.
- Use correctly indented lists where appropriate.
- Avoid excessive capitalisation.
- Be careful when copy-and-pasting between different formats. For instance, text which looks fine in a PDF document may transform itself into a chaotic mess (by losing its formatting) when transferred into an email or a Word document.

Clarity summary

These considerations will help focus your mind on writing well.

- When starting to write a letter or document, ask yourself:
  - What am I trying to say?
  - What words will express it?
  - Could I make it shorter?
- Keep sentences as short as possible. If you can cut words out without affecting the meaning of the sentence, do it. For example, try writing 'although' instead of 'in spite of the fact that'.
- Try to have only one main idea per sentence.
- Paragraphs should start with the main idea, then deal with subordinate matters.
- The writing should move logically from one idea to the next.
- Avoid negative structures. For example, 'not unreasonable' should be simply 'reasonable'.
- Use precise language and terminology. Avoid ambiguity.

- Use active verbs rather than nominalisations. For example, do not write 'we are in opposition to that idea'. Write 'we oppose that idea' instead.

- Never use a long word where a short one can be used. For example, avoid words like 'notwithstanding' where simple words like 'despite', 'still' or 'even if' can be used instead.

- Do not use a foreign phrase or jargon if you can think of an ordinary English word that means the same thing. For example, do not write *modus operandi* when you can write *method*.

- Use terms of art with care. Differentiate between terms of art and jargon. **On all fours** can be replaced with other words, but **bailment** and *patent* cannot.

- Try to produce text that looks as if it has been written by a human being. Break any of the rules above if necessary to achieve this aim.

7.3 CONSISTENCY

7.3.1 Synonyms

Legal English is full of synonyms. It is therefore all too easy to start writing about something using certain words, and then later on in the document or letter start using other words to describe it. This can lead to lack of clarity or to ambiguity. It is crucial to be consistent in your use of terminology.

For example, if you start off with **buyer** and **seller**, do not start using **vendor** and **purchaser** later in the document. Never mix parts of different pairs: e.g. **landlord** and **lessee**, **vendor** and **buyer**.

7.3.1.1 Example of mixed terminology

Here is an example of a sentence that mixes terminology:

The defendant has in its response to the claimant's letter informing said company of the patent implied that it would not consider the plaintiff's patent rights valid.

In this sentence, it appears that four parties are mentioned: the defendant, the claimant, the 'said company' and the plaintiff. However, on close reading it becomes clear that the defendant and the 'said company' are the same thing, as are the plaintiff and the claimant.

The meaning of the sentence is further obscured by dubious syntax that makes it difficult to grasp which of the parties is doing the 'informing' mentioned in the sentence and which is doing the 'implying' mentioned after the word 'patent'.

The sentence can be clarified by making the terminology consistent and by rearranging the syntax in order to connect the verbs with their subject:

In its response to the claimant's letter informing it of the patent, the defendant implied that it would not consider the claimant's patent rights valid.

A list of commonly used near-synonyms   7.3.1.2

Here are some examples of commonly used near-synonyms for legal concepts used in legal documents. There are subtle differences in meaning or usage between them.

- **Assign** is mostly used in relation to intangible property, such as rights under a contract. It may also be used in relation to tasks or duties (e.g. 'the task of drafting the statement was assigned to Mary'). The word **transfer** is generally used in relation to tangible property, such as land and other physical items, or to the sale of the assets of a company.

- **Breach** is used in relation to contractual violations, while **infringement** is used in relation to the violation of rights (particularly intellectual property rights). **Violation** is used in relation both to rights (particularly human rights) and contracts.

- **Clause** is frequently used in relation to specific contracts, while **article** is more often used in EU legislation and overarching or framework agreements/terms and conditions.

- **Contract** is generally used in relation to a specific written contract with legal effect, while **agreement** may also be used in a more general sense to refer to loose understandings or oral agreements (which may or may not have legal effect).

- **Landlord** and **tenant** are used in relation only to the lease of real estate, while **lessor** and **lessee** may also be used in relation to the lease of other types of property (e.g. machinery or vehicles).

- **Liability** and **obligation** – and their verb forms **liable** and **oblige** or **obligate** – are very hard to separate, but in essence **obligation** is generally used to refer to a specific duty under a contract or legal provision. For example, 'X is obligated to deliver the goods to Y'. On the other hand, **liability** generally refers to legal consequences. For example, 'If Y fails to pay the invoices as they fall due, Y shall become liable to pay penalty interest on the outstanding amount at a rate of 10% per annum'.

In a nutshell, breach of an obligation may lead to legal liability.

- **Undertake** is generally used to indicate a commitment to do a certain thing and to accept the legal consequences of doing so ('X undertakes to deliver the goods to Y by 5 June'), while **assurance** refers to a collateral promise given by a third party.

- **Void** and **invalid** mean that something is not legally binding and has no legal effect, while **ineffective** can be used to refer to something that fails to achieve the required legal aim.

7.3.2   Defined terms

The problems caused by the difficulties in choosing and adhering to the most appropriate term can be dealt with in part by using defined terms. However, defining too many terms can be counter-productive, especially if the matters to which the definitions refer only appear once or twice. A definition is only needed if the meaning of the word or phrase is unclear and cannot be ascertained from the context.

When creating a definition, ensure:

1 that it has a clear and specific meaning and is not therefore open to divergent interpretation;

2 that its meaning is not, however, too narrow in scope, as this can lead to absurd or unintended meanings in certain contexts;

3 that it is used in the same sense throughout the document as that provided by the original definition; and

4 that it does not include an obligation (see the discussion on separating obligations from definitions at 12.2.3).

The dangers of putting in too many definitions can be summarised as follows:

- The document becomes more difficult to read and use.

- Creating and amending the document is more difficult: the author is more likely to make mistakes.

- Over-rigid definition of the meaning of certain words may lead to absurd or unintended conclusions.

- Over-defining can be self-defeating: often the attempt to include everything leads to something important being left out. A court might then take the view that the omission must have been deliberate (in the light of the fact that everything else in the contract is rigidly defined). As a result, the use of definitions can actually lead to loopholes in the document.

As a general rule:

- If a definition is only going to be used once, it should be omitted altogether.

- If it is only going to be used within a single paragraph, article or clause, only define it in that paragraph, article or clause.

- If it's going to be used throughout the text, define it in a definitions clause near the beginning of the text.

EFFECTIVENESS   7.4

When drafting legal documents or letters, clarity and consistency are worth nothing if the document is not actually legally effective.

Effectiveness checklist   7.4.1

The following checklist will help focus your mind on how to achieve legal effectiveness and relates particularly to the drafting of legal documents such as contracts.

1 Does the language you use correctly state a condition, obligation, authorisation or limitation? See section 12.1.

2 Does it state it in such a way that it is clear to whom or what it relates? A key point here is to avoid the passive – i.e. do not write **a meeting must be called if**…, but '**the Managing Director must call a meeting if**…'.

3 Does it state it in such a way that it is enforceable (1) under the terms of the document itself, and (2) by reference to the law that governs the document?

4 Have you set clear time limits for the performance of any obligation?

5 Is it in conflict with any other terms of the document?

6 Does the document clearly state what will happen in the case of breach of any obligation? It is important to define the nature of the innocent party's rights and the nature of the penalty that will be imposed on the breaching party.

7 Are the obligations, authorisations, conditions and discretions actually capable of being exercised in practice? A key point here is to be careful with precedent legal documents – if used, they must be adapted rigorously to the deal in hand.

8 Is it precise enough? In particular, set clear timeframes rather than using words like ***forthwith***; specify precise standards rather than using formulations like ***to a reasonable standard***; state enforceable obligations rather than using formulations like ***use their best endeavours to***, etc.

7.4.2   Beware of adjectives

Adjectives should be used with great care, particularly in legal documents. The reason for this is that their meaning can vary greatly according to the context and the writer's intention. They do this to a markedly greater extent than occurs with nouns and verbs, the meaning of which is usually reasonably well fixed. Consider the following typical legal phrases, paying particular attention to the adjectives shown in bold:

- *The Company is entitled to make such changes as it considers* **necessary** *and* **prudent***.*

- *In the event of default, the agreement shall be terminated* **forthwith***.*

- *The Distributor shall* **promptly** *return all documents upon* **reasonable** *request by the Company.*

- *The Company must deliver goods of* **satisfactory** *quality, and must replace all* **defective** *parts free of charge.*

It can be seen that the general effect of using these adjectives is to make the meaning of the sentences less precise. When is a change 'necessary'? How soon is 'forthwith'? How quickly is 'promptly'? When is quality 'satisfactory'? It may be that these words have defined meanings in the law on which the relevant document is based or in the sector to which the document relates – but this is a matter that needs to be verified. Lack of clarity on such issues may lead to unnecessary disputes between the contracting parties.

Consequently, when drafting a document in which obligations need to be precisely specified, adjectives should be avoided where possible. Instead of writing that changes may be made when 'necessary' or 'prudent', define the circumstances in which changes may be made. Instead of using words like 'forthwith' or 'promptly', specify exact time limits. Instead of stipulating that goods must be of 'satisfactory' quality, provide a detailed quality specification. In addition, consider the use of defined terms to fix the meaning of any words that might otherwise have an ambiguous or indeterminate meaning.

However, as discussed at 7.3.2, in some cases attempts to define everything narrowly may be undesirable or self-defeating. The use of adjectives can be useful where the parties wish to create some leeway in the interpretation of obligations, or where it is not essential – or feasible – to define every obligation in detail. For this reason, adjectives are useful in framework agreements where the precise nature of specific obligations will be defined in further agreements made in relation to a particular transaction. In such cases it is important to have a clear understanding of how a particular adjective might be construed by the courts.

Finally, never use any word unless you are sure (1) that you know all its possible legal meanings, and (2) that it can only have one meaning in the context in which you have used it.

EXAMPLES OF BAD STYLE AND ANALYSIS   7.5

Here are some examples of bad style, together with analyses of what is wrong with them and suggested solutions.

Example 1: waiver   7.5.1

Text   7.5.1.1

In the event that there is a waiver of the indemnity provisions by the vendor, a letter confirming the waiver must be produced by the vendor's solicitor for the purpose of inspection by the purchaser.

Problems   7.5.1.2

This sentence is too long for its content. Its meaning should be capable of being understood at a single glance, but this is not the case. The main problems are (1) that the wordiness of the sentence obscures its meaning, and (2) that it contains unnecessary stipulations.

Solution   7.5.1.3

The following changes should be made:

1 Reduce phrases to words: 'in the event that' can be reduced to 'if'.

2 Change nominalisations to verbs: 'waiver' can be changed to 'waive'. This allows us to get rid of 'there is a waiver of' and replaces it with 'waives'.

3 Correct the structure of the sentence. As currently drafted, the order of the sentence is verb (waive) – object (indemnity provisions) – subject (the vendor). In order to create a subject-verb-object structure, 'vendor' should be mentioned first.

4 Remove the unnecessary stipulations. The phrase 'for the purpose of inspection by' is unnecessary, since it can be assumed that the purchaser will read the letter. The phrase 'a letter confirming the waiver must be produced' can be changed to the shorter and more familiar term 'confirmed in writing'.

7.5.1.4   Redrafted version

If the vendor waives the indemnity provisions, this must be confirmed in writing to the purchaser by the vendor's solicitor.

7.5.2   Example 2: settlement

7.5.2.1   Text

The first case was settled for £200,000, the second piece of litigation was disposed of out of court for £239,500, while the price of the agreement reached in the third suit was £55,500.

7.5.2.2   Problems

This sentence is too long and contains inconsistent terminology ('settled', 'disposed of out of court' and 'price of the agreement', as well as 'case', 'piece of litigation' and 'suit') to describe the same things.

7.5.2.3   Solution

The following changes should be made:

1   In all three cases, the term 'settled' should be used to indicate that agreement was reached between the parties without the need for a full court hearing.

2   In all three cases, the term 'case' should be used to refer to the dispute between the parties.

3   The sentence should be phrased so that 'settled' is used as a verb applying to all three cases.

7.5.2.4   Redrafted version

The first case was settled for £200,000, the second for £239,500 and the third for £55,500.

7.5.3   Example 3: exclusion clause

7.5.3.1   Text

The exclusion clause is already null and void by reason of the prior order and direction of the court. This being the case, the exclusionary clause can have no further force or effect.

Problems

The problems here are (1) repetition between the two sentences, and (2) unnecessary words.

Solution

The following changes should be made:

1   The second sentence adds nothing to the meaning of the whole and should be deleted.

2   The phrases 'null and void' and 'order and direction' can be shortened to 'void' and 'order', respectively, since in both cases the additional words add nothing to the meaning.

3   The phrase 'by reason of' should be changed to a less pretentious equivalent, such as 'due to' or 'as a result of', and 'order of the court' can be shortened to 'court order'.

Redrafted version

The exclusion clause is already void due to the prior court order.

Example 4: offer of settlement

Text

My client is willing to settle this case for £75,500, to be paid to your client, and your client must immediately return the blueprints and specifications and must remove all his equipment from the property. Moreover, my client insists upon having replacement of the entire section of fence that your client took down, the replacement to be at your client's expense.

Problems

This is an offer to settle a case on specified terms. The main problem here is that the precise nature of the terms is not set out in a clear way.

Solution

The following changes should be made:

1   A form of tabulation should be introduced so that the terms of the offer are clearly delineated.

2 Unnecessary and repetitive wording (such as 'moreover', 'insists' etc.) should be removed.

3 Nominalisations (i.e. 'having replacement of') should be changed to active verbs.

7.5.4.4   **Redrafted version**

My client is prepared to settle this case for £75,500, provided that your client:

> *returns the blueprints and specifications;*

> *removes all his equipment from the property; and*

> *replaces at his own expense the entire section of fence he took down.*

7.5.5   **Example 5: personal injury**

7.5.5.1   **Text**

Mr Brown hit the windscreen of the car with his head, but as it was composed of celluloid, he was unhurt.

7.5.5.2   **Problems**

The only problem with this sentence is that it is unclear whether it is Mr Brown's head or the windscreen that is composed of celluloid.

7.5.5.3   **Solution**

In order to remove the ambiguity in the sentence, we must clarify that it is the windscreen that is composed of celluloid. This can be done by replacing 'it' with 'windscreen'.

7.5.5.4   **Redrafted version**

Mr Brown hit the windscreen of the car with his head, but as the windscreen was composed of celluloid, he was unhurt.

What to avoid

AMBIGUITY

Ambiguity occurs when writing can be interpreted to mean more than one thing, and these things are in conflict with each other.

Ambiguity should be distinguished from vagueness, which arises when a certain piece of text is not certain or precise in meaning. While ambiguity is almost always undesirable in legal drafting, a degree of vagueness can be permissible and even helpful in certain circumstances. First, the use of less than precise wording may offer a useful means of overcoming disagreement between the parties to an agreement over the scope of the provision at issue. Second, attempting to draft at a too detailed level can result in accidental omission of something that should have been covered.

In ordinary English usage, a conflict of meaning may not be fatal if one meaning seems more likely than another. However, in legal English, especially in contract-drafting, it can be disastrous. A key reason for this is the literalist approach taken by common law lawyers to the interpretation of legal text, which means that words and phrases are interpreted by reference to their literal meaning rather than according to the purpose and effect that may be assumed from the wider context in which they appear. In the worst-case scenario, a slightly misplaced comma may end up costing thousands of dollars.

There are many reasons why ambiguity occurs, but here are some of the main offenders:

1 Use of a word that has more than one meaning in the context.

Many English words have a number of different meanings depending on the context in which they are used. This is a natural feature of the language. Take, for example, the word ***following*** in these sentences:

*Please refer to the **following** paragraph.*

AND

*There is a car **following** us.*

It can be seen that the meaning of the word is very different in each sentence. However, this is not a problem because the context tells us which meaning applies. In the first sentence, the 'following paragraph' means the next paragraph. In the second sentence, 'a car following' means a car in pursuit (i.e. behind 'us').

Sometimes, however, the context does not clearly indicate which meaning applies. Consider this piece of legal verbiage:

Even if the company sells the product, if it does not usually sell this particular product in the usual course of business it may not be held liable.

The problem here is **may**, which either refers to a possibility (e.g. 'I may read those documents this afternoon, or I may not. It depends on how long the court hearing takes') or to an entitlement (e.g. 'The purchaser may inspect the goods at the seller's warehouse'). So, depending on how one reads this sentence, it either means that there is a possibility that the company will not be held liable or that there is no entitlement to hold it liable. Neither of these options makes perfect sense and each is in conflict with the other.

The solution is to turn **may not** into **cannot**. Thus:

Even if the company sells the product, if it does not usually sell this particular product in the usual course of business it cannot be held liable.

2 Unclear pronoun reference.

The use of pronouns is an excellent way to avoid clumsy repetition of nouns, but this technique can result in confusion if carelessly handled. For example:

John drafted the contract for the client during the meeting itself and he then read it through carefully.

The problem here is that since we don't know the gender of the client, the 'he' referred to in the sentence may either be John or the client.

The key issue, obviously, is to ensure that it is clear which noun each pronoun is supposed to replace. If there is a possibility of doubt, use a proper noun instead. For example:

John drafted the contract for the client during the meeting itself and the client then read it through carefully.

3 Poor punctuation.

Punctuation can have a drastic impact on the meaning of a sentence. Consider these two sentences:

The judge said the accused was the most evil man he had ever encountered.

AND

The judge, said the accused, was the most evil man he had ever encountered.

In the unpunctuated sentence above, the word order dictates the natural subject–object relationship. The judge is the subject of the sentence. The use of punctuation changes this around to create a radically different meaning.

The point to bear in mind is that punctuation is not just window-dressing used to make sentences look tidy. In many cases it can dictate the meaning of the sentence – and should therefore be used with great care.

4 Separation of parts of a verb phrase.

The meaning of English sentences can in many cases be changed completely by altering the word order. For example:

My client has discussed your proposal to fill the drainage ditch with her partners.

This sentence probably means that the client has discussed with her partners the proposal to fill the drainage ditch – but it is capable of being interpreted to mean that the client is considering throwing her partners into the drainage ditch.

The ambiguity in this sentence is caused by the separation of the verb phrase 'discussed with' from its object ('her partners'). By reuniting these parts of the whole phrase, the real meaning of the sentence becomes clear:

My client has discussed with her partners your proposal to fill the drainage ditch.

5 Dangling participles.

A participle is a word formed from a verb that has some of the characteristics of an adjective. In the present tense, they always end in **-ing**. It should not be left 'dangling' as it is in the following sentence:

Drafting the contract, the assignment clause became unusually problematic.

The problem here is that because 'drafting' is not securely connected to anything else in the sentence, it appears that the assignment clause must be drafting the contract. This is obviously ridiculous. The problem can be resolved by introducing a subject:

When Laurence was drafting the contract, the assignment clause became unusually problematic.

6 Incorrect placement of noun modifiers.

In this context, a modifier denotes a word or phrase that clarifies the meaning of another word or phrase. For example, in the phrase **complicated sales agreements** the modifier is 'complicated' and the noun is 'sales agreements'.

Problems arise when a sentence contains more than one modifier or noun and it is unclear how these relate to one another. Here is an example involving two nouns and one modifier:

complicated sales agreements and litigation

The question that arises here is whether the litigation is also complicated.

Furthermore, it is now not so clear that 'sales' is strictly part of the noun, since it could also modify 'litigation'. Therefore, in order to clarify the phrase, we need first to decide whether 'complicated' and 'sales' modify both 'agreements' and 'litigation' (and if so, also clarify the nature of the connection, if any, between the agreements and the litigation) or only 'agreements', and then adopt one of the following solutions:

1 Both nouns modified:

complicated sales agreements and ensuing litigation

OR

complicated sales agreements and complicated sales litigation

2 'Sales agreement' modified only:

complicated sales agreements, and litigation

8.2 SEXIST LANGUAGE

8.2.1 Personal pronouns

It is inappropriate in modern legal and business English to use the personal pronouns **he** or **his** or **she** or **her** to refer to a hypothetical person whose sex might be either male or female – for example, one introduced by a genderless title (e.g. **the buyer**, **the manager**, **the lawyer**).

To some extent this problem can be avoided by using one or more of the gender-neutral pronouns and adjectives set out below:

- any
- anybody
- anyone
- each
- every
- everybody
- nobody

- none
- no one
- some
- somebody
- someone

However, these words do not get us terribly far. The main problem is that English, unlike a number of other languages, has no gender-neutral singular personal pronouns (except **one**, which is too formal and abstract for most situations encountered in practice).

A good workaround is to use the plural possessive form **their** even when writing about a single person. Although this is not strictly logical, the **Oxford English Dictionary** permits the use of this form as 'belonging or associated with a person whose sex is not specified'.

In this way, the writer can avoid using sexist language. For example, instead of writing:

Every competent lawyer must ensure that his legal knowledge is kept up to date.

Write instead:

Every competent lawyer must ensure that their legal knowledge is kept up to date.

Other methods can also be employed to avoid using **he** or **his**. These include:

- Deleting the pronoun reference altogether if possible. For example, 'the nominated delegate must sign the document as soon as it is delivered to him': delete **to him**.

- Changing the pronoun to an article like **a** or **the**. For example, 'the lawyer's task is to assist the client with his case' can be changed to 'the lawyer's task is to assist the client with the case'.

- Using **who**, especially when **he** follows **if**. For example, 'if he does not pay attention to detail, a finance officer is worse than useless' can be changed to: 'the finance officer who does not pay attention to detail is worse than useless'.

- Repeating the noun instead of using a pronoun. For example, 'When considering the conduct of negotiations, the delegate should retain an objective view. In particular, he [insert **the delegate**] should…'.

- Use the plural form of the noun. For example, instead of writing 'a lawyer must check that he has all the relevant papers before attending court', write 'lawyers must check that they have all the relevant papers before attending court'.

- Use the infinitive form of the verb, including 'to' (e.g. 'to perform', 'to draft' etc.). For example, instead of writing 'the lawyer agrees that he will draft the contract', write 'the lawyer agrees to draft the contract'.

- Use a combination of the techniques above. In particular, the plural and a relative pronoun can be successfully combined to change a sentence like 'if a client does not pay his invoices, he cannot expect the lawyer to carry out further work for him' to 'clients who do not pay their invoices cannot expect their lawyers to carry out further work for them'.

- If all else fails, use the passive form. For example, instead of writing 'he must deliver the files to X', write 'the files must be delivered to X'. However, note that this is not a perfect solution, since the passive form makes it unclear who is responsible for delivering the files to X. Therefore, it should only be used if the identity of the parties has already been established in a previous sentence, or if it is not necessary or important to attribute responsibility for undertaking the actions to a particular person or persons.

8.2.2 Terminology

In addition to paying attention to the use of personal pronouns, it is also important to ensure as far as possible that the terminology used is not gender specific. This applies particularly to words ending in -**man**. For example, consider using **chair** instead of **chairman**, **firefighter** instead of **fireman** and **drafter** instead of **draftsman**.

It should be remembered, however, that there is a limit to the extent to which the English language can reasonably be manipulated to remove all possible traces of gender discrimination. There is a balance to be struck between avoiding the use of gender-specific language and making your English sound like normal language. Another way of looking at this is that while the English language is in a state of constant development that reflects broader changes in the world and in attitudes, getting too far ahead of the arc of change may result in linguistic usage that seems artificial and unfamiliar. This will particularly be the case if, in retrospect, it becomes clear that the arc of change drifted off its anticipated trajectory (leaving behind it a fast-melting residue of hastily discarded neologisms).

Equally, avoiding gender-specific language in English writing by carefully avoiding certain words and phrases is only one aspect of gender equality. Changing underlying attitudes is, arguably, the more important issue.

A particular problem arises in respect of words for which the only gender-neutral equivalent involves the use of -**person** or **person**-. Words such as

personpower, ***warehouseperson*** and ***foreperson*** (instead of ***foreman***) should be avoided where possible.

Some examples of old-fashioned terms and suggested non-sexist alternatives are set out below.

Old-fashioned term	Non-sexist equivalent
air hostess/stewardess	flight attendant
anchorman	anchor
businessman	business executive, manager, entrepreneur, business professional
cameraman	camera operator, photographer
chairman	chair
craftsman	artisan
deliveryman	courier, messenger, delivery driver
draftsman	drafter
fireman	firefighter
foreman (in the workplace)	supervisor
foreman (of a jury)	presiding juror
freshman	fresher, first-year student
headmaster	head, principal
juryman	juror
mankind	humankind/humanity
man-made	synthetic, manufactured
manpower	workforce, personnel
ombudsman	ombuds
policeman/policewoman	police officer
postman/mailman	postal worker, mail carrier
salesman	sales representative
spokesman	representative

statesman	political leader
statesmanship	diplomacy
the common man	the average person
warehouseman	warehouser
workman	worker

8.3   CONSTANTLY LITIGATED WORDS

Two words and phrases commonly used in English legal drafting have produced constant litigation: *best endeavours* and *forthwith*.

Best endeavours

Best endeavours (and its variant *best efforts*) is often used in contracts to indicate that parties have promised to attempt to do something. The use of the phrase usually suggests a compromise in which neither party is prepared to accept a clear statement of their obligations. It denotes making every practicable effort to achieve the desired result without actually guaranteeing to achieve it.

The problem with the phrase is that there are no objective criteria by which best endeavours can be judged. It is easy to conclude that someone has used 'best endeavours' to ensure that something is done if the result is that the thing is done. It is very hard to make the same judgment if, despite certain efforts having been made, the thing is not done.

The phrase poses particular problems in professional undertakings (such as 'X promises to use its best endeavours to obtain the title deeds') because of the vagueness it introduces into the obligation undertaken. For this reason, the Law Society of England and Wales has warned solicitors against giving a 'best endeavours' undertaking.

Despite the points raised above, best endeavours clauses do have their place in circumstances where it is impossible or unwise to give an absolute obligation. See 11.3.4 for a specimen best endeavours clause.

Forthwith

Forthwith causes problems because it is too open-ended to introduce any certainty into the contract. According to the context, 'forthwith' could mean a matter of hours or a matter of weeks.

Everything depends on the context. For example, in one English case 'forthwith' was held to be within 14 days. In another it was held that notice entered on a Friday and given the following Monday was not given 'forthwith'. In yet another, the duty to submit a claim 'forthwith' was held not to arise until a particular state department had the basic information to allow the claim to be determined.

For these reasons, it is preferable to specify a precise time and date by which something must be done if time is of the essence in an agreement.

FALSE WORD PAIRS

Many English words look and sound alike but can have very different meanings. Typical examples include **principal** and **principle**, **affect** and **effect**, and **disinterested** and **uninterested**. In some cases – as in **prescribe** and **proscribe** – the meanings may in fact be opposite.

It is important to be aware of the more common of these false pairs – the consequences of confusing them could be disastrous. For more information on this subject, see the glossary of easily confused words at the back of the book.

PROBLEM WORDS AND PHRASES

Certain words and phrases cause problems, either because they have a number of meanings or because it is unclear to writers when one word should be used instead of another. It may not be possible to avoid them – particularly since many such words are extremely useful (when used correctly) – but care should be taken when using the following words, among others.

Only

Only, when used as an adverb, has four meanings:

1 It can be used to mean 'nothing or no one else but' ('only qualified lawyers are able to draft these documents').

2 It can also be used to mean 'with the negative result that' ('she arrived at court early, only to find that the hearing had been delayed').

3 A further meaning is 'no longer ago than' ('it was only on Thursday that the document arrived').

4 Lastly, it can mean 'not until' ('we can finalise the contract only when the document arrives').

The positioning of this word in a sentence is of critical importance. The meaning of the whole sentence can change profoundly according to where it is placed. Here are some examples:

- *Only the claims that were heard in court concerned trademark infringement* means that other claims that were not heard in court did not concern trademark infringement.

- *The only claims that were heard in court concerned trademark infringement* means that no other claims were heard in court except for those concerning trademark infringement.

- *The claims that were heard in court concerned only trademark infringement* means that the claims that were heard in court did not concern anything other than trademark infringement.

- *The claims that were heard in court only concerned trademark infringement* means that the claims that were heard in court did not concern anything except trademark infringement, with the additional possible implication that the fact that they did not concern anything except trademark infringement means that the situation was less serious than might otherwise have been the case.

Generally, **only** should be placed immediately in front of the word or phrase that it qualifies.

8.5.2　Fewer or less?

These words are often used incorrectly, even by native speakers of English.

Fewer should be used with plural nouns, as in 'handle fewer cases' or 'there are fewer emails in my inbox today'.

Less should be used with nouns referring to things that cannot be counted, as in 'there is less work to be done today'. It is incorrect to use less with a plural noun ('less cases', 'less emails').

8.5.3　Can or may?

Can is mainly used to mean 'to be able to', as in the sentence 'Can you translate from German into English?', which means, are you able to translate from German into English?

May is used in connection with entitlement or discretion. For instance, in ordinary language when asking to be allowed to do something, may is used in sentences such as 'May we leave now?'. In legal text, **may** is used in sentences like 'X may use the facilities provided by Y' – i.e. X is entitled to use the facilities provided by Y and may use them at his or her discretion.

Hence, **may** is both more polite than **can** in non-legal usage, and more appropriate in legal texts because its emphasis is on permission and entitlement, which fits in with the way in which legal texts work.

Imply or infer?

8.5.4

Do not confuse the words **imply** and **infer**. They can describe the same situation, but from different points of view.

If a speaker or writer **implies** something, as in 'he implied that the manager was a fool', it means that the person is suggesting something though not saying it directly.

If you **infer** something from what has been said, as in 'we inferred from his words that the manager is a fool', this means that you come to the conclusion that this is what they really mean.

Also

8.5.5

'Also' is a useful word and it is commonly used in conjunction with verbs in legal text. However, it is often put in the wrong place in sentences.

It is worth bearing these considerations in mind:

1   If possible, avoid starting a sentence with 'also'.

For example, try to avoid formulations like 'Also the purchaser is bound by this obligation'. Write instead, 'The purchaser is also bound by this obligation'.

2   Put it before the verb to which it relates instead of after.

For instance, write 'the lawyer must **also** report to the client on a regular basis', instead of 'the lawyer must report **also** to the client on a regular basis'.

The purpose of putting 'also' before 'report' in this case is that doing so makes it clear to the reader that reporting to the client on a regular basis is the additional duty the lawyer must fulfil. On the other hand, in the second example ('the lawyer must report also to the client on a regular basis') the reader gains the impression that the lawyer is being asked to report to the client as well as some other unidentified person on a regular basis.

8.5.6   Specially or especially?

Especially and *specially* are sometimes confused. Their meanings are close but not exactly the same. In brief, both can mean 'particularly' but *especially* is generally a synonym for 'in particular'. For example:

She was pleased with the performance of all the team members, especially Karen for her handling of the Wyatt case.

Meanwhile, *specially* can be used to mean 'for a special or specific purpose'. For example:

She had the machine specially built for this job.

8.5.7   Save

Save usually means (1) to rescue from harm or danger (e.g. 'the lawyer's advice saved the client from signing a grossly unfair contract'); or (2) to make and keep safe – i.e. to record or deposit for future reference (e.g. 'I saved the contract on a memory stick').

However, it can also be used to mean 'except'. It is frequently used in this sense in legal documents. For example:

No warranties are given save as to those set out in Schedule 3.

8.5.8   Client or customer?

Traditionally, the word *customer* is associated with the purchase of uncomplicated tangible items on which very little advice is required (e.g. bricks, timber, garden furniture, groceries), while the word *client* is associated with the purchase of professional services that largely consist of advice and have little or no tangible aspect (e.g. financial consultancy, legal advice, tax planning).

Consequently, businesses that provide professional services (e.g. lawyers, accountants, financial advisers) are generally said to have clients, while businesses that sell products (e.g. wholesalers and retailers of groceries, bricks, garden furniture etc.) have customers.

However, sometimes businesses that provide professional services worry that what they sell may be viewed as excessively intangible and airy and thus possibly dispensable. Therefore, they may be tempted to adopt the word *customer* to give an impression of being tangible, robust and down-to-earth.

Similarly, businesses that provide apparently uncomplicated items often worry that their business may appear unsophisticated – and they may also realise that there is money to be made in cultivating an ongoing relationship with the purchaser (e.g. in offering after-sales services, etc.). Accordingly, they adopt the word **client** to give the impression that they are selling more than just a tangible product and that they seek an ongoing and mutually beneficial relationship with the purchaser of their goods.

In accordance with/according to   8.5.9

These very similar phrases appear with almost unbelievable frequency in legal texts, and in such a wide variety of contexts that it is very hard to tell them apart.

However, they do have slightly different meanings – and sometimes these differences are of crucial importance.

In a nutshell, 'in accordance with' is used to indicate that the matter referred to has mandatory effect. It means roughly the same as 'in compliance with'. For instance:

The work must be carried out in accordance with the client's specific instructions.

Whereas 'according to' generally indicates reportage. It tells the reader that the matter referred to is derived or reported from a certain source. For instance:

According to my lawyer, I could claim substantial damages for this infringement.
In case this explanation is not entirely clear, consider the following sentences:
According to the weather forecast it will rain tomorrow.

OR

In accordance with the weather forecast it will rain tomorrow.

The first of these sentences is correct – it is reportage that simply tells us what the weather forecast said. But the second – 'in accordance with the weather forecast' – indicates that the weather forecast actually governs the weather, which is clearly not the case.

Confusion may arise in situations in which both expressions can be used, but with different emphasis. Compare:

Rent shall be paid in accordance with paragraph seven of the lease agreement.

AND

Rent shall be paid according to paragraph seven of the lease agreement.

The difference between these sentences is that the first tells us that paragraph seven governs the way in which rent is paid, while the second tells us where to find the obligation to pay rent (i.e. in paragraph seven).

FALSE COLLOCATIONS

One of the most difficult aspects of English usage is achieving idiomatic mastery of collocations.

8.6.1   What's a collocation?

Collocations are expressions that consist of two or more words that frequently appear together. These may involve adjectives and nouns (e.g. *a derisory offer* or *a binding contract*), verbs and nouns (*to fulfil obligations* or *to cast aspersions*), or adverbs and nouns (*legally valid* or *wholly fraudulent*).

Some collocations are relatively flexible – i.e. the verb, adverb or adjective part of the phrase may be replaced by another word to produce a broadly similar meaning. For example, in the phrase *to fulfil obligations*, the word 'fulfil' could be replaced by 'meet' without altering the meaning of the phrase.

Other collocations are less flexible. Consider, for example, the relatively common phrase *to cast aspersions*. An aspersion is a disparaging or damaging remark. It is always said to be 'cast' (not made, thrown, spoken etc.). Another example is the common phrase *to hold discussions*. Here, discussions are generally 'held' (not 'made', 'carried out' etc.).

You can usually get around the danger of constructing a false collocation by using another phrase altogether, or even a single word. The phrase *to cast aspersions* could be replaced by *to make disparaging remarks*, and *to hold discussions* may in most cases be reduced to *to discuss*. However, the use of unfamiliar pairings of words will instantly appear subtly wrong to a native English speaker.

8.6.2   Legally fixed collocations

The situation becomes even more difficult when it comes to phrases that can be regarded as legally fixed as a result of legal tradition. In other words, generations of lawyers have become accustomed to referring to specific legal processes using a certain form of words to the extent that it becomes quite difficult or even impossible to deviate from this form of words without creating legal uncertainty.

This issue is particularly noticeable when dealing with verb and noun collocations that describe the ways in which certain legal events or processes are begun and ended. For example, contracts may be *entered into* or *executed*, and later *terminated* or *rescinded*; but they cannot be *begun* and then *cancelled* or *ended*.

In order to illustrate this point, here is a table showing a few of the collocations used to describe how certain legal matters or entities are terminated.

Verbs used	Nouns used
abolish annul	law (particularly a restrictive or archaic law) contract (relatively archaic usage) marriage (when the marriage is not legally valid)
cancel	order (e.g. for the purchase of goods – not a court order) meeting appointment
discharge	obligation (i.e. to carry it out) duty (as for obligation) invoice (i.e. to pay) contract (when the contract is legally completed) from liability (a synonym for release)
dismiss	application (e.g. to court) appeal (to court) employee (from employment)
dissolve repeal	company, partnership act/statute (or part thereof) law
repudiate	contract (i.e. by failure to fulfil its terms)
rescind	contract (i.e. termination due to breach) authorisation (i.e. to cancel)
revoke	order (i.e. court order) power of attorney permission authorisation licence

terminate	contract
	employment
wind down	project, operation
wind up	company
withdraw	offer
	permission
	support

8.6.3   A short list of legally relevant collocations

Here are a few examples of collocations in common use in legal English:

abide by a contract/decision/agreement
adhere to a contract/standard/principle/rule
adjourn a meeting/hearing/case
assign rights
authorised representative
award damages (i.e. by a court)
basic principle
binding contract
binding obligation
breach a contract/law/statute
break/keep/make a promise
bring up a subject/issue/matter
cancel an order (e.g. an order for the purchase of goods – not a court order)
cast aspersions
claim damages
clarify an issue
compelling reason
comply with the law
contractual breach
contributory factor
copyright protection
derisory offer
detrimental effect
dismiss a case/appeal/employee
draw up a contract/list/schedule
enter into a contract/discussion/negotiations
establish a cause/firm/company

estimated costs
exclusive agent/distributor/contract
exercise discretion
flagrant breach
foreseeable future
fulfil criteria/obligations
give/grant/obtain permission
grant permission
handle a complaint
hold a discussion
honour a commitment
incur liability/risk/penalty/costs
infringe copyright/rights/a patent/a trademark
irrevocably appoint
launch a scheme/initiative
legally valid
make a complaint/contribution/mistake/recovery/proposal/suggestion
managerial position
negotiate a settlement
pass a law/test
provide an explanation/a reference/a solution
public domain
put down a deposit
reasonable control
reasonable costs
relevant issue
rescind a contract
satisfy/meet requirements/conditions/criteria
substantial amount/increase/decrease
terminate a contract
weighty problem/matter
wholly fraudulent
written notice/request

British and American English

British and American English can be differentiated in three main ways:

1 Differences in language use conventions: meaning and spelling of words, grammar and punctuation differences.

2 Vocabulary. There are a number of important differences, particularly in business terminology.

3 Differences in the ways of using English dictated by the different cultural values of the two countries.

It is necessary to choose between British or American English and then apply the conventions of the version you choose consistently. If you muddle up British and American standards, it implies that you do not understand that they are different.

9.1 DIFFERENCES IN LANGUAGE USE CONVENTIONS

Here are some of the key differences in language use conventions.

1 Dates. In British English the standard way of writing dates is to put the day of the month as a figure, then the month (either as a figure or spelled out) and then the year. For example, 19 September 1973 or 19.09.73. The standard way of writing dates in American English is to put the month first (either as a figure or spelled out), then the day of the month, then the year. For example, September 19th 1973 or 9/19/73. Commas are also frequently inserted after the day of the month in the USA. For example, September 19, 1973.

2 **o** and **ou**. In British English, the standard way of writing words that might include either the letter **o** or the letters **ou** is to use the **ou** form. For example, *colour*, *humour*, *honour*, *behaviour*. The standard way of writing such words in American English is to use only **o**. For example, *color*, *humor*, *honor*, *behavior*.

3 **Through**. In American English, the word **through** (or, in very informal use, **thru**) can be used to mean **until**. For example, 'September 19th thru October 1st' would be in British English '19 September until 1 October'.

4 Hyphens. Hyphens are often used in British English to connect prefixes with the main word. For example, *pre-emption*, *pre-trial*, *co-operation*. They are less common in American English. For example, *preemption*, *pretrial*, *cooperation*.

5 **z** or **s**? In British English, **s** is generally used in such words as **recognise**, **authorise**. The letter **z** is used in American English in such words as **recognize** or **authorize**. However, it is not incorrect to use **z** in such words when using British English as standard (but be consistent).

Note, however, that some words must always end in **-ise** whether you are using British or American English standards. These include:

advertise	advise
arise	comprise
compromise	demise
despise	devise
disguise	enfranchise
excise	exercise
franchise	improvise
incise	merchandise
premise	revise
supervise	surmise
surprise	televise

6 **l** or **ll**? In American English, a single **l** is used in such words as **traveled** or **counseled**. In British English, **ll** is used (e.g. **travelled**, **counselled**).

Note, however, that in British English, some words that end in a double **ll** lose one **l** when a suffix is added: **skill** becomes **skilfully**, **will** becomes **wilfully**. In American English, the double **ll** is retained: **skill** becomes **skillfully** and **will** becomes **willfully**.

7 **-re** or **-er**? In American English, the **-er** ending is used in words like **theater**, **center**, **meter** and **fiber**. In British English, these words are spelt **theatre**, **centre**, **metre** and **fibre**.

8 **oe** and **ae**. Some scientific terms retain the use of the classical composite vowels **oe** and **ae** in British English. These include **diarrhoea**, **anaesthetic**, **gynaecology** and **homoeopathy**. In American English, a single **e** replaces the composite vowel: **diarrhea**, **anesthetic**, **gynecology**, **homeopathy**.

9   *-e* or *-ue*? In British English, the final silent *-e* or *-ue* is retained in such words as ***analogue***, ***axe*** and ***catalogue***. In American English, it is omitted: ***analog***, ***ax*** and ***catalog***.

10 *-eable* or *-able*? The silent *e*, produced when forming some adjectives with a suffix, is generally used in British English in such words as ***likeable***, ***unshakeable*** and ***ageing***. In American English, it is generally left out: ***likable***, ***unshakable*** and ***aging***. The *e* is, however, sometimes used in American English where it affects the sound of the preceding consonant: ***traceable*** or ***manageable***.

11 *-ce* or *-se*? In British English, the verb that relates to a noun ending in *-ce* is sometimes given the ending *-se*. For example, ***advice*** (noun)/***advise*** (verb), ***device***/***devise***, ***licence***/***license***, ***practice***/***practise***. American English uses *-se* for both the noun and verb forms of these words. It also uses *-se* for other nouns that in British English are spelt *-ce*, including ***defense***, ***offense***, ***pretense***.

12 Prepositions. In American English, it is acceptable to omit prepositions in certain situations. In British English, this habit is less common. For example, an American lawyer might find a certain clause in a contract to be 'likely enforceable'. A British colleague would be more likely to say that it was 'likely to be enforceable'. An American civil rights activist might 'protest discrimination', while his British colleagues would 'protest against discrimination'.

13 ***Have*** and ***got***. In American English it is quite acceptable to use the word ***got*** without ***have*** in sentences like 'I got two tickets for the show tonight'. In British English, it is more usual to say 'I've got two tickets for the show tonight'.

14 ***Gotten***. ***Gotten*** is a proper word in American English, but is only used as an Americanism in British English, except in certain phrases such as 'ill-gotten gains'.

15 ***While*** or ***whilst***? Both ***while*** and ***whilst*** are used in British English. In American English, ***while*** is the right word to use, and ***whilst*** is regarded as a pretentious affectation.

16 Grammatical abbreviations. American authors generally put a comma (,) after the abbreviations ***i.e.*** and ***e.g.*** (as recommended by the ***Chicago Manual of Style***), while British authors generally do not.

17 Use of dots in abbreviations. In American English dots are usually inserted between the different parts of abbreviations that use uppercase. This is not the case in British English. Hence 'U.S.A.' but 'UK'.

VOCABULARY

Here are some key vocabulary differences.

Ordinary words and phrases

British	American
aerial (TV)	antenna
aluminium	aluminum
anti-clockwise	counter-clockwise
at weekends	on weekends
aubergine	eggplant
autumn	fall
banknote	bill
bill	check
biscuit	cookie
braces	suspenders
building society	savings and loan association
calibre	caliber
camp bed	cot
car bonnet	hood
car park	parking lot
car windscreen	windshield
caravan	trailer
cheque (bank)	check
chips	french fries
cinema	movie theater
clerk (bank)	teller
clever	smart

cling film	plastic wrap
cooker	stove
cosy	cozy
courgette	zucchini
crisps	potato chips
crossroads/junction	intersection
dialled	dialed
dived	dove
draught	draft
dressing gown	bathrobe/housecoat/robe
dual carriageway	four-lane highway
estate agent	realtor/real estate agent
film	movie
flat	apartment
flyover	overpass
frying pan	skillet
fuelled	fueled
full stop (punctuation)	period
give way	yield
grey	gray
ground floor	first floor
high street	main street
holiday	vacation
increase (of money)	hike
lent	loaned
lift	elevator
lorry	truck

maize/sweetcorn	corn
manoeuvre	maneuver
meet	meet with
metre	meter
motorway	highway, freeway, expressway, throughway
mum	mom
muslin	cheesecloth
nappy	diaper
oblige	obligate
ordinary	regular, normal
pants	underpants
pavement	sidewalk
petrol	gasoline, gas
plough	plow
post	mail
power point	electrical outlet
programme	program
property (land)	real estate
quarters (three-quarters)	fourths (three-fourths)
queue	line, line-up
rationalisation (personnel)	downsizing
riding (horses)	horseback riding
ring road	beltway
rivalled	rivaled
rowing boat	rowboat
sceptical	skeptical
sizeable	sizable

skilful	skillfull
sombre	somber
stand (for election)	run
starter	appetizer
storey (of building)	story, floor
stupid	dumb
sweet shop	candy store
tap	faucet
tartan	plaid
terraced house	row house
till	checkout
towards	toward
transport	transportation
trainers	sneakers
travelled	traveled
trousers	pants or slacks
tyre	tire
underground (or tube train)	subway
upmarket	upscale
vest	undershirt
waistcoat	vest
work out (problem)	figure out
Yours faithfully	Respectfully yours/Yours truly
Yours sincerely (letter)	Sincerely yours

Business and legal terminology

Note that some of these terms are not exactly equivalent and there may be cases where they can be used interchangeably. For example, 'competition law' is often understood as a wider concept than 'antitrust law', and a large number of US terms (e.g. 'par value') are in relatively common use in British legal English.

British	American
articles of association	bylaws
called to the bar	admitted to the bar
competition law	antitrust law
balance sheet	statement of financial position
bills	notes
bonus or scrip issue	stock dividend or stock split
company	corporation
creditors	payables
debtors	receivables
depreciation	amortization
employment law	labor law
exceptional items	unusual items
flotation	initial public offering (IPO)
indemnify	hold harmless and indemnify
land and buildings	real estate
maintenance	alimony
nominal value	par value
ordinary shares	common stock
preference shares	preferred stock
profit and loss account	income statement
provisions	allowances
receivership	chapter 11 bankruptcy

shareholders' funds	stockholders' equity
share premium	additional paid-in capital
solicitor	attorney, lawyer
stocks	inventories
theft	larceny
turnover	revenues
undistributable reserves	restricted surplus

9.3

DIFFERENCES RELATED TO CULTURAL VALUES

There are a number of differences between British and American English that relate to the different cultural values of the two countries. For example, British English contains a number of frequently used metaphors relating to football ('scoring an own goal') and cricket ('a sticky wicket'), while American English uses metaphors relating to baseball ('in the ballpark').

The two versions of the language also have certain tendencies that are worth bearing in mind. These are not absolute, since individual writers have their own styles that may incorporate aspects of both British and American tendencies. However, in general:

- British English tends to react more slowly to new words and phrases than American English. American English enthusiastically adopts new usages, some of which later pass into general use (e.g. **corporate citizen**, **social performance**), and some die out or become less fashionable after a short period in fashion (e.g. **synergy**).

- British English has a slight tendency to vagueness and ponderous diction. American English (at its best) tends to be more direct and vivid.

- American English tends to be more 'slangy' than British English.

- Both American and British English are keen on euphemisms. In British English, these are often used for humorous purposes (e.g. **to be economical with the truth**) or to smooth over something unpleasant. In American English they may also be used for reasons of modesty (thus **lavatory** or **WC** becomes **restroom** or **bathroom**), to make something mundane sound important (thus **ratcatcher** becomes **rodent operative**) or to cover up the truth of something unpleasant (thus civilian deaths in war become **collateral damage**).

● American English has a tendency to lengthen certain existing words in an effort to give them greater weight. This is particularly the case with some nouns that are capable of being given an alternative *-tion* ending. Thus, **transport** becomes **transportation** and **documents** becomes **documentation**.

STRUCTURE OF CONTRACTS

There is generally no legal requirement for a contract to follow a particular format or layout. The exact structure used will vary according to the kind of document being drafted. However, most modern commercial contracts prepared by lawyers follow a similar structure.

There are obvious advantages in having a structured and standard layout that is familiar both to lawyers and to parties to the contract. The aim in all cases should be to produce a document that is laid out in a clear and logical way, thus making it as easy as possible to read and understand.

As a rough rule, the structure of a typical commercial contract is as follows:

- The names and addresses of the parties
- Recitals
- Definitions
- Conditions precedent
- Agreements
- Representations and warranties
- Boilerplate clauses
- Schedules
- Signatures
- Appendices

These brief headings are considered in the notes below.

10.1.1 The names and addresses of the parties

The first section of the contract usually sets out the full names and postal addresses of all the parties to the contract. This section may also specify that a shortened name will be used in the remainder of the contract to denote each of the parties. For example:

Pan-Oceanic Shrimp Packers plc (hereinafter referred to as 'the Company')

The words 'the Company' will then be used in the remainder of the contract in place of Pan-Oceanic Shrimp Packers plc.

Recital

The recital is often referred to as a non-operative part of the contract since it has no specific legal effect. The purpose of the recital is to explain to the reader the background to the transaction. If necessary, the recital also sets out certain facts that may influence the way in which a court might interpret provisions of the contract.

For example, the background to an exclusion clause might be clarified by relating the decision of both parties to impose the risk of loss on one party rather than the other because this is more economical from an insurance viewpoint.

If it is vital to the contract that the content of the recital be treated as an integral element of the substantive parts of the contract, an express clause to this effect should be included in the contract.

Recitals are generally introduced with the word **whereas**, and comprise a narrative written in the present tense:

Whereas

The Company is engaged in the manufacture of the Products, and the Distributor wishes to distribute the Products in the territory of Anyland.

Definitions

The definitions section contains a list of terms used later in the contract. A definition is given for each term, which represents the way in which the drafters of the contract wish the term to be interpreted as a matter of law. Here is an example:

'Execution date' means 5 October 2020, the date of execution of this Agreement.

Often the definitions section needs to be read in conjunction with another section of the agreement. For example, a definition may simply state as follows:

'Licence' has the meaning assigned to that term in Section 4.3 of this Agreement.

When a definition appears several times within a single clause but not elsewhere in the contract, it is usually more convenient to insert the definition in brackets in that clause and omit it from the definitions section. Here is an example of this type of definition drawn from a confidentiality clause:

The Employer and the Employee acknowledge that as a result of this employment relationship, the Employee will be in possession of confidential customer information, trade secrets, technical data and know-how relating to the products, processes, methods, equipment and business practices of the Employer and its clients (hereinafter 'Confidential Information').

When a definition is only used once in the text, it is unnecessary and should be deleted. The full name of the thing defined should be used instead.

The definitions form part of the substance of the contract since they prescribe that certain words and phrases shall mean certain things. It is best to state directly what these words and phrases shall mean rather than resorting to phrases such as 'where the context so admits', since this creates potential for ambiguity.

When drafting a contract, it is often convenient to insert definitions throughout the agreement, as necessary, and then to remove these once the contract has been drafted, then edit and arrange them in a suitable order in the initial definitions section.

See also the discussion of defined terms at 7.3.2.

10.1.4   Conditions precedent

Conditions precedent are conditions that have to be satisfied before the agreement comes into force. They are generally viewed as being outside the main terms of the contract.

One important consequence of this fact is that these conditions are therefore not subject to the ***parol evidence rule***. This rule states that where all the terms of a contract are contained in a written document, no external evidence may be added to it to vary the interpretation to be given to the contract. Since the conditions precedent are not regarded as forming part of the main terms of the contract, the parol evidence rule does not apply. Consequently, it follows that external evidence can be added to vary the interpretation of such clauses.

A contract may stipulate that if a specified future event occurs during the term of the contract then it will be terminated. This type of stipulation is sometimes known as a ***condition subsequent***.

10.1.5   Agreements

The agreements section contains the rights and obligations of the parties. This part reflects the heart of the deal struck between the parties. The drafting of the clauses will therefore depend upon the particular facts of the case at hand. In a simple sale of goods contract, the seller will promise to sell and deliver goods of a certain description and quality. The buyer will promise to pay for them.

In addition, this part of the contract will contain various clauses covering what happens if the seller fails to deliver or the buyer fails to pay.

Representations and warranties

The representations and warranties section contains promises by one or other party that a given statement or set of facts is true. A representation is a statement of fact made by one contracting party to the other that induces the other to enter into the contract. A warranty is a contractual promise and if such a promise is broken, the innocent party will be able to claim damages.

Boilerplate clauses

Boilerplate clauses are standard clauses that are inserted as a matter of course into certain types of agreement. They relate to issues that are to do with the way in which the contract works rather than the heart of the deal itself. These include clauses dealing with **service of notices** (the means by which documents that relate to the contract must be sent) and **assignment** (whether and on what basis the parties can transfer the contract to other parties), together with many other types of clause.

Schedules

If the contract contains certain very detailed agreements or information, the parties often prefer to put this in schedules set out at the end of the contract, instead of cluttering up the main part of the contract with a mass of detail. For example, detailed price lists for various kinds of goods sold under the contract are usually placed in a schedule.

It should be noted that the stipulations contained in the schedules do form part of the substantive agreement between the parties.

Signature section

The signature section comes after the schedules and before the appendices. Witnesses are not required for most kinds of contract. All parties to the contract are required to sign the document as evidence of their agreement to its terms.

The parties' names are usually printed together with the date of the contract, and the parties must then add their signatures to the contract. It is common practice for contracts to be produced in **duplicate**. This means that two copies of the contract are made – one for each party – and the parties each sign both copies of the contract.

Appendices

Appendices usually contain documents that are referred to in the contract. These may simply be put there because they are useful reference material for the parties. They do not necessarily form part of the substantive agreement between the parties. For example, in a contract for the sale of machine parts by one company to another, the appendices to the contract might contain detailed drawings or specifications for the machine parts for illustrative purposes.

10.2   PRINCIPLES OF INTERPRETATION

10.2.1   The textual approach

10.2.1.1   The nature of the approach

The basic method of interpretation traditionally used by common law lawyers is known as the **textual** or **literal** approach. This approach is based on the idea that the meaning and effect of a contract or piece of legislation should be determined solely from the words of the text itself and not from any external evidence.

This method contrasts with the approach to interpretation traditionally taken in civil law jurisdictions. In such jurisdictions, the **purposive** or **teleological** approach is used. This is based on the idea that the meaning and effect of a contract or piece of legislation should be determined taking account of the object and purpose of the contract or piece of legislation and the intentions of the parties (if a contract) or intention of the drafter (if legislation).

The effect of this approach on the drafting of contracts is that common law lawyers tend to draft contracts in a way that seeks to cover any possible thing that might go wrong in the contract, no matter how remote. This of course leads to long and complicated documents, and is made worse by the fact that many common law countries (particularly the USA and to a lesser extent the UK) have lightly regulated free-market economies in which parties' freedom to contract is little affected by legal rules. In such climates there is greater need for remedies and dispute-resolution methods to be specifically agreed between the parties in the contract itself.

10.2.1.2   Relevance for the drafter

The relevance of this literal approach for the drafter using English is twofold. First, if you are using American or British templates for your English language drafting but the governing law applicable to the document you are creating does not fall within the common law tradition, it is quite likely that a large number of the provisions will be redundant. It may therefore be necessary to cut or heavily amend a number of the clauses contained in the template.

Second, if you are drafting in English and the document being created will be governed by law falling with the common law tradition, it will be necessary to take a highly pedantic approach. In the common law tradition, even such matters as the placing of a comma can acquire profound legal significance.

For example, in one Australian case the court had to look at a workers' insurance policy that described the employer's business as 'Fuel Carrying and Repairing'.

The question the court had to decide was whether the policy covered an employee who was injured when driving the employer's vehicle carrying bricks. The court interpreted the policy as if it read either 'Fuel, Carrying, and Repairing' or 'Fuel Carrying, and Repairing'. Litigation could have been avoided if a comma had been inserted in the first place.

Specific rules of interpretation   10.2.2

In addition to the basic approach outlined above, some specific rules of interpretation are used in common law jurisdictions. These are briefly outlined below.

The document must be read as a whole   10.2.2.1

This rule provides that when a reader is seeking to interpret the meaning of a particular clause in a contract, this should not be done without taking into consideration what the rest of the contract says. The exact meaning of a part of the contract should become clear once the whole document has been read.

Contra proferentem rule   10.2.2.2

This rule provides that if an ambiguity in a contract cannot be resolved in any other way then it must be interpreted against the interests of the party that suggested it.

For example, if a problem arises concerning the extent of cover provided in an insurance contract and one interpretation favours the insurer and the other the insured party, the court will use the interpretation that favours the insured party.

Noscitur a sociis rule   10.2.2.3

Noscitur a sociis is Latin meaning 'it is known by its neighbours'. The ***noscitur a sociis*** rule states that if the meaning of a phrase in a contract is unclear by itself, its meaning should be gathered from the words and phrases associated with it.

10.2.2.4   *Ejusdem generis* **rule**

Ejusdem generis is Latin meaning 'of the same kind'. The ***ejusdem generis*** rule applies when a list of specific items belonging to the same class is followed by general words; the general words are treated as confined to other items of the same class.

Therefore, if a list reads 'cats, dogs, and other animals', the phrase 'other animals' will be interpreted as meaning other ***domestic*** animals only.

The phrase ***inter alia*** (including but not limited to) is often used to avoid this presumption being made – it indicates that the list is not exhaustive, but merely illustrative. See the *Glossary of Foreign Terms Used in Law* for an example of usage.

10.2.2.5   *Expressio unius est exclusio alterius* **rule**

Expressio unius est exclusio alterius is Latin meaning 'the inclusion of one is the exclusion of another'. The ***expressio unius est exclusio alterius*** rule states that when a list of specific items is not followed by general words, it is taken as exhaustive. For example, 'weekends and public holidays' excludes ordinary weekdays.

10.2.3   **Golden rules of interpretation**

Two rules of interpretation are sometimes referred to as golden rules on account of their overriding importance. These are:

10.2.3.1   **Words should be given their ordinary meaning**

This rule provides that when reading a contract one should stick to the ordinary and grammatical sense of the words being used. There are two exceptions to this:

- Where the ordinary meaning of a word leads either to absurdity or inconsistency with the rest of the document, the meaning should be modified in the light of the intentions of the parties to avoid such absurdity or inconsistency.

- Technical words should be given their technical meanings.

Consistent terminology

This rule is often stated as follows:

Never change your language unless you wish to change your meaning, and always change your language if you wish to change your meaning.

The basic point here is that if you have used one word to refer to a particular concept, you should stick to it consistently throughout the document. If you change to a different word, there is a risk that this will be interpreted to mean a different concept. For this reason, defined terms are often used in commercial contracts as a means of maximising consistency of terminology and fixing the meaning of words.

Contract clauses
Types and specimen clauses

11.1 OVERVIEW

As discussed above, there is no legal requirement for contracts to follow a particular format or layout, but it is customary for modern commercial contracts to do so.

The notes below set out the different sections of a typical commercial contract and the kinds of clauses (and provisions that may be included within clauses also dealing with other issues) that might be included in each section. Example clauses are given in respect of those provisions.

This is not intended as an exhaustive list. Furthermore, not all of the types of clauses and provisions set out below will be relevant to every type of commercial contract. However, the contents of the following subsections can be used as a rough checklist for drafters who wish to check that they have covered the most obvious aspects of the contract being prepared. Note, however, that the example clauses given are fairly simply worded, and may therefore not be appropriate for more complicated contractual situations.

11.2 DEFINITIONS

Here are some definitions that commonly appear in contracts. In practice, the nature or scope of the definitions used vary widely depending on the subject-matter of the contract, the governing law and the way in which the contract is designed to work.

Affiliates: the term 'affiliates' refers to individuals or companies connected with a party to the contract.

Charges: the term 'charges' refers to fees, costs and payments to be made under the contract or incurred by one of the parties, or to legal charges (e.g. mortgages) on property etc.

Commencement date: the date on which the agreement comes into effect, or the obligations under the agreement commence.

Completion: the term 'completion' can mean either the formal coming into effect of the contract or the completion of work to be done under the contract.

Exclusive, non-exclusive and sole: where these words have particular meanings; e.g. as applicable to agency or distribution agreements.

Expressions of time (months, years, etc.): the way in which the terms 'month' or 'year' etc. should be interpreted.

Force majeure: the circumstances under which the parties may be released from their obligations under the contract (see below).

Intellectual property: the extent and nature of the intellectual property dealt with and to be protected by the parties under the contract. This may be defined by means of a general definition in the definitions section cross-referenced to a schedule in which the various aspects of intellectual property to be protected are defined and itemised in detail.

Interpretation: the way in which the parties should interpret references to legislation (i.e. to include future amendments); gender (i.e. references to 'he' may also include 'she' and vice versa); singular and plural forms of words used in the contract; headings etc.

Parties: the names to be used in referring to the parties in the contract (e.g. expressions such as 'Employer' and 'Employee', or 'Company' and 'Distributor' may be used in place of the parties' full names).

Price: the payment terms and interest rates applicable.

Sub-contracting: the identification and role of particular sub-contractors that will carry out aspects of the work agreed between the parties in the main contract.

Territory: definition of the territory to which the contract applies.

MAIN COMMERCIAL PROVISIONS 11.3

Acknowledgements 11.3.1

These clauses indicate the existence of a legal relationship or that a person has not relied on certain statements or facts. Here is an example:

Party A acknowledges that Party B has assigned certain R&D contracts with Party C to Part A ('R&D Contracts').

Vocabulary: to 'assign' means 'to transfer', and 'R&D' means 'research and development'.

Appointment 11.3.2

In this clause, one party appoints another party to carry out specified tasks or fulfil a specified role. It is important to ensure that the clause is clear about who is being appointed, what they are being appointed to do, whether and how much they will be paid for doing it and how long the appointment is to last.

Here is an example, in which one party appoints another to provide certain services.

Party A hereby appoints Party B to provide haulage services in the Territory for the Term in return for the Payments, and Party B accepts such appointment.

Vocabulary: 'haulage' means 'transportation', usually by lorry. The 'Territory' refers to a specific geographical area defined elsewhere in the contract, and the nature of the 'Payments' will also be defined elsewhere in the contract.

11.3.3 Audit and records

This type of clause is needed where payments under the contract are calculated by reference to a variable factor (e.g. extent of work done or sales received) and provides a right of audit – i.e. a right to carry out an official inspection of financial records – to the party that will receive such payments. The clause should deal with such questions as what records may be examined, whether copies may be made of them, how long the right to inspect will continue for and who bears the costs of the audit etc.

The example clause below empowers the authorised representatives of each party to inspect certain records.

The authorised representative of each party shall be entitled at that party's expense to inspect and audit the books, accounts and records relating to the subject-matter of the contract, the times at which such inspection shall take place to be agreed between the parties in advance of each inspection.

Vocabulary: the 'subject-matter' of the contract means the deal the contract is designed to put into effect, and 'in advance of' means before.

11.3.4 Best endeavours

This provision is generally contained within another clause, and it creates a qualified obligation whereby a party must demonstrate a high level of commitment and effort towards achieving a certain result, but is not absolutely obliged to achieve it (e.g. 'A shall use its best endeavours to sell the Products as specified in Appendix II'). Generally speaking, this kind of formulation should be avoided if it is possible to indicate specific and absolute obligations.

While this is a useful provision in circumstances where a certain result is intended but cannot be guaranteed, it is notoriously difficult to enforce (see discussion in section 8.3).

Here is an example of a best endeavours clause relating to dispute resolution.

If the unresolved dispute is having a material and adverse effect on the Project, the Parties shall use their best endeavours to achieve an expeditious resolution of the dispute.

Vocabulary: 'material' in this context means 'significant', and 'adverse' means 'harmful'. The word 'expeditious' is frequently used in legal contexts to mean 'quick'.

Commencement   11.3.5

This provision is generally contained within another clause and indicates when performance of the obligation contained in that clause is to start. Particular care should be taken in drafting where the commencement date is different from the date of the contract or where different parts of the contract commence on different dates.

The example clause below stipulates the commencement date in a fixed-term contract.

This agreement shall commence on [insert date] ('the Commencement Date') and continue for a period of [__] months unless terminated earlier by either party under the provisions of Clause [__].

Completion   11.3.6

This provision is generally contained within another clause to indicate when certain defined activities are to take place. Care should be taken to ensure that the meaning of the word 'completion' is clear and unambiguous in the contexts in which it is used.

This example clause provides a definition for the term 'Completion Date'.

The 'Completion Date' means the date of actual completion of the matters detailed in clauses [__] and Completion shall be construed accordingly.

Vocabulary: the word 'construed' means 'interpreted'. 'To construe' is to interpret.

11.3.7   Conditions precedent and subsequent

This provision is generally contained within another clause.

Here is an example of a condition precedent in relation to the grant of a patent.

The obligations contained in paragraph [___] of this contract shall not come into effect until the day after the date on which Party A receives formal notification from the Patent Office that a patent has been granted.

Vocabulary: the phrase 'come into effect' means 'to become legally valid'.

11.3.8   Consent

This provision is generally contained within another clause and has a variety of meanings:

1   That a contracting party is responsible for obtaining various consents necessary for the contract to proceed.

2   That a party is warranting that the necessary consents have been obtained.

3   That a party may not take certain steps unless the consent of the other party has been obtained.

The main issue to be considered when drafting such a provision is whether the requirement for consent should be made subject to a provision that it cannot be reasonably withheld.

Here is an example of a clause prohibiting assignment of the contract by either party in the absence of written consent from the other party.

This contract and all the rights under it may not be assigned or transferred by either party without the prior written consent of the other party.

Vocabulary: the phrase 'prior written consent' means 'agreement given in writing before assignment of the contract occurs'.

11.3.9   Consultation

This clause generally takes the form of a stipulation that one party must consult with another party before taking certain actions (note that this does not amount to an obligation to obtain the other party's consent, but is more onerous than a mere obligation to inform the other party). The drafting of this kind of clause should take into account the question of what actually qualifies as proper consultation, how much time should be allowed for this process to take place and in what form the advice should be given etc.

The clause set out below stipulates a general duty to consult and consider recommendations made by the other party.

Party A shall consult with Party B and give good faith consideration to any recommendations made by Party B.

Vocabulary: the phrase 'good faith consideration' means 'genuine consideration'. In other words, Party A must give genuine thought to recommendations made by Party B.

Currency   11.3.10

This clause stipulates the currency in which payments are to be made under the contract, and is often contained in a payments clause. The clause should also specify whether payment can only be made in that currency, how and when the currency is to be converted and who bears the risk of the currency exchange rate changing between the date of the agreement and the date on which payment is in fact made.

Here is a simple clause specifying the currency and manner of payment.

All sums payable under this contract by Party A to Party B shall be paid in euros by direct bank transfer to Party B's bank account number [insert number] held at [insert name and address of bank].

Deposits and part payments   11.3.11

This clause stipulates when, under what circumstances and in what amounts deposits or part payments are to be made in respect of purchases handled under the contract.

The example clause given below provides that one party must pay a non-returnable deposit to the other party.

Party A shall pay to Party B a deposit in the sum of [__] within seven (7) days of the date of signature of this agreement. If Party A fails to pay the balance of the Contract Price by [insert date] or seeks to terminate the Order, Party B may retain all of the deposit.

Vocabulary: a 'deposit' is a preliminary payment made in the purchase of an item, which may or may not be returnable if the purchase is not completed. In this case, the deposit is not returnable if Party A does not pay the rest of the agreed price or tries to terminate the order.

11.3.12   Exclusive, non-exclusive and sole

See note at 11.2. This provision may be contained within a main commercial clause or may also be a stand-alone clause.

Here is a clause granting an exclusive licence to sell certain products.

Party A hereby grants Party B, subject to the provisions of this contract, an exclusive licence to manufacture, use and sell the Licensed Products in the Territory.

Vocabulary: an exclusive licence is one granted to only one party (as opposed to a non-exclusive licence). Therefore, under this clause Party B is the only one able to manufacture, use and sell the Licensed Products in the specified territory.

11.3.13   Indexation

This provision gives a means by which the parties can adjust prices for goods and services or salaries or wages in order to take account of the effects of inflation. It should stipulate the method of calculation, the index used and whether notice should be given in case of increases etc. Such a provision is often contained within a payment clause.

The example clause given below is taken from a UK contract and provides a means of increasing a salary automatically by reference to the retail prices index (which is the primary consumer price index used in the UK).

On each anniversary of the Commencement Date, the Salary specified in clause [__] shall be increased by the percentage by which the Retail Prices Index has increased during the preceding year.

Vocabulary: 'preceding' means 'previous'.

11.3.14   Interest

This provision specifies whether interest should be charged on late payments of contractual debts, at what rate it should be charged and whether any other rights are obtained by the party receiving payment. It is often contained in a payments clause.

The clause set out below simply provides for the payment of interest at a specified rate on invoiced amounts paid late.

All sums payable by Party A to Party B under this contract shall be paid against invoice within [insert time period] of the date of invoice, and in the event of late payment all sums due shall bear interest at the rate of [insert percentage] per month.

Vocabulary: the expression 'paid against invoice' means that Party B must send an invoice to Party A stating the amount to be paid and the date on which payment must be made, and Party A must pay as stated in the invoice.

Net sales value   11.3.15

This provision is usually contained within a payments clause, where payments are calculated by reference to the amount of a party's sales of goods (e.g. in agency and sales agreements). The word net indicates that certain items (VAT, insurance etc.) may be deducted from the amount actually charged to the customer.

The example given below shows how the net sales value definition can be applied in a payments clause.

The Licensee shall pay to the Licensor a royalty being a percentage of the Net Sales Value of all the Licensed Products sold by the Licensee.

Vocabulary: the word 'royalty' means a payment made to an author or patent holder in respect of the use or sale of published work or products.

Options   11.3.16

An 'option' is a contractual right for one party (the 'option holder') to elect to bring into force a certain term of a contract. Options often relate to the purchase of land or shares or to take a licence (e.g. in relation to intellectual property). They generally continue for a specified term and are exercisable on pre-agreed terms.

An option clause should include a clear statement of what the option holder receives on exercising the option. It should also cover the questions of whether the option is exclusive or not, whether a lockout agreement (an agreement not to negotiate with a third party during the period of the negotiations) is being created, what payment is to be made for the option, how the option may be exercised etc.

The provision set out below is taken from an option clause in a franchise agreement, and provides the franchisee with a right of first refusal where the franchisor indicates its aim to grant a franchise to a third party in respect of a further retail outlet.

In the event that the Franchisor wishes to grant to a third party a franchise for a new Outlet in the Designated Territory during the term of this contract the Franchisor shall notify the Franchisee in writing of such desire, following which the Franchisee shall have 90 days from the date of such notice in which to notify the Franchisor in writing that it shall exercise the Option in respect of such Outlet failing which the Franchisor shall be at liberty to grant a franchise to a third party for such Outlet.

Vocabulary: a 'franchise' is a licence given to a trader (the franchisee) enabling them to manufacture or sell a named product or service in a particular area for a stated period. The franchise is granted by the franchisor to the franchisee.

11.3.17   Payment terms and interest

This clause provides relevant stipulations about payment, including: when payments are to be made; the method of calculation; retention of title; whether VAT is included; by what method payment is to be made; whether interest is to be added; the currency of payment; any deductions; whether time is of the essence; what statements or receipts are required etc.

Here is a simple clause that merely records that payments are to be made without deductions of any kind.

Payments made under this contract shall be made without deductions (including taxes or charges). If the applicable law requires any tax or charge to be deducted before payment, the amount due under this agreement shall be increased so that the payment made will equal the amount due to [specify party] as if no such tax or charge had been imposed.

Vocabulary: 'deductions' are amounts subtracted from the sum to be paid before payment of that sum.

11.3.18   Receipts

This provision is usually contained in another clause (e.g. payment clause) and is necessary when a party is required to acknowledge that it has received something. It is important to ensure that the payment for which a receipt is required is sufficiently identified in the relevant provision.

The example clause below imposes a duty on the payee to issue receipts to the payer in respect of the amounts paid under a certain clause of the contract.

Party B shall issue a written receipt to Party A within seven (7) days of receipt of each payment received under clause [__] of this contract, confirming the amount of payment made and the date on which it was received.

Vocabulary: a 'receipt' is a document acknowledging that a specific payment has been made.

11.3.19   Reporting

This clause is used when a party is required to make regular reports to the other parties about its activities under the contract (as in a consultancy or agency agreement). It should stipulate what information is provided, in what form it should be provided, the rights of the recipient etc.

In the clause below, one party agrees to provide specified sales information to the other party, which extends to details of competing products.

Party B shall supply such reports, returns and other information as Party A from time to time requests, including sales forecasts and information with regard to products competing with or likely to compete with the products marketed by Party A in the Territory.

Vocabulary: the expression 'from time to time' usually means 'periodically' or 'at any particular time'.

Retention of title   11.3.20

Under a provision for retention of title, a seller of goods seeks to retain ownership of the goods, even after delivery to the buyer, until they have been paid for. Such a clause should ensure full title is retained, clearly identify the goods and indicate what the purchaser may do with the goods etc. This type of provision is usually contained in a payments clause.

The clause below specifies that the buyer does not own the goods until they have been paid for, but at the same time clarifies that the risk in the goods passes to the buyer at the time of delivery.

Ownership of the goods that are the subject of this contract shall not pass to the Buyer until they are fully paid for, but the risk in the goods shall be borne by the Buyer from the date of delivery by the Seller or its agents to the Buyer.

Vocabulary: the word 'borne' is the past participle of 'bear' and here means 'carried by the specified party'. In other words, in this context if anything happens to the goods, the responsibility for this is the Buyer's.

Set-off and retention   11.3.21

This provision is usually contained in payments clauses. 'Set-off' generally means 'deduction'. It occurs when party A to the contract is obliged to pay party B a sum of money, but party B also owes party A a smaller sum. In such a situation, it may be agreed that party A will deduct from the sum to be paid to party B the amount that party B owes to party A. 'Retention' generally means 'holding back'. For example, a contract may provide that a sum is not to be paid until the contract work is successfully completed.

The example clause below simply records that set-off is not permitted.

Party B agrees with Party A throughout the term of the contract not to set-off for any reason any money payable by Party B to Party A for supplies of products under the contract.

11.3.22   Sub-contracting

This clause deals with whether sub-contracting of the work required under the contract is allowed at all; on what terms it might be allowed, whether there is a duty to consult the other party and the situations in which particular obligations and requirements are laid upon sub-contractors (e.g. as to intellectual property rights).

The example clause below provides that sub-contracting is permitted but must be personally supervised by the Contractor.

All work undertaken or services provided by the Contractor, or by any sub-contractor appointed by the Contractor, under the terms of this contract, shall be done or performed by, or under the personal supervision and direction of, the Contractor.

11.3.23   Time of the essence

Where a term of a contract is said to be 'of the essence', breach of that term will usually entitle the other party to terminate the contract (i.e. delays are regarded as a fundamental breach of the contract). Provisions to this effect will usually form part of another clause, and should indicate the consequences of failing to meet the time limits stipulated.

The example clause set out below provides that time is of the essence with respect to the dates and periods set out in the contract or to any other dates and periods agreed between the parties. The result of this is that delays in the performance of obligations past these time limits will be treated as fundamental breaches of the contract (giving rise to the right to terminate the agreement) instead of minor breaches (giving rising only to a possible claim for damages).

Time shall be of the essence of this contract both as regards the dates and periods specifically mentioned and as regards any dates and periods that may be substituted for them by agreement in writing between the parties.

Vocabulary: the phrase 'substituted for' means 'to replace with'. In this clause if the agreed dates and periods are changed by agreement between the parties, time will still be of the essence in relation to the new dates and periods.

SECONDARY COMMERCIAL PROVISIONS

Capacity

'Capacity' refers to whether a person or legal entity has the legal right to enter into a contract. A provision on this issue is usually contained in another clause, and its purpose is to indicate that various documents that may be signed under the contract (e.g. notices, approvals, variations of contract) may only be signed by an authorised representative of a party.

In the clause given below a party warrants that a certain person has authorisation to sign documents on its behalf.

The Company warrants that its duly authorised representative [insert name] has the necessary authority to enter into this contract on the Company's behalf.

Vocabulary: the word 'warrants' in this context means to make a legally binding statement.

Confidentiality

A confidentiality clause allows one or both parties to protect the confidentiality of sensitive information. Such a clause should identify the information to be covered, which parties are bound by the clause, what the confidential information can be used for, to what extent it can be disclosed (e.g. to employees or third parties) and whether there are any exceptions to the requirement of confidentiality etc.

The short clause set out below provides a general duty of confidentiality in respect of information shared as a result of the contract.

The parties to this contract shall at all times keep confidential all information acquired in consequence of this contract, except for information to which they may be entitled or bound to disclose by force of law or where required to do so by regulatory agencies.

Vocabulary: the expression 'by force of law' means 'as a result of a legal requirement'. Therefore, in this clause if either a binding legal provision stipulates that information must be disclosed, or a court orders such disclosure, then such disclosure must be made.

Consequences of termination

In many cases, certain rights or obligations contained in the contract may continue to exist or come into existence after the contract has ended. The contract may contain a clause on this subject. This clause should indicate which provisions survive termination, how long they survive for, whether any payments are to be made, whether termination of this agreement impacts on other related agreements or whether any new rights are granted on termination etc.

The clause below specifies which clauses shall survive termination of the contract.

No term, other than clause [insert clause or clauses that will survive termination], shall survive expiry or termination of this contract unless expressly agreed in writing between the parties.

Vocabulary: the expression 'expressly agreed' means 'specifically agreed'. In other words, there must be specific agreement between the parties on that particular issue.

11.4.4   Cumulative remedies

This type of clause provides that remedies provided for under the contract are in addition to any other rights or remedies a party might have. The aim of such a clause is to prevent a party from arguing that only one of a possible range of remedies can be used.

The clause below provides that both parties may use the full range of legal remedies and rights available to them under the applicable law.

Any remedy or right conferred on either party for breach of this contract shall be in addition to and without prejudice to all other rights and remedies available to it under the applicable law.

Vocabulary: the use of the phrase 'without prejudice' in this clause means that the fact that a party has used a remedy granted under the contract does not prevent them from using other remedies.

11.4.5   Disclaimers

A disclaimer is used by a party to a contract in order to disclaim (i.e. avoid) responsibility for a particular fact or situation. Such a provision is often used in the context of warranties to indicate an understanding that no legal liability arises in a context where it might otherwise arise.

Here is a simple clause in which the purchaser of goods acknowledges that it has inspected the goods to be sold and entered into the contract on that basis rather than on the basis of representations made by the Vendor. This acts as a disclaimer on the Vendor's part for any possible liability arising from misrepresentation.

The Purchaser agrees that the goods to be sold have been inspected by [him/her] or on [his/her] behalf and [he/she] has entered into this agreement on the basis of such inspection and not in reliance on any representation or warranty made by or on behalf of the Vendor.

Vocabulary: the phrase 'on his/her behalf' means that the inspection is carried out by another person on the instruction of the Purchaser.

Exemption clauses

Commercial contracts invariably contain provisions that seek to exclude or limit liability (collectively known as exemption clauses). These are discussed in further detail in section 12.3.

The example clause below seeks to exclude liability for one party's failure to deliver goods or provide services by the dates specified in the contract, or for any damage caused to the other party as a result of failing to deliver the goods or provide the services by those dates.

While Party A will endeavour to meet estimated dates for delivery of the goods and performance of services specified in Schedule II, Party A undertakes no obligation to deliver or perform by such dates, and Party A shall not be liable for any damage resulting from any failure to deliver or perform by such dates however caused.

Vocabulary: the phrase 'undertakes no obligation' means 'accepts no obligation'. The word 'liable' means 'to be legally responsible for'.

Expiration and termination at will

This type of provision is used in fixed-term contracts to specify the date on which the contract automatically expires and is generally contained in the termination clause. It may also provide that the contract may be terminated earlier by one or more of the parties by notice to the other parties.

The clause given below provides that the contract terminates on a fixed date if it has not been terminated prior to that under any other applicable provision of the contract.

Subject to any earlier termination under clause [__], this contract shall continue in force until the [__] of the Commencement Date when it shall terminate automatically by expiry.

Vocabulary: the phrase 'terminate automatically by expiry' means that when the specified date is reached, the contract is no longer valid, and no action is required by either party to achieve this.

11.4.8   **Force majeure**

Under common law, where a contract becomes impossible to perform or can only be performed in a manner substantially different from that originally envisaged, then performance is excused under the doctrine of frustration.

The purpose of a force majeure clause is therefore to define the circumstances in which performance may be excused. This may either be done by setting out a long list of such circumstances (but see the **exclusio unius est exclusio alterius** rule at 10.2.2.5) or by merely referring to 'circumstances beyond the control of the parties' etc.

The clause sets out below that no liability applies in respect of breaches of contract caused by circumstances beyond the reasonable control of the parties, and incorporates an extension of time for performance in the event of delay being caused by force majeure events.

Neither party shall be liable for delay in performing or failure to perform obligations under this contract if such delay or failure results from events or circumstances beyond its reasonable control. Such delay or failure shall not constitute a breach of this contract and the time allowed for performance shall be extended by a period equivalent to that during which performance is so prevented.

Vocabulary: the phrase 'circumstances beyond reasonable control' means circumstances over which the parties cannot for legal purposes be expected to have control, even if it might theoretically be possible for them to influence such circumstances.

11.4.9   **Indemnities**

An indemnity consists of an undertaking given by party A to party B that party A will make good any losses suffered by B arising from claims made against B by a third party in specified situations.

The wording 'hold harmless' is often used in contracts to indicate that the party giving the indemnity will not sue the other party for recovery of its losses. The clause should indicate what the indemnifying party will be responsible for, whether there are any limits on the amount to be paid, what the indemnity covers, whether other persons are covered by the indemnity etc.

In the clause below Party A provides a general indemnity to Party B in respect of any breach of warranties given in the contract.

Party A undertakes to indemnify Party B and keep Party B fully indemnified against all losses, liabilities, costs and expenses arising out of the breach of the [above warranties] or out of any claim made by a third party which if substantiated would constitute such a breach.

Vocabulary: the phrase 'losses, liabilities, costs and expenses' covers a variety of slightly different types of financial loss. The word 'losses' means losses in income caused by the breach of warranty, 'liabilities' means legal obligations (which may also be financial) brought about by the breach, 'costs' means legal costs and 'expenses' means financial outlay necessitated by the breach.

Insurance

This clause generally includes warranties as to the level and scope of insurance cover held by a contracting party and may also include obligations on a party to ensure against certain risks. The drafting should take account of whether the party requires insurance in the circumstances of the contract, what kinds of incidents are to be covered by the clause, what level of cover is required and for how long etc.

The clause set out below provides a warranty that valid insurance is in place in relation to the subject-matter of the contract.

The Vendor warrants that:

insurance policies are in force in respect of the Assets to their full reinstatement value and against all other risks and liabilities (including but not limited to product liability and consequential loss of profits); and

to the best of the Vendor's knowledge and belief there are no circumstances that could lead to any such insurance being revoked or not renewed in the ordinary course of events.

Vocabulary: 'reinstatement' is roughly a synonym for 'replacement'. 'Product liability' refers to defects in the products caused by the manufacturing process. The phrase 'to the best of the Vendor's knowledge' means 'as far as the Vendor knows'.

Warranties

Warranties are statements of fact that the party giving the warranty asserts to be true, breach of which will usually lead to the other party being entitled to claim damages.

They include standard warranties as to a party's ability to enter into an agreement as well as detailed warranties regarding the quality of the goods or services that form the subject-matter of the contract. It is common for the party giving the warranty to limit the warranty to matters within its knowledge (using the formulation 'to the best of his/her knowledge, information and belief').

The clause below provides a warranty about the quality of the goods to be supplied under the contract. It should be noted that Party B's acceptance of designs that are provided to it is not in itself sufficient to relieve Party A of liability for defects in the products.

Party A warrants that all goods delivered under this contract shall be free from defects in material and workmanship, conform to applicable specifications and drawings and free from design defects and suitable for the purposes intended by Party B. Party B's approval of designs provided to it by Party A shall not relieve Party A of its obligations under any provision of this contract including the warranty contained in this clause.

11.5   BOILERPLATE CLAUSES

11.5.1   Agency and partnership

Commercial contracts sometimes include provisions stating that one party cannot bind the other parties or act on their behalf except where this is specifically provided for in the contract. The purpose of such provisions is to prevent an assumption arising, in respect of a long-term business relationship, that an agency or partnership relationship may have arisen.

The clause set out below simply asserts that no partnership exists under the contract.

Nothing in this contract shall be deemed to constitute a partnership between the parties.

Vocabulary: see 6.9 for an explanation of the meaning of 'deemed', and 10.1.7 for an explanation of the meaning of 'boilerplate clause'.

11.5.2   Agents for service

In some cases, a party may require that documents issued by a court or some other party in relation to a court case should be served upon (i.e. sent in a legally prescribed or agreed manner) someone other than the party concerned. A clause may be included in a commercial contract that specifically provides that this is agreed between the parties in the event of future legal proceedings.

The clause set out below authorises an agent to accept service on Party A's behalf and specifies the details of that agent for the benefit of the other parties.

Party A irrevocably appoints [insert name] at present of [insert address] to receive on its behalf service of proceedings issued out of the courts in any action or proceedings arising out of or in connection with this contract.

Vocabulary: the word 'irrevocably' means that the appointment cannot be revoked (i.e. cancelled).

Amendment or variation   11.5.3

This type of clause normally deals with the issue of whether and to what extent the parties may amend an agreement, and the procedure to be followed if amendment takes place. The clause will typically specify who is entitled to make amendments, with whom they must be agreed, the manner in which they are to be made and whether amendments may be made to the whole contract or only to specified parts of it.

The clause set out below provides that there is no automatic right to make amendments or variations to the contract, and therefore these may only be made with the written consent of both parties.

No amendment or variation to this contract shall take effect unless it is made in writing and signed by the authorised representatives of each of the Parties.

Announcements   11.5.4

The purpose of this clause is to control the extent to which and the manner in which information is released into the public domain about an existing contract or about negotiations to enter into a contract. This is particularly important for public companies (where the information could affect the share price), as well as to companies subject to close regulatory control or media scrutiny.

Such a clause will usually state whether announcements are allowed, who is entitled to make them, whether the consent of other parties is required, whether the wording of the announcement needs to be agreed etc.

The clause below provides that announcements may only be made if both parties agree to them or they are necessary for legal reasons. The clause also imposes a duty on the parties to consult each other prior to the announcement.

No announcement of any kind shall be made in respect of the subject-matter of this contract except as specifically agreed between the parties or if an announcement is required by law. Any announcement by either party and so required by law shall only be issued after prior consultation with the other party.

11.5.5   Arbitration and ADR (alternative dispute resolution)

The purpose of an arbitration clause in a contract is to enable the resolution of disputes between the contracting parties by an impartial third party or panel acting in a judicial manner.

Clauses on this issue generally address issues including whether an expert should be used in the arbitral proceedings, the duration of the arbitration agreement, the number of arbitrators to be used, the method of appointment of the arbitrator(s), the language and law to be used in the arbitration proceedings, whether the decision reached in arbitration should be final (i.e. should the clause exclude the possibility of further appeal to the court?) etc.

The clause below provides for arbitration to be carried out by the International Chamber of Commerce in accordance with the relevant rules.

Any dispute or claim arising out of this contract shall be referred to the International Chamber of Commerce ('ICC') in Paris for resolution in accordance with the ICC Conciliation and Arbitration Rules.

11.5.6   Assignment and novation

These terms refer to the transfer of a party's rights and obligations to another party. 'Novation' arises where a party assigns both rights and obligations under the contract to a third party, giving rise to a new contract between the transferee and the other party to the existing contract. Such an arrangement requires the consent of the transferor, the transferee and the other contracting party. Clauses dealing with assignment and novation generally state whether assignment is permitted, who is entitled to assign, what can be assigned, whether the consent of the other party is needed and in what form etc.

The clause below provides that there is no automatic right to assign any part of the contract to a third party, and therefore such assignment may only be made if the other party gives consent.

Neither Party may assign, delegate, sub-contract, charge or otherwise transfer any or all of its rights and obligations under this contract without the prior written consent of the other Party.

Vocabulary: the word 'charge' in this context means 'to provide as a security on a loan'.

11.5.7   Costs and expenses

The word 'costs' is generally used to refer only to legal fees. Expenses form a slightly different category and generally refer to expenditure involved in dealings with regulatory authorities (e.g. registrations and application costs) or to incidental expenses such as transport costs.

The usual rule is that unless the contract specifies otherwise, the parties bear their own costs and expenses incurred in negotiating and preparing a contract. However, they may provide otherwise in a specific clause to this effect, which may specify the costs and expenses involved, who is to be responsible for paying them, when they are to be paid and the consequences of failing to pay.

The clause below simply confirms that each party will bear its own costs and expenses in relation to drawing up the contract.

Each party shall bear its own legal costs and other costs and expenses arising in connection with the drafting, negotiation and execution of this contract.

Vocabulary: the word 'execution' in this context means signature of the contract and any other actions required to make it legally valid.

Further assurances 11.5.8

After completing a transaction, the parties may be required to take further steps in order, for example, to comply with statutory or regulatory requirements. For instance, it may be necessary to execute further documentation to give effect to certain parts of the contract. The purpose of a further assurance clause is therefore to secure the relevant party's agreement to carry out whatever further action is needed to implement the contract.

The clause below confirms that the parties will, if necessary, carry out such further actions as are necessary to put the purposes of the contract into effect.

Each party agrees to execute, acknowledge and deliver such further documentation and do all such acts as may be necessary to carry out and put into effect the purposes of this contract.

Language 11.5.9

English is frequently used in international transactions. However, in many cases contracts are prepared in more than one language. In such contracts it is advisable to insert a clause regulating such issues as which language version is the authoritative version, which language should be used for amendments to the contract, which law should be used and whether documents relevant to the contract should be translated into English.

The clause below may be used where the contract is drawn up entirely in English. It provides that the contract may be translated into other languages but that the English text remains the authoritative version.

This contract is made only in the English language. It may be translated into any language other than English, provided that the English text shall in any event prevail.

Vocabulary: the word 'prevail' in this context means that the English text takes precedence over texts in any other language.

11.5.10   Law and jurisdiction

This type of clause usually specifies which legal system applies to the contract or disputes arising from it and may also stipulate which court should hear the matter. In formulating such a clause, it is important to consider whether the drafting of the contract in general will be binding under the law to be specified in the clause.

The clause set out below provides that the contract will be governed by Finnish law and that the Finnish courts have exclusive jurisdiction in relation to any claims arising from it.

The validity, construction and performance of this contract shall be governed by Finnish law, and the Parties agree to submit to the exclusive jurisdiction of the Finnish courts in respect of any claim arising under this contract.

Vocabulary: the word 'construction' in this context means 'interpretation'. 'Exclusive jurisdiction' means that no other court is entitled to hear cases arising out of the contract.

11.5.11   Notices

This type of clause specifies the means by which the parties to the contract are to communicate with each other when certain events under the contract occur.

Usually, a notices clause will provide that the parties must send formal notices to one another in specified circumstances, including where they intend to terminate the contract or to exercise options or powers contained in the contract. The clause will stipulate whether the notice should be given in writing, the means by which it must be delivered, to whom it must be given and what time period must elapse before it becomes effective.

The clause below provides that notices must be served by first-class post and shall be treated as having been received at the time that it would normally have been received by post. Of course, it is also possible to agree that notices may be served by other means, either in place of or in addition to the post (e.g. personally, by email etc.).

All notices and other communications made under this contract shall be in writing and shall be deemed to have been duly given if sent in a letter by first-class or airmail pre-paid post addressed to that party (at the party's last known address or place of business or that party's registered office or the address of that party set out at the head of this contract [or any alternative address notified by that party in accordance with this clause]) and any notice so given shall be deemed to have been received (unless the contrary is proven) at the time at which the letter would be delivered under normal postal conditions.

Waivers

11.5.12

The term 'waiver' refers to a situation in which one party to a contract agrees not to insist on the exact performance by the other party of obligations contained in the contract. A concession of this type should be made in a formal document, which therefore amounts to a variation of the contract (though in certain situations an 'implied waiver' can arise as a result of the conduct of the parties).

The purpose of a waiver clause is to regulate the circumstances under which a waiver may occur. Such a clause will usually clarify that failure to exercise a right under the contract, or delay in exercising it, does not amount to a waiver of that right. It may also specify that a waiver of performance under a term of a contract does not constitute a waiver of any future breach of that term or any other term.

In addition, a waiver clause may incorporate provisions setting out the conditions under which a waiver may take place.

Here is a simple clause that stipulates that failure or delay in exercising a contractual right shall not constitute a waiver of that right or of any other right under the contract.

No failure or delay by any party to exercise any right, power or remedy shall operate as a waiver of it, nor shall any partial exercise of such right, power or remedy preclude any further exercise of it or of any other right, power or remedy.

Vocabulary: the word 'preclude' means 'prevent'.

Whole agreement

11.5.13

In formal legal terms, a binding contract may be formed in writing, involving one or more documents, or orally, or by a mixture of written documents and oral statements. It is therefore important for the parties to clarify either that the contract consists of the final written agreement alone or specify what other documents or statements should also be included.

The clause set out below clarifies that all the terms of the agreement between the parties are contained in the written contract and excludes the validity of any prior agreement between them. It also seeks to exclude liability for misrepresentation.

This contract contains the whole agreement between the parties and supersedes and invalidates any prior written or oral agreement between them, and the parties confirm that they have not entered into this contract on the basis of any representations that are not expressly incorporated in this contract.

Vocabulary: 'supersedes' means 'replaces', and 'expressly' means 'specifically'.

OPERATIVE LANGUAGE

As a rough rule, the functions of contractual language can be summarised using the acronym COAL (conditions, obligations, authorisations, limitations). These functions require different words and phrases, as set out below.

Conditions

Conditions can take different forms. For example:

1 When something ***must*** be done before something else ***may*** be done (condition precedent). For example:

   The consent of X must be obtained before the terms of this agreement may be implemented.

2 When an option to do something is linked to the performance of an obligation. In this context expressions such as ***provided that***, ***on condition that*** and ***subject to*** are frequently used. For example:

   This agreement may be renewed for a further period of two years subject to X having carried out the duties specified in section 7 to the satisfaction of Y.

3 When certain criteria must be fulfilled in order to qualify for a particular benefit, position, bonus etc. In such circumstances, words such as ***fulfil***, ***satisfy*** and ***meet*** are used in conjunction with words like ***criteria*** and ***conditions***. For example:

   Applicants must meet the criteria set out in Schedule II in order to be eligible to apply for this post.

4 When something provided under a contract must be of a certain quality, fit for a certain purpose or fulfil certain requirements. For example:

   The components supplied by the Seller shall be fit for the purpose for which the Buyer intends to use them.

12.1.2   Obligations

12.1.2.1   Will and shall

In legal usage (though not necessarily in 'normal' usage) **will** refers to the future and indicates intention, whereas **shall** indicates an imperative. Thus 'he will go' means that he intends to go, while 'he shall go' means that he is obliged to go.

Therefore, in legal documents drafted in the third person, obligations that will come up in the future are often expressed using **shall**. For example:

X shall deliver the Goods to Y on 5 November 2021.

At the time of writing, 5 November 2021 is in the future and X is obliged to deliver the Goods (a defined term, hence the capital 'G') to Y on that date.

12.1.2.2   When 'shall' is not required

While **shall** does not necessarily imply the future, in practice its use is generally not required when there is no element of futurity in the agreed obligation. Here is an example:

A hereby grants B an exclusive licence to manufacture, use and sell the Licensed Products in the Territory.

In this clause, the absence of the word **shall** indicates in practice that there is no element of futurity in A's obligation to grant the licence to B – it becomes an obligation at the point the document is executed. If it were included, the implication would be that the grant of the licence will happen at some unspecified point in the future. The lack of certainty about exactly when the licence will be granted would therefore undermine the effectiveness of the clause.

The word **hereby** is used essentially to emphasise this point but can be omitted without loss of meaning.

12.1.2.3   Alternatives to shall/shall not

Must is a good replacement for shall when expressing the imperative. For example:

If X becomes a party to this agreement, he shall [must] immediately pay to Y…

However, some take the view that **must** has an unnecessarily bossy feel to it, and accordingly prefer to use **shall** in its place.

Undertake is sometimes used as a straightforward synonym for **shall** but is more commonly used to indicate a more complex situation involving agreement to do something and acceptance of the associated legal consequences (usually of failure to do it). For example:

X will endeavour to meet estimated dates for delivery of the Goods to Y but undertakes no obligation to deliver by such dates, and X shall not be liable for any damage resulting from any failure to deliver by such dates.

Endeavour is used to express an obligation to attempt something without being committed to achieving it – as in the example above.

Authorisations   12.1.3

Authorisations refer to those situations in which a party is allowed to do something but is not obliged to do that thing.

The word **may** is very commonly used in such circumstances, but should be treated with care since it has a number of meanings:

- to express a possibility that something may be done ('the Company may purchase further products in the future';
- to indicate that one has a discretion to do that thing ('either party may assign the benefits under this contract on three months' written notice to the other party');
- to indicate a wish ('the parties intend that the signature of this contract may signal the beginning of a mutually beneficial cooperation between them').

The following words are generally used in the contexts suggested:

- 'is entitled to' indicates a party's right ('X is entitled to use the office premises');
- 'is not entitled to' indicates that a party does not have a right ('X is not entitled to use the office premises');
- 'may' indicates a party's discretion to do something ('X may use the office premises');
- 'may not' indicates that a party does not have discretion to do something ('X may not use the office premises').

12.1.4   Limitations (restrictions)

Limitations – which may also be referred to as **restrictions** – refer to things that may be done, but only with permission or to a certain extent. For instance, a speed restriction in a city does not stop you driving your car in the city, but is designed to ensure that you keep to a certain speed limit when doing so.

12.1.4.1   Permission-based limitations

When drafting limitations based on permission, the key words are **without** and **unless**, which allow the drafter to create the limitation in different ways. For example:

Unless the Lessor gives express permission, no building work may be carried out at the Site during weekends.

OR

No building work may be carried out at the site during weekends without the Lessor's express permission.

12.1.4.2   Extent-based limitations

Extent-based limitations take a number of forms – temporal, geographical, as to scope of activities, applications and responsibilities – though time limitations are perhaps the most frequently encountered of these. Words and phrases typically found in this context include **by**, **no later than** and **remains open until**:

The goods shall be delivered no later than/by 5 April 2021.

This offer remains open until 5 April 2021.

The word **within** is particularly useful in this context, as it can mean **inter alia** 'no later than' in a temporal context ('within 14 days'), no further than in a geographical context ('within a 12-kilometre radius') or not outside a particular business sphere ('within the clothing retail sector'). It is particularly encountered in anti-competition clauses:

X may not establish a business in competition with Y within six months of the termination of the Contract.

12.1.5   Operative language table

The table below offers an at-a-glance guide to operative language for contractual purposes, with examples of usage.

Conditions	Obligations/ Prohibitions	Authorisations	Limitations
provided that (e.g. 'The contract may be extended for further periods of two years provided that the sales targets are fulfilled.')	**shall** (e.g. 'X shall deliver the goods to Y by 17 May 2021.')	**may** (e.g. 'X may use the facilities provided by Y.')	**within** (e.g. 'A shall pay to B a deposit in the sum of EUR 10,500 within seven (7) days of the date of signature of this agreement.')
on condition that (e.g. 'The agent is entitled to the bonus specified in clause 4(a) on condition that the threshold sales levels set out in clause 6 are met.')	**must** (e.g. 'The consent of the Bank must be obtained before the share transfer may proceed.')	**may not** (e.g. 'X may not use the facilities provided by Y.')	**by** (e.g. 'A shall pay the sum of EUR 10,500 to B by 4 June 2021.')
subject to (e.g. 'A hereby grants B, subject to the provisions of this contract, an exclusive licence to sell the Licensed Products in the Territory.')	**is not required to** (e.g. 'X is not required to fulfil the criteria set out in Schedule II.')	**is entitled to** (e.g. 'The Company is entitled to alter the price of the goods on giving three months' written notice to the Distributor.')	**no later than** (e.g. 'A shall pay the sum of EUR 10,500 to B no later than 4 June 2021.')
shall/must...may (e.g. 'The consent of the Bank must/shall be obtained before the share transfer may proceed.')	**undertakes** (e.g. 'A undertakes to indemnify B against all losses, liabilities, costs and expenses arising out of the breach of the above warranties.')	**is not entitled to** (e.g. 'X is not entitled to use the facilities provided by Y during weekends and public holidays.')	**without** (e.g. 'Neither Party may assign any of its rights under this contract without the prior written consent of the other Party.')

fulfil/meet/satisfy the criteria/ conditions (e.g. 'In order to qualify for such price reduction the Buyer must satisfy the criteria/conditions set out in Schedule I.')	**must not** (e.g. 'A must not use the facilities provided by Y without Y's express written permission.')		**until** (e.g. 'This offer remains open until 6 December 2021.')
	shall not (e.g. 'Ownership of the goods that are the subject of this contract shall not pass to the Buyer until they are fully paid for.')		**unless** (e.g. 'Unless the Lessor gives express permission, no building work may be carried out at the Site during weekends.')
	shall endeavour to/shall use its best efforts to (e.g. 'A shall endeavour to/ use its best efforts to meet estimated dates for delivery of the goods specified in Schedule II.')		
	NB This is a 'soft' obligation since A is only required to attempt to meet the estimated dates for delivery but does not have to commit to doing so.		

***NB* No operative language where** (1) no element of futurity (e.g. 'X hereby appoints Y as its sole distributor'), or (2) for definitions (e.g. '"Execution Date" means 31 May 2021').

TROUBLESHOOTING ISSUES

The notes set out below should be read in the context of the general notes on drafting contained in Chapter 7. See in particular the guidance on problematic long sentences under 7.2.3.1.

Avoid sandwiches

The heading above is not a dietary recommendation, but refers to a bad drafting habit in which the purpose of criteria being outlined does not become apparent until the end of the paragraph in which they appear.

Here is an example of how **not** to do it:

Applicants shall by 20 July 2021 (1) supply an up-to-date CV; (2) fill out and return the application form; and (3) complete the competence test, in order to be considered for the advertised position.

The problem here is that being considered for the 'advertised position' is the purpose of the criteria, but this does not become apparent until the end of the sentence. This makes it more difficult to grasp the purpose of the criteria than need be the case.

Here is a better version:

In order to be considered for the advertised position, applicants shall by 20 July 2021 provide the following: (1) an up-to-date CV, (2) a completed application form and (3) a completed competence test.

The use of the phrase 'provide the following' in this version further streamlines the drafting by creating a springboard for the three criteria listed. In other words, each limb of the criteria completes the opening phrase.

12.2.2 **Avoid faulty springboards**

In drafting terms, a 'springboard' is a phrase used to introduce lists of criteria or rules in contractual or legislative drafting. These lists come in four different types:

1 lists of short items;

2 lists in which each item completes the introductory sentence;

3 lists in which all items are complete statements in their own right without a grammatical link to the introductory sentence;

4 lists in which one or more of the items consists of more than one sentence.

The notes below cover (2), since this is the most problematic category. It requires: an introductory colon, no initial capitals, a semi-colon after each item and a full stop at the end. Here is an example:

A shall transmit to B by 31 December 2021:

>   *all relevant data relating to Unit 5;*

>   *all relevant data relating to Unit 6;*

>   *information about any changes made to such data.*

This example works in formal terms because it respects the rules outlined above. A typical mistake made in this situation is to put initial capitals for each item. This is incorrect because each item completes the introductory sentence, which means that the whole should be regarded as a single unbroken sentence. Separating the items onto different lines does not change this. You would not write, for instance:

A shall transmit to B by 31 December 2021 All relevant data relating to Unit 5.

It works in substantive terms because the verb 'transmit' can be used with the nouns 'data' and 'information' – i.e. both data and information can be transmitted. A typical mistake made on this point is to forget the scope of the meaning of the verb used in the springboard sentence when drafting the items that follow. For example:

A shall transmit to B by 31 December 2021:

>   *all relevant data relating to Unit 5;*

all relevant data relating to Unit 6;

information about any changes to such data;

the hardware currently stored in Unit 7.

The problem here is that the 'hardware' mentioned in item (4) cannot really be 'transmitted', since transmission is usually used only in connection with intangible items. There are two possible solutions. The first is to use a more general word (e.g. 'send') in the springboard sentence:

A shall send to B by 31 December 2021…

The second is to omit the verb phrase ('transmit to B') from the springboard sentence and use different verbs in the items that follow as appropriate. For instance:

A shall by 31 December 2021:

(1) transmit to B all relevant data relating to Unit 5

…

(4) transport to B the hardware currently stored in Unit 7.

This second solution is less satisfactory than the first, since it is necessary to find a different verb for each item and remember to add 'to B' in each case. However, it can be useful in long lists covering a range of different issues where it would clearly be impossible to relate all the items to a single verb.

Separate obligations from definitions

12.2.3

When drafting definitions, care should be taken that the definition given merely declares what a particular word or phrase is intended to mean and does not contain any obligations.

Here is an example of a definition that has become merged with an obligation:

'Completion Date' means 8 October 2021, on which date Party A must pay the purchase price in respect of the Property to Party B and relieve Party B of liability for all rates and taxes payable on the Property.

This is bad drafting, because it results in hiding the obligation in a part of the document where the reader does not expect to find it. The contract will remain legally valid, but time will be wasted trying to locate the obligation. The second part of the sentence should be detached from the definition and reformulated as a separate contractual term, as follows:

12.2.3.1 Definition

'Completion Date' means 8 October 2021.

12.2.3.2 Payment

On the Completion Date Party A must pay the purchase price in respect of the Property to Party B and must relieve Party B of liability for all rates and taxes on the Property.

12.2.4 Differentiate conditions and promises

It is important not to confuse the function of conditions and promises in the drafting of contracts.

A **condition** is an event that must occur before performance of a certain obligation occurs. A **promise** is the means by which a party binds itself to the performance of that obligation.

These two functions must be clearly differentiated in the drafting of a contract, since failure to do so will frequently result in the ultimate obligation being unclear. Here is an example of this problem:

Party A shall deliver the Products to Party B on 13 August 2021. The Products shall be fit for the purpose notified to Party A by Party B. Party B shall pay Party A the sum of $110,000 by 13 September 2021.

Here, the fitness of the products for the notified purpose is a condition, while the other parts of the clause (the obligation to deliver the products and pay for them) are clearly promises. The mixture of these different functions makes it unclear whether Party B has to pay for the products even if they are not fit for the purpose. The solution is to place the fitness-for-purpose condition in a separate clause and separate the delivery and payment obligations – resulting in three different clauses.

12.2.5 Avoid use of 'and/or'

The formulation 'and/or' is frequently used in the drafting of legal documents but can in certain situations lead to ambiguity. The reason for this is that the use of 'and' and 'or' together is often contradictory. The usual remedy is to use one of the words but not both.

Here is an example of a problem caused by using 'and' and 'or' together:

Party A must provide the necessary equipment and/or the financing necessary to purchase the necessary equipment.

The use of 'and/or' in this sentence makes it appear that Party A does not have a choice in what it provides, while in reality it is entitled to provide either the equipment or the financing, but not both. Therefore, the word 'and' should be omitted.

Conversely, in the following sentence, 'or' should be omitted because it is clear that both parties have equal entitlement:

Party A and/or Party B may use the Premises.

Use a clear numbering system

A number of different numbering systems are used in Anglo-American legal documentation. No one system is best – the choice is a matter of personal preference or company policy. However:

- In all cases consistency in the use of numbering is crucial: once a particular system has been chosen, it should be logically applied.

- In order to ensure the user-friendliness of the document it is best not to descend beyond the third level of numbering (e.g. 1[2][a] or 3.3.1) unless this is absolutely necessary. Instead of subdividing further, it may be better to structure the document in a different way.

Three of the most common systems are illustrated in the table below.

Arabic/Roman system	Decimal system	Partial combination
1.	1.	1.
2.	2.	2.
3(1)	3.1	3.1
(2)	3.2	3.2
(3)(a)	3.3.1	3.3(a)
(b)	3.3.2	(b)
(c)(i)	3.3.3	(c)(i)
(ii)	3.3.3.1	(ii)
(iii)(A)	3.3.3.2	(iii)(A)
(B)	3.3.3.3	(B)
(C)	3.3.3.3.1	(C)

12.2.7 Avoid excessive cross-referencing

It is often necessary to create cross-references between one clause and another in a legal document (often using formulations such as 'subject to the provisions for termination contained in clause 5.1'), where one obligation cannot be read in isolation from another. A good example of this is where a clause dealing with the basis on which a commercial contract involving ongoing obligations can be renewed includes a reference to a clause that deals with the basis on which it can be terminated. In this situation, cross-referencing is necessary because the alternative would be to duplicate the content of the clause that is referenced. This would be bad drafting partly because duplication in itself entails the risk of creating confusion in the reader's mind and partly due to the risk of discrepancies creeping into the duplicated versions.

However, excessive cross-referencing should also be avoided. The main reasons for this are as follows:

- It makes the document difficult to read and understand, since the reader is constantly having to alternate between different clauses to grasp the overall meaning of a provision (and for the same reason it makes the document difficult to create).

- There is increased scope for errors in the preparation and amendment of the document. A typical error in this respect is that having created a reference in one numbered clause to another numbered clause, the drafter changes the number or content of the clause referred to without making a corresponding change to the reference.

The following considerations may be useful when deciding whether and how to insert a cross-reference in a text:

- Is the cross-reference necessary? Does it make the text easier to understand?

- Does the cross-reference indicate the subject-matter involved? For example, it is better to write 'subject to the provisions governing assignment laid down in clause 15' than 'subject to clause 15'.

- As a rule of thumb, avoid cross-references to provisions that do not themselves contain the subject-matter in question but simply contain a further cross-reference to yet another provision.

- In the event that it is necessary to create an external cross-reference (i.e. to a different document), ensure that this document is accessible to the relevant parties.

DRAFTING EXEMPTION CLAUSES

In most commercial contracts, either party to a contract may seek to avoid incurring liability for certain breaches of the contract (**exclusion clause**), or may specify that their liability for such a breach will be limited in some way (**limitation clause**). The term 'exemption clause' refers to both of these situations, and such clauses may be designed to fulfil a variety of purposes, including the following:

- Allowing a party unilaterally to vary the nature of its obligations under the contract.

- Limiting a party's remedies in the event that another party breaches the contract.

- Imposing restrictions on the circumstances in which a party is entitled to exercise contractual remedies.

- Limiting liability to a specified sum of money ('liquidated damages' clause).

- Excluding liability for certain types of loss (e.g. indirect and consequential losses – see below).

- Excluding liability altogether.

Exemption clauses are interpreted using the **contra proferentem rule**, which states that where the words of the clause are ambiguous, they will be interpreted in the way least favourable to the party relying on them. This rule is applied strictly in the case of exclusion clauses (particularly where they seek to exclude liability for negligence) and less strictly in the case of limitation clauses.

Such clauses are often the subject of dispute between parties to a contract and the courts are regularly called upon to interpret their meaning. Therefore, parties should take care in deciding what liability they wish to exclude or limit, and in ensuring that the contract accurately reflects their intentions. Particular care should be taken in differentiating between:

1   **direct loss**, i.e. loss that arises naturally and directly from the breach of contract; and

2   **indirect or consequential loss**, i.e. loss that was reasonably contemplated because of special circumstances going beyond the ordinary course of things and known by the parties at the date of the contract.

A problem arises here from the use of clauses that seek to limit 'indirect or consequential loss'. Parties often use this phrase in the mistaken belief that they are excluding all potential liability for loss of profit, whereas in fact it will only cover the second situation outlined above. For example, loss of general trade due to delay in delivery of goods will usually be direct loss since in most commercial situations this cannot be classified as 'special circumstances'.

Here are some pointers aimed at ensuring that your exemption clauses are drafted in such a way as to ensure that you have limited your liability in accordance with your aims.

- Exclusion or limitation clauses should be drafted in plain English and should explicitly state what liability is to be excluded or limited.

- It is important to evaluate what potential losses could be classified as direct and what losses could be classified as indirect or consequential and then carefully draft the exclusion or limitation clause accordingly.

- In particular, if loss of profits is to be excluded they should be excluded in clear terms, distinct from any separate exclusion of indirect or consequential losses.

- Always remember that clauses excluding or limiting recovery of indirect or consequential losses may not exclude claims for loss of profits.

Wording such as 'no liability for indirect or consequential losses such as loss of profits' or 'loss of profits or other indirect or consequential losses' should be avoided. Both involve the risk that loss of profits considered to be 'direct' will not be excluded.

An example of a simple exemption clause is set out in section 11.4.6.

12.4 STRUCTURING A CLAUSE

Each clause in a document should deal with a separate issue. The typical structure of a clause is as follows:

- definitions of terms used only in the clause;

- the basic proposition;

- exceptions to the basic proposition;

- any restrictions on the scope of the exceptions.

If the clause contains a number of sentences that deal with different areas of the main topic of the clause, these should be split into separate sub-clauses. Where the clause is long and complex, such sub-division is essential.

When drafting a clause, the drafter should also consider whether that clause has any bearing on, or overlaps with, the terms of another clause in the document, and if necessary take the following steps:

- Eradicate any duplication or contradiction in the stipulations set out in different clauses. Ensure that each clause clearly deals with a separate issue.

- Create explicit linkages between the clauses (e.g. 'this clause takes effect subject to the provisions of clause 7').

Detailed provisions such as timetables or formulae can be placed in a separate clause or in a schedule to the document and then cross-referenced.

LAYOUT AND DESIGN   12.5

The use of clear, readable English and a logical document structure should be complemented by user-friendly document design. The aim of document design should be to help readers find their way around the document. In this way, the document will be simpler to understand.

Here are a few suggestions on improving the layout and design of your documents:

- Use a readable font in an appropriate size (generally between 10 and 12 points, with 12 being standard).

- Use between 45 and 70 characters per line.

- Use plenty of white space – break up slabs of text, use wide margins around the text, double-space all text and use generous spacing between clauses.

- Use headings. Give each main clause a bold heading. If possible, give subsidiary clauses headings in italics.

- Use italics rather than underlining to emphasise text.

- Use properly indented lists where appropriate.

- Put citations in footnotes rather than having them interrupt the flow of the main text.

- Don't justify the right margin.

- Use a cover sheet for any document over five or six pages long.

- Avoid excessive capitalisation.

CHECKLIST

This checklist can be used when drafting or evaluating business contracts and other documents.

Before drafting the document

- Have you got all the information you need?
- What is the main aim of the document?
- What are the main facts that form the basis of the document?
- What is the applicable law and how will it affect the drafting?
- Are there any useful **precedents** (generic legal documents on which specific legal documents can be based) that could be used for the draft?

Content

- Do the terms of the document reflect the intentions of the client or – if a contract – the bargain struck between the parties?
- If the document is a contract, does it contain fair mutual obligations?
- Does the document make provision for things that might go wrong in the future?
- Does the drafting of the document provide protection if something does go wrong?
- If the document is a contract, does it provide a dispute-resolution mechanism in case something goes wrong?

Language

- Is the language used in the document clear and coherent?
- Are there any ambiguities?
- Is terminology used in a consistent way?
- Are the spelling and punctuation correct?
- Will the reader understand the contract?

- Have the following been removed:
  - ○ irrelevant language;
  - ○ jargon;
  - ○ excessive use of capitals;
  - ○ unnecessary definitions;
  - ○ unnecessary use of foreign terms?

Law

- Is the document legally effective?
- Does it fulfil all formal requirements (if applicable)?
- Are any clauses in the document illegal?
- How will the governing law interpret its terms in the event of breach?

Accuracy

Is all factual matter contained in the document accurate? In particular, take note of:

- dates;
- time limits;
- names and addresses;
- prices;
- identification numbers;
- references to other sections or schedules;
- information contained in schedules.

Structure

- Does the document have a logical structure?
- Does each paragraph contain just one main idea?
- Does the order of sentences and paragraphs make sense?
- Are there links between one paragraph and the next?
- Are there links between sentences in each paragraph?

Presentation and layout

- Is the font size big enough (12 points)?
- Are the lines the right length (45 to 70 characters per line)?
- Is there enough white space in the document?
- Have headings been used for main clauses?
- Have properly indented lists been used where appropriate?

Correspondence, memoranda and essays

LETTER-WRITING CONVENTIONS

Overview

Correspondence written in English in legal contexts is subject to fewer formal conventions than is the case in various other languages. Comparatively few set phrases are routinely included, and greater emphasis is placed on substance than rigid observance of formalities and habits of style. The introduction of email and other forms of messaging has increased this tendency. However, certain conventions do exist, as discussed below, and provide a convenient framework that aids effective and professional communication.

Beginning a letter

When beginning your letter, note the following conventions:

- *Dear Sir* opens a letter written to a man whose name you do not know.

- *Dear Sirs* is often used to address a firm where at least one of the members of the firm is male. However, *Dear Sir or Madam*[1] is arguably a better alternative, since it does not assume that the person who opens the letter will be a man.

- *Dear Mesdames* (extremely formal and rarely used) is used to address a firm where all the members are female.

- *Dear Madam* is used to address a woman, whether single or married, whose name you do not know.

- *Dear Sir or Madam* (or *Dear Sir/Madam*) is used to address a person when you do not know their name or sex.

When you know the name of the person you are writing to, but do not know them well, the salutation takes the form of *Dear* followed by a courtesy title (i.e. Mr, Ms, Miss, Mrs etc.) and the person's surname.

Note

1 This approach was taken up, for example, by Freshfields Bruckhaus Deringer, one of Britain's most prestigious law firms, in 2016. The firm uses 'Dear Ladies and Gentlemen' in the US.

In business correspondence, 'Mr' is the standard title to be used when writing to a man, and 'Ms' is the standard title to be used when writing to a woman. 'Ms' is almost always preferable to 'Mrs' or 'Miss' (1) for reasons of gender equality, since, as with 'Mr', it does not involve a differentiation based on marital status; and (2) because the recipient's marital status has no business relevance. Individual recipients may of course indicate that they prefer a different form of address, but by default correspondence to female recipients should utilise 'Ms'.

Initials or first names are not used with courtesy titles, e.g. **Dear Mr Smith**, NOT **Dear Mr J Smith** or **Dear Mr John Smith**. Persons who you know well can be addressed using just their first name, e.g. **Dear John**.

In British usage, a comma after the salutation is optional, i.e. **Dear Mr Smith**, or **Dear Mr Smith**.

In American usage, it is customary (1) to put a dot after the courtesy title (e.g. Mr., Ms.); and (2) to put a colon after the salutation (e.g. **Dear Mr. Smith:**).

13.1.3   Ending a letter

If the letter begins **Dear Sir**, **Dear Sirs**, **Dear Madam**, **Dear Mesdames** or **Dear Sir or Madam**, the ending should be **Yours faithfully**.

When writing to American firms, **Respectfully yours** (very formal) or **Yours truly** (less formal) should be used. However, in general American lawyers take a more relaxed approach to such formalities than their British colleagues.

If the letter begins with a personal name, e.g. **Dear Mr Jones**, **Dear Mrs Brown** or **Dear Ms Porter**, it should end with **Yours sincerely**. The American equivalent is **Sincerely** or **Sincerely yours**.

A letter to someone you know well may close with a number of different informal phrases. Examples include:

- With best wishes
- Best wishes
- With best regards
- Best regards
- Kind regards
- Kindest personal regards
- Best

Avoid closing your letter with old-fashioned phrases, e.g. **We remain, sir, your obedient servants**.

Commas after the complimentary close are generally not used in legal letters. The complimentary close is usually placed on the left, aligned under the rest of the letter.

Reference table (letter endings)

The table below provides a quick guide to ending your letters, according to the title used in the opening.

Title Used	Status	Ending (UK)	Ending (US)
Mr	married or unmarried male	Yours sincerely	Sincerely
Mrs (rarely used in business and legal contexts)	married female	Yours sincerely	Sincerely
Miss (rarely used in business and legal contexts)	unmarried female	Yours sincerely	Sincerely
Ms	married or unmarried female	Yours sincerely	Sincerely
Sir	male – name not known	Yours faithfully	Yours truly/ Respectfully yours
Madam	female – name not known	Yours faithfully	Yours truly/ Respectfully yours
medical/academic/ military e.g. Dr/Professor/ General	these titles do not change whether addressing a male or female	Yours sincerely	Sincerely
None (Dear Bill/ Dear Susan etc.)	Irrelevant	Best regards	Best regards

Abbreviations used in letters

13.1.4

A number of abbreviations may be used at the foot of a letter. Here are some examples:

- **Enc./Encl**. indicates that documents are enclosed with the letter. If there are a number of these, it is usual to list them.

- **pp** means *per procurationem* (meaning, in essence, 'for and on behalf of') and is used if someone other than the writer has signed the letter on the writer's behalf.

- **cc** means carbon copy. Carbon copies are almost never used nowadays but were in common use in the pre-photocopier era, during which an additional sheet of paper could be placed underneath the sheet being typed or written on and would retain an imprint of the typing or writing, thus providing a record of it. The term survives as an abbreviation used to indicate that copies are sent to named individuals other than the named recipient.

- **bcc** means blind carbon copy. This abbreviation is used when other people have been sent copies but you do not want the recipient to know this. The abbreviation is written on the copies only and not on the original version that is sent to the recipient.

The abbreviation **FAO** is sometimes seen in the address printed on the envelope. It means 'for the attention of' (e.g. **FAO the Managing Director**).

13.2 LETTER-WRITING STYLE

13.2.1 Planning

The main aims of legal correspondence in all cases are clarity and accuracy. However, the style of correspondence will differ slightly according to whom the correspondence is being written for. When writing to another lawyer, the writer can assume that legal jargon and terms of art will be understood and do not need to be explained. When writing to clients and other third parties, this assumption cannot be made. Care should be taken to explain legal technicalities in terms that a layperson can understand.

In all cases, start by thinking about what you are going to say and how you are going to say it. Ask yourself these questions:

- What am I trying to say?

- Who am I trying to say it to?

- What do they need to know?

- What sort of tone should I adopt?

- What words will express what I am trying to say?

- How will I structure what I am going to say?

- How can I divide my writing into manageable sections?

- Could I make it shorter?

Structure

General considerations

The most important thing to remember when writing a letter or email is to consider the reader. The content and style of your letter or email will be affected by the following considerations:

- Who is going to be reading it?

- How much do they understand about the subject-matter of the letter? (i.e. the content is likely to differ if you are dealing with (1) a client or (2) an expert in a particular field.)

- What do they need to know?

- How much background information do they need?

- Do you need any information from them?

- What sort of tone should you adopt?

Whoever you're writing to, you should ensure that your letter or email is:

- as short as possible but not shorter (if you try to use too few words the letter may become cryptic;

- clearly written;

- clearly set out; and

- appropriate in tone.

First paragraph

The opening sentence or paragraph is important as it sets the tone of the letter and creates a first impression.

If you are replying to a previous letter, start by thanking your correspondent for their letter:

Thank you for your letter of 4 May 2020.

If you are writing to someone for the first time, use the first paragraph to introduce yourself, the subject of the letter, and why you are writing:

We act on behalf of Smith Holdings Ltd and write concerning the lease on 22 Fairfields Avenue, Farnley Trading Estate.

13.2.2.3 Middle paragraphs

The main part of your letter will concern the points that need to be made, answers you wish to give or questions you want to ask. The exact nature of these will depend very much on the type of letter being written.

13.2.2.4 Final paragraph

At the end of your letter, if it is to a client or a third party, you should indicate that you may be contacted if your correspondent requires further information or assistance. If appropriate, you might also indicate another person in your office who may be contacted if you are absent. It is not usual to do this in a letter to another lawyer acting for another party in a case, however.

Here is an example of a typical letter ending:

Please do not hesitate to contact me, or my assistant John Bowles, if you require any further information.

13.2.3 Tone

It is important to try to strike the right tone in your letter. The right tone in most cases is one of professional neutrality. On the one hand, you should avoid pompous, obscure language. On the other hand, you should avoid language that is too informal or colloquial.

At all times, and particularly when writing to parties on the other side of a case from your client, you should avoid any tinge of personal animosity. This is important because although lawyers often find themselves in the position of having to threaten people or organisations with legal action on behalf of clients, the lawyer must ensure that basic standards of professional courtesy are adhered to at all times.

When seeking the right tone, certain things should be avoided:

1 Contractions. A contraction is when a word is shortened using an apostrophe, e.g. 'I can't and I won't'. This is too informal for most legal contexts.

2 Slang. This should be avoided, (1) because using it is unprofessional, and (2) because it may not be understood. Always use the correct, formal term, e.g. not a **fake** but a **charlatan**.

3 Expressions, proverbs, common metaphors. Again, these are both unprofessional and may not be understood. Always state precisely what you mean rather than resorting to an expression. For example, do not write **he**

was as mad as a wet hen when he heard the news, but *he was angry when he heard the news*.

4   Throwaway informality. It is important to retain a quality of professional gravity in the tone of your writing. Therefore, do not write *it's all sorted to go*, but (e.g.) *the matter has been satisfactorily resolved*.

EMAILS

Introduction to emails

It is often thought that emails are a less formal medium than letters. This is true up to a point but may be a dangerous belief for lawyers. Do not allow the informality of writing emails to lead you to forget the importance and possible sensitivity of the information you may be communicating.

Remember that an email is just as permanent as a letter and may be printed out and referred to in the future. Remember also that the exchange of emails leaves an easily traceable trail in both correspondents' inboxes. For these reasons, the same high standards of professionalism should be adhered to when writing emails as one would follow when writing letters.

There are several areas of legal communication where more traditional forms of correspondence may still be the most suitable. These include the following:

1   To communicate information or send documentation that is confidential.

2   As noted above, to send documents or communications that require a signature.

3   For personal or sensitive communications. Email has a slightly perfunctory, impersonal feel to it. Therefore, it is usually not suitable for any communication where a personal touch is required, e.g. messages of congratulation, condolence, complaint (or a response to a complaint).

Email writing style

Although email has been one of the most popular means of business communication for more than two decades at the time of writing, its ease of use and informality still give rise to a degree of uncertainty as to the writing style and conventions that should be followed in business situations.

In legal work, while email correspondence may tend towards informality, it should follow the same principles as any other form of business correspondence.

Here are some tips:

- Write a clear and informative heading in the subject line. Avoid leaving the subject line blank or writing uninformative headings ('Hi', 'Hello' etc.) as this will increase the chances of the email being regarded by the recipient as possible spam or virus mail and thus being deleted.

- In general, email messages follow the style and conventions used in letters. For example, you can use salutations such as **Dear Mr Archer** or **Dear Gerald** and complimentary closes such as **Yours sincerely**. However, if you know the recipient well, or if you are exchanging a series of messages with one person, you may dispense with the salutation and complimentary close altogether.

- Make a clear mental division between personal messages and messages written in the course of legal work. In a message written in the course of legal work, the same rules of writing apply as for a letter: write clearly and concisely, pay attention to the accuracy of factual information and legal advice given and observe high standards of professional courtesy; consider audience, purpose, clarity, consistency and tone.

- Use correct grammar, spelling, capitalisation and punctuation, as you would in any other form of correspondence. In particular, while it is useful to have a working knowledge of the latest email acronyms (see 13.3.3 below), it is inadvisable to use them in emails sent for work purposes. The reasons for this are first that they may not be understood – or they may be misinterpreted – by the recipient; and second that their use may undermine your professional credibility.

- Do not write words in capital letters in an email message. This can be seen as the equivalent of shouting and therefore have a negative effect. If you want to stress a word, put asterisks on each side of it, e.g. *urgent*.

- Keep your email messages short and to the point. People often receive a lot of emails at work, so conciseness is especially important.

- In general, limit yourself to one topic per message. This helps to keep the message brief and makes it easier for the recipient to answer, file and retrieve it later.

- Check your email message for mistakes before you send it, just as you would check a letter.

See the answer key for an example email.

Email abbreviations

The following – and many other – abbreviations are often found in emails and other informal communications.

This list is offered for recognition purposes only. It should not be taken as a recommendation to use the abbreviations contained in it, because (with the possible exception of such old favourites as ASAP, BR, BTW, FAQ, FYI, POV and TOC) most of them are extremely informal. They are therefore not suitable for most email correspondence conducted at work, and should never be used in letters.

Abt = about
AFAIC = as far as I'm concerned
AFAIK = as far as I know.
ASAP = as soon as possible.
BFN = bye for now.
BR = Best regards.
BTW = by the way.
CID = consider it done.
COB = close of business.
C/w = comes with.
DU = don't understand.
ETA = estimated time of arrival.
ETD = estimated time of departure.
FAQ = frequently asked questions.
FUD = fear, uncertainty and doubt.
FYI = for your information.
IAW = in accordance with.
ICBW = I could be wrong.
IMO = in my opinion.
IOW = in other words.
ITYS = I told you so.
LOL = laughing out loud.
NRN = no reply necessary.
OIC = oh I see.
OTOH = on the other hand.
POV = point of view.
P/w = password.
QFE = question for everyone.
TBA = can mean 'to be advised', 'to be announced' or 'to be agreed'.
TBC = to be continued.
TOC = table of contents.
Vm = voicemail.
W/e = weekend OR week ending.

| 13.4 | **LANGUAGE FOR LETTERS AND EMAILS** |

The list below covers some of the major language functions you, as a legal professional, are likely to perform when writing a letter or email. For each function, language suggestions are given.

The first line (saying 'hello')

Dear Mr Jones/Dear Sirs

OR

[informal email only] Hello/Hi David

Confirming client's instructions

During our meeting you told me that…

OR

You instructed me as follows…

OR [*informal*] It was interesting to hear about…

Referring to the previous email/letter

Thank you for your email/letter of 9 January about/concerning…

OR

I/we write with reference to your letter of 9 January about/concerning…

Acknowledging letter and promising to write later

I/we acknowledge receipt of your letter of 9 January to which I/we will provide a substantive response shortly.

Referring to theme of a message received

You informed me/us that…

OR

I/We note the points you raise with regard to…

OR

[*informal*] It was interesting to hear about…

Explaining why you are writing

I am/We are/writing to…

Referring to something

With regard/respect to…

Expressing doubt

I/we have certain reservations about…

OR

I/we remain unconvinced by your argument that…

Asking for clarification of issues

I/we have a number of queries about…

OR

I/we should be grateful if you could clarify/provide further information about…

Expressing certainty

Clearly/obviously/undoubtedly…

Giving advice

My/our advice on this matter is as follows.

Refuting an allegation

Your client's allegation that… is entirely denied by our client.

Disagreeing on a point of law or fact

[***strongly***] I/we entirely disagree with your analysis/statement to the effect that…

[***tentatively***] I/we are unable to agree entirely with your analysis/statement to the effect that…

Prefacing a statement of legal opinion

[***strongly***] It is clear that the correct analysis of the facts/applicable law is…

[***tentatively***] It seems to me/us that the correct analysis of the facts/applicable law is…

Stating a position

It is our [client's] position that…

Making an offer

Our client has instructed us to put forward the following offer: [***list***]

OR

Our client is prepared to settle this matter on the following terms: [*list*]

Accepting an offer

Our client is prepared to accept the offer set out in your letter of…

Rejecting an offer

Our client is unable to accept the offer you have made…

OR

[*more forcefully*] The offer you have made is not acceptable…

OR

[*conditionally, with counteroffer*] Our client is unable to accept the offer you have made in its current form. However, if you/your client were prepared to [*insert counterproposal*] then it may be that he/she might be prepared to reconsider the matter.

Setting deadlines

This offer will remain open until 29 April 2021.

Making a threat to take certain action by a specified date

[*strongly*] We have our client's instructions that unless full payment is received by 14 January, we should issue legal proceedings…

[*tentatively*] If payment is not made by 14 January, our client will have to consider instructing us to issue legal proceedings…

Issuing a rebuke to the other party's lawyers

[*sarcastically*] With the greatest of respect, your statement that…is not credible…

[*politely*] We take the view that your statement…

Giving good news

I/we am/are pleased to be able to…

Giving bad news

Unfortunately, I/we have to tell you…

Asking somebody to do something for you

I/we would appreciate it if you would/could/might…

Showing willingness to do something for somebody

I/we would be glad to…

Asking for an immediate response

I/we would greatly appreciate you giving this matter your immediate attention.

OR

[*where a deadline is necessary*] This matter is urgent. We should be grateful to hear from you no later than close of business on 22 May.

Clarifying what action is to be taken

I/we will now take the following steps: [*list*]

OR

We must now take the following action: [*list*]

Requesting further information

I/we should be grateful if you could provide us with the following information/documentation: [*list*]

Requesting clarification

I/we require clarification of the following issues…

OR

I/we would like to hear a little more about the following issues…

Confirming an agreement

As discussed on the telephone on 9 January, it is agreed that…

OR

We confirm that we have reached agreement [concerning the question of…] between us on the following terms: [*list*]

Making a suggestion

I/we would like to suggest/propose that…

Offering further help

If I/we can be of any further assistance, please do not hesitate to contact me/us.

Promising to get back with further help

I/we will be in touch again shortly.

Thanking for help

I/we would like to take this opportunity to thank you for your assistance.

Closing remarks

Please do not hesitate to contact me if you have any queries or require further information.

13.5 CHECKLIST

The following self-editing checklist may be useful when drafting letters and emails.

Purpose:

- What is the purpose of the communication?
- Have I adapted the style and content to suit the reader's needs?
- Have I dealt with the issues?
- Have I answered all the questions?
- Have I answered them in enough depth?

Content:

- Is the information accurate?
- Is it relevant?

Humanity:

- Will my tone produce the desired response?
- Is it friendly, courteous, helpful, frank, forceful?

Layout:

- Is the layout appropriate for the purpose and content?
- Is it set out in manageable blocks?

Structure:

- Are the sentences short enough?
- Does the order of sentences and paragraphs make sense?

- Does each paragraph contain just one main idea?
- Is there a link between each paragraph and the next?
- Are there links between the sentences in each paragraph?
- Does the whole letter have a clear and logical structure?

Language:

- Have I used plain language, i.e. clear, concise and correct language that can be easily understood by the reader?
- Have I used active verbs instead of nominalisations wherever possible?
- Have I omitted words and phrases that are:
    - Infrequently used
    - Inelegant
    - Redundant
    - Unnecessarily technical
    - Verbose
    - Vague?
- Is the grammar appropriate for the purpose?
- Are the punctuation and spelling correct? See 14.2 and 15.4.2 for example letters.

MEMORANDA

13.6

General points

13.6.1

Memoranda (usually known as **memos**) are written internal communications that advise or inform staff of new policies, procedures, events or decisions. They are usually quite formal and impersonal in style.

Memos may be addressed to one other person or to a number of persons. They may be put on a noticeboard for everyone to see or circulated in internal mail.

Layout

13.6.2

Firms often use headed paper for memos. This gives less information about the firm than the letterhead for external correspondence but indicates which department has issued the memo.

A memo should state at the top of the first page:

- the person(s) to whom it is addressed;
- the author;
- the date;
- the subject.

Important points or long lists of points are usually best presented using bullets (•) or numbers.

13.6.3 Content

A typical memo might be structured as follows:

- The memo should have an appropriate title – one that accurately reflects the contents, and preferably one for which a file can easily be selected.
- The first paragraph of the memo may be used to explain the background to the issue that the memo refers to.
- The main part of the memo should be used to explain concisely:
  - what is going to happen;
  - why it is going to happen;
  - when it is going to happen;
  - how it will affect people;
  - who will be affected.
- The next part of the memo should explain what should be done by anyone affected.
- The last part of the memo should advise staff where they can go for an explanation and how to communicate their comments or complaints.
- The memorandum should be signed by the writer.

See the answer key for an example memorandum.

13.7 ESSAYS

This section contains tips on writing university law essays and is therefore primarily aimed at students. Those whose days of study appear to be behind them may therefore skip over it, unless they wish to indulge in a little harmless and nostalgic *Schadenfreude*.

General observations

Here are five thoughts on how to approach the writing of law essays, with particular reference to exams.

1 Examiners are, on the whole, not sadists. They want you to succeed and, while you will have to demonstrate a proper understanding of the subject in order to do so, they are not trying to trick you. Therefore, each question should be treated as an opportunity to show what you know by correctly identifying the relevant subject area or areas, demonstrating your knowledge of the key principles and legal sources, and showcasing your argumentation skills. Giving a definitive answer to the question posed is the least important consideration, mainly because there almost certainly isn't one single correct answer. That said, it is important to answer the question actually asked, not the one you would like the examiner to have asked, and to focus on it consistently throughout the essay.

2 Following from the above, it is usually possible to achieve a pass level by correctly identifying the relevant subject area and providing a coherent and logical answer that demonstrates fair knowledge and understanding of the key legal sources and principles and sets forth a defensible argument. A higher-level answer will contain a sophisticated argument, demonstrate a comprehensive knowledge of the relevant legal sources and principles, convincingly address potential counterarguments and draw on current legal practice and research.

3 Law exam questions tend to fall into two basic categories. The first of these is a 'problem' question. This will typically contain a scenario that will be similar to, but not exactly the same as, one you have studied and may be loosely modelled on a well-known case. Questions of this type often invite the candidate to advise one or more of the persons mentioned in the scenario and usually require specific answers to a number of questions. The key to answering such questions is to identify the relevant legal issues inherent in the scenario and to exclude any that are irrelevant. It is best to answer each point of the question directly without writing a lengthy introduction or conclusion. The second category is the 'discussion' question. These typically offer a proposition (which may, for example, be a quotation from a famous judgment or academic commentary), which you are invited to discuss. Questions of this type call for an essay constructed along traditional 'beginning, middle and end' lines that sets out a clear and independent argument addressing the question asked.

4 It pays to put together an essay plan before starting to write. Even in an exam situation where time is limited and the temptation to start writing immediately can be overwhelming, it is worth forcing yourself to spend five minutes of your writing time noting down the relevant points and legal principles that

will inform your essay and establishing its structure. If done properly, this will improve the clarity of your essay, safeguard against the problem of writing yourself into a dead-end and allow you to keep control of your timekeeping: if you know what you want to say before you start writing, you will have enough time to get it down on paper. It will also help ensure that (where there is a choice of questions) you don't attempt to answer a question on a topic that you have not prepared thoroughly.

5 It also pays to use up-to-date legal sources and follow legal news. Law changes all the time, so law textbooks go out of date very quickly. Ensure that you are using the very latest edition of each textbook and supplement your understanding of the subject area by reading online articles and blogs and talking to your lecturers.

13.7.2 Content and structure

As noted above, the category of question you are dealing with has a bearing on the structure that should be adopted. The notes below set out the traditional 'beginning, middle and end' structure that is appropriate for discussion questions in exam situations.

The detailed requirements for longer essays (e.g. coursework and dissertations) are separately established by, and may vary marginally between, each university. Longer essays usually follow a sophisticated structure and typically include the following: an abstract summarising the main lines of the argument, a table of contents, chapter divisions, headings and sub-headings, footnotes or endnotes that indicate the legal sources referred to and a bibliography.

13.7.2.1 Beginning

Before starting to write, ensure that you have identified the legal topic at issue, the key points that need to be discussed in the body of the essay and how they apply to the question.

The introduction should generally be kept short, and in respect of a problem question it may be better to go straight to the different elements of the problem. In a discussion question the introduction should identify the relevant legal area, set out the question to be answered, indicate the key issues and strands of your argument and possibly preview your conclusion.

13.7.2.2 Middle

The middle section should be used to analyse the legal issues by reference to legal principles and sources (the applicable statutory and case-law together with current research and scholarship), address potential counterarguments and clarify the interrelationships between the different legal issues involved. This last point is critical to the establishment of a persuasive argument because if the interrelationships are not clearly established, the result may be a list of disconnected points. A hierarchy usually emerges – i.e. generally speaking, one issue is decisive, and the others support it but are not decisive in themselves. When analysing case law, there is usually a key judgment, which is generally to be found in the case in which the relevant court first dealt with the issue at hand in a comprehensive manner. This should be addressed first before moving onto discussion of other cases that qualify and clarify the judgment in that case.

For example, in an essay dealing with the issues of measures having equivalent effect to a quantitative restriction under EU law, one would typically start by noting that Article 34 TFEU prohibits 'quantitative restrictions and all measures having equivalent effect'. You would then look at the key case – i.e. the Court of Justice of the European Union's judgment in *Dassonville*[2] – and follow this with a discussion of more recent cases that qualify the *Dassonville* ruling. It is worth noting that in case law references the legal principle articulated in the judgment is crucially important, but the facts of the case usually aren't. Therefore, there is nothing to be gained by 'telling the story' of the case (although remembering it can sometimes help keep the case in your mind). If there is space, you should also engage with opinions expressed in recent academic articles in reputable journals on the issue in question.

Care should be taken to indicate the breaks or continuities between the various topics covered in the middle section and to create a logical flow comprehensible to the reader. This can be done either by dividing them into separate paragraphs or inserting headings, or by signposting transitions using the discourse markers discussed in section 7.2.7.

Conclusion

13.7.2.3

The conclusion can be kept quite short. It reiterates the question outlined in the beginning paragraph and summarises how you have answered it by noting the main points made in the body of your essay and showing how these contribute towards the overall solution you propose. No new points or argument should be introduced at this stage.

Note

2 Judgment of 11 July 1974, *Dassonville*, C-8/74, ECLI:EU:C:1974:82

Checklist

The following checklist may be useful when writing and editing law essays.

1 Is your essay clearly organised and structured? Use clear headings and subheadings and utilise a coherent internal structure. Ensure that any style rules used in the institution at which you are studying have been followed.

2 Is your essay grammatically correct and clearly written? Check syntax and spelling using a spellchecker where possible. Ensure that the meaning of each sentence is clear and that it has a logical connection to those that precede and follow it.

3 Have you checked through the paper and corrected any errors? Always review your work if there is time to do so. In an exam situation, try to allow five minutes for this.

4 Is the referencing accurate and relevant? Do the cases and legislation referenced back up the points being made? Are they up to date and relevant? Using recent sources is a useful way of indicating your engagement with the issues relevant to the question.

5 Is your analysis coherent and consistent? Select an effective method of organising your essay (e.g. chronologically or in order of importance) and stick to it. Ensure that you answer the question rather than simply seeking to demonstrate your general knowledge of the applicable area of law.

6 Does your essay demonstrate evidence of original analysis and insight (backed up by authority)? Is it well argued? Avoid simply citing references or academic articles – engage with the opinions expressed in them and express your own.

7 Does the conclusion reflect upon the points discussed in the middle of the essay and provide an answer to the question?

8 Does the essay contain plagiarism? If you have copied from other sources without acknowledgement, this will be spotted and will inevitably entail serious consequences. This is particularly the case in respect of essays created on a computer, which can be run through an online plagiarism detector program in minutes. Ensure that all quotations from academic articles etc. are correctly identified and referenced in footnotes.

Applying for a legal position

HOW TO APPLY

Types of application

There are basically three kinds of job applications that you can make:

- An application for a specific advertised position.

- An application to a recruitment consultant to register your details in case a suitable position arises.

- An unsolicited application – i.e. a general application to a firm in circumstances where no specific position has been advertised.

The kind of letter or email you write will depend on the kind of application you make, but in all cases you should:

- Find out whether the application must be made on a special application form, or through an internet platform, or by sending in your curriculum vitae (CV) and a covering letter.

- Find out the name and job title of the person to whom you should send your application. Many job applications are disregarded because they are not addressed to a particular person. The larger law firms have human resources departments, which deal with job applications. If it is not clear to whom an application should be addressed, phone or email the human resources department to find out.

- Do your research. Find out as much as possible about the firm or organisation you are applying to before sending your application. In this way you can (1) save yourself the trouble of sending out any applications that stand little chance of success, and (2) adapt your application to the needs of the particular firm or organisation to which you are writing.

- Remember to quote any reference numbers mentioned in the advertisement.

When applying for a legal position, always ensure that your letter and CV (or application form) are free from grammatical errors and spelling mistakes. Lawyers are trained to pay attention to detail, and mistakes will make a very poor impression.

14.1.2   Application for a specific advertised position

Your letter should have a beginning, middle and end. Generally, the terms **vacancy**, **post**, **position** or **appointment** are used instead of **job** in advertisements.

In the beginning of your letter, explain what you are applying for and mention any documents that you have enclosed. For example:

I wish to apply for the commercial lawyer vacancy advertised in this month's edition of Legal News. *I enclose a copy of my curriculum vitae or the relevant application form duly completed.*

Use the middle of the letter to state what appeals to you about the position you are applying for, and why you think that you would be particularly well suited to it. You can use this part of the letter to (1) demonstrate knowledge about the firm or organisation to which you are writing, and (2) give some indication of your expertise and experience. For example:

This position is of particular interest to me as I know that your firm is well known for its work with IT companies. I have had over three years of experience in IT law in my current position and am keen to develop my expertise in this area further.

At the end of the letter, offer to supply more information if necessary:

I look forward to hearing from you. However, if there is any further information you require in the meantime, please let me know.

14.1.3   Application to a recruitment consultant to register details

The main purpose of this application is to indicate what kind of position you are seeking and what kind of previous experience you have. However, it is important to make a good impression on the recruitment consultant to whom you write, since the consultant is only likely to put your name forward to firms looking for new employees if they have confidence in your abilities.

When dealing with recruitment consultants it is important to remind them periodically that you are still looking for work. Most consultants have large databases of people who have, at one time or other, registered their details, and those who have been silent for a long period of time tend to be forgotten. Phone the recruitment consultant either shortly before or shortly after you have sent them or uploaded your details and let them know exactly what you are looking for and why you are a suitable candidate. If possible, agree a plan of action with the consultant. After this initial conversation, if you hear nothing for a week or so, phone again to check on progress. Resist the temptation to fire off an email instead of phoning – emails are easier to ignore than phone calls.

Your initial application should state what kind of position you are looking for, the geographical area in which your ideal job would be located and the salary range you are seeking. Additionally, be sure to refer to any documents that you have enclosed or uploaded. For example:

I am looking for a position as an assistant commercial lawyer, mainly specialising in company commercial matters, in a large commercially oriented law firm. Ideally, I would like to remain in the London area, but would be prepared to consider relocating for an exceptional position. I am looking for a salary in the region of £45,000–£55,000 per annum.

You should then state any particular qualities or experiences you have that will make you especially attractive to employers. For example:

I have had over five years of experience in the field of company commercial law and also have significant experience in IT law. I am fluent in German and spent one year during my current employment working at the firm's branch office in Munich, where I headed the company commercial department.

At the end of your letter, you should indicate that you will be proactive in pursuing your job search. A suitably worded ending will communicate to the recruitment consultant that you are a serious applicant worthy of being strongly marketed to prospective employers. For example:

If there is any further information you require, please let me know. I am keen to pursue this matter vigorously and will telephone on Friday 12 June to discuss progress with you. I can be contacted at any time on my mobile at: 033 987 3192.

An unsolicited application   14.1.4

When sending an unsolicited application, you should start by asking whether the firm you are writing to might have a vacancy that you could fill. For example:

I am writing to enquire whether you might have a vacancy in your company commercial department for an assistant lawyer. I enclose a copy of my curriculum vitae.

If someone associated with the firm you are writing to suggested that you write to them, mention this in your opening:

I was recommended by Clive Enright, who has a long association with your firm, to contact you regarding a possible position in your company commercial department.

In any event, you should then explain why you are applying to the firm – state what it is about the firm that particularly attracts you and why you would be a suitable employee for the firm. For example:

I am particularly interested in the possibility of working for your firm since I note that it has strong expertise in the field of intellectual property. I have three years' post-qualified experience working in the commercial department of my present firm and have primarily focused on patent and industrial design rights. I am keen to further my expertise and experience in this area.

At the end of the letter, offer to supply more information if necessary:

I look forward to hearing from you. However, if there is any further information you require in the meantime, please let me know.

14.2 **SPECIMEN APPLICATION LETTER**

Here is a specimen application letter written in response to a specific advertised position. The applicant starts off by referring to the job advertisement. She goes on to expand on her present duties and gives other information she believes to be relevant to the post. She explains why she is applying for this particular vacancy and demonstrates knowledge of the firm to which she is applying. If she gives her current employers as referees on her CV, she could also mention that she would prefer Bowen & Stanmore not to approach them until after an interview.

12 Wakely Road
Cambridge
CB2 1AP

16 September 20_

Ms G Tilton

Human Resources Coordinator
Bowen & Stanmore
1 Grawley Avenue
Oxford
OX1 4BE

Your Ref: GT 334/07

Dear Ms Tilton,

I wish to apply for the vacancy advertised in *Legal News* on 10 September 20__ for an assistant commercial lawyer. I enclose a copy of my curriculum vitae.

I am currently employed as an assistant solicitor at Parton & Rice in Cambridge and have had four years of post-qualified experience, primarily in company commercial and IT law. In addition to handling a substantial caseload, I am also heavily involved in helping to coordinate my firm's marketing strategy with regard to IT clients. I am particularly interested in the position on offer since I am aware that your firm has extensive expertise in this area.

I speak fluent German and use the language daily in the course of my work.

If there is any further information you require, please contact me. I look forward to hearing from you.

Yours sincerely,

Michelle Hathaway

Enc. CV

APPLICATION FORMS AND CVS

General points

Application forms are mainly embedded in online platforms nowadays. While this offers a convenient way of completing the form, one drawback is that it is sometimes difficult to get an overview of the details you have completed as you click through the various stages of the process. Therefore, it can often be useful, if it's possible, to print off the whole form at the outset and prepare the more complex parts of your application offline.

Some firms or organisations prefer a CV, which is known as a ***resume*** in American English. A CV should contain your personal and working history.

Curriculum vitae (CV)

There is no single and uniform way of constructing a CV. They vary widely from country to country, sector to sector and role to role, and styles change quickly over time. Therefore, the notes below represent one approach but, depending on where you are applying, in what business area and for what role, another approach may work better. A wide range of CV templates are available for download, at a price, from the Internet. Some organisations may require you to use a specific CV template in order to apply for positions with them.

There are various ways of presenting information in a CV. Traditionally, the sequence was name, address, contact details, education, qualifications, work experience, referees and interests. However, it is now more common to begin with brief personal details, followed by a short profile or description of yourself (sometimes also called a career summary). After that, the most important information is recent employment history, and skills and qualifications.

In the interests of completeness, you should account for all years since leaving school, but if the information is irrelevant to the position you are applying for or is some years old, you should summarise it as briefly as possible.

These days, it is unnecessary to mention marital status, children, age, health or current salary, although this may vary according to the laws and customs in different countries. Here is a simple CV for a fairly experienced commercial lawyer.

	Anna Hampton
Address	33 Bromwell Street Road
	Oxford
	OX4 7TR
Telephone	01865 774582
Mobile	032 973 1429
Email	anna.hampton@eelpies.com
Profile	I am a motivated and confident five-years-qualified commercial lawyer with strong experience in company commercial and IT law. I have in-depth experience of supervising and coordinating a team of lawyers and legal assistants, and excellent communication and research skills. I take an innovative and proactive approach to resolving complex issues.
Employment (2015–present)	Cranford & Marchand, London
	Assistant lawyer, company commercial department
	Caseload comprised company commercial and IT matters. Worked on several large merger cases under the supervision of the partner in charge of the department. Helped build up the IT law practice and was personally involved in supervising, coordinating and training a team of junior assistant lawyers.
2013–15	Bracewell & Frank, Manchester
	Trainee
	Undertook a training contract, gaining experience in company commercial, commercial property, commercial litigation and criminal litigation departments.
2012	Rechtsanwälte Lindner, Düsseldorf
	Legal assistant
	Assisted with trademark litigation matters, provided research support, interviewed clients and carried out legal translation work.
Qualifications	Diploma of Legal Practice, College of Law 2013
	LLB, University of Bristol (2:1) 2011
	A levels in German (A), French (B) and Geography (B), Irondale College Exeter 2010
Key skills	Fluent German (CEFR C2) and French (CEFR C1)
	Advanced Microsoft Word skills
	Driving licence

ATTENDING AN INTERVIEW

Here are a few pointers on attending an interview

- Make sure you know in advance where the venue for the interview is and how you are going to get there. Leave yourself plenty of time – arriving late and/or flustered will create a bad impression.

- Look the part. When applying for most legal positions, you will be expected to be smartly but conservatively dressed.

- Do your research. Find out as much about the firm or organisation to which you have applied, and the position you are seeking, as possible.

- Review your application. Be prepared for things you have mentioned in your application to be brought up and questioned by the interviewer. Therefore, do not mention anything in your application unless you are prepared to discuss it in detail and support it with evidence.

- Be prepared for difficult questions. Always answer all questions frankly and fully. Try to discern the underlying objective of the interviewer in asking certain questions: the purpose of the question may be more to encourage you to demonstrate your skills and motivation than to elicit a literal and factual answer. The following are interview favourites:

    - 'Where do you see yourself in five years' time?': the interviewer is testing your ambition, sense of purpose and career planning.

    - 'Why do you want to work for us?': the interviewer is checking for motivation *and* your understanding of the position on offer.

    - 'Tell me about yourself': the interviewer is checking mainly for confident self-presentation and for your ability to present relevant information succinctly.

    - 'Why do you want to leave your current job?': the interviewer is looking for positive motivation. Never say that you want to leave in order to obtain a better-paid position or that your job is boring (even if either of those are true), and avoid direct criticism of your present or past employers or colleagues.

● If you do not get the job after being interviewed, do not be scared to telephone the firm to which you applied to ask the reason for this. If there is something in your style of presentation that you can correct, it is worth learning about it. Most reasonable firms are prepared to discuss with candidates over the telephone the reason why they were rejected.

This chapter contains four different legal texts together with exercises on each. An answer key for the exercises can be found at the back of the book. These exercises supplement the chapter-specific exercises available on the companion website at www.routledge.com/cw/haigh

15.1 CASE STUDY: CONCORDIA BUS CASE (2002)

15.1.1 Legal summary (competition law)

Competition law includes a mixture of political and economic objectives. It aims to perfect the common market by preventing undertakings from imposing practices that undermine the removal of barriers to trade. The central issues are consumer protection, market efficiency (avoidance of monopolies) and fair competition (including such matters as the prohibition of subsidies by national governments and the application of competition rules to non-EU companies trading within the EU).

The case summarised below is a competition law case under the EU legal system and is largely concerned with the application of the principle of equal treatment, a key concept of EU law.

The principle of equal treatment requires that comparable situations must not be treated differently and that different situations must not be treated in the same way, unless such treatment is objectively justified. This principle has proved important in relation to public procurement directives within the EU.

The decision reached in the case indicates that the principle of equal treatment does not preclude taking into account the criteria of protection of the environment merely because only a limited number of undertakings can comply with those criteria.

15.1.2 Case summary and exercises

The Concordia Bus case involved a referral by the Finnish Supreme Administrative Court to the European Court of Justice for a preliminary ruling on a point of competition law. Read the summary and then do the exercises on it below.

On 27 August 1997 Helsinki City Council decided to introduce tendering (1) _____ for the entire urban bus network. By letter of 1 September 1997, the city's purchasing unit called for tenders for operating the network. According to the (2) _____, the contract would be (3) _____ to the undertaking whose tender was economically most advantageous overall to the city. Three categories of criteria would be used to assess this: the overall price asked for operation, the quality of the bus (4) _____, and the operator's quality and environment programme.

On 12 February 1998 the commercial service committee chose HKL-Bussiliikenne, since it had obtained the greatest number of points overall. Another company, Concordia Bus Finland Oy Ab, which came second, appealed to the Competition Council (*Kilpailuneuvosto*), arguing in particular that it was unfair and (5) _____ to award additional points for a bus fleet with nitrogen oxide emissions and noise level below certain limits. It said that points had been awarded for using a type of bus that only HKL-Bussiliikenne was in fact able to offer.

The Competition Council (6) _____ that the contracting (7) _____ was entitled to define the type of bus fleet it wanted, and also found that all the competitors had the possibility of acquiring buses powered by natural gas. It therefore concluded that it had not been proved that that criterion discriminated against Concordia.

Concordia appealed to the Supreme Administrative Court (*Korkein hallinto-oikeus*) to have the Competition Council's decision (8) _____. The Supreme Administrative Court decided to (9) _____ the proceedings and refer several questions to the Court of Justice for a preliminary ruling.

The most important of those questions was whether the Community legislation, correctly interpreted, allows a municipality that organises a tender procedure for the operation of an urban bus service to include operators' ecological and quality management in the comparison of tenders.

On this point, the Court of Justice ruled that, where the contracting authority decides to award a contract to the tenderer whose tender is the most economically advantageous, it may take ecological criteria into consideration, provided that those criteria:

- are connected with the subject-matter of the contract;

- do not give the contracting authority an unrestricted freedom of choice;

- are (10) _____ mentioned in the contract documents or the tender notice; and

- comply with all the fundamental principles of Community law, in particular the principle of non-discrimination.

The Court of Justice also said that the principle of equal treatment does not prevent the taking into consideration of criteria for protection of the environment merely because the transport operator to whom the contract is awarded is one of the few undertakings able to offer a bus fleet that meets those criteria.

15.1.1.1 Exercise 1: terminology

Complete the gaps numbered (1) to (10) in the text above with one of the choices set out below in respect of each number.

1 deceptively, progressively, cautiously, stealthily

2 tender notice, tender announcement, tender notification, tender documentation

3 given, handed over, passed, awarded

4 ranks, fleet, squadron, team

5 discriminative, discriminating, discriminatory, biased

6 acknowledged, admitted, took the view, had the opinion

7 person, provider, team, entity

8 squashed, quashed, thrown out, cancelled

9 stop, halt, stay, adjourn

10 clearly, definitely, unequivocally, expressly

15.1.1.2 Exercise 2: draft a memorandum

Draft a short memo providing answers to the following questions.

1 What criteria did Helsinki City Council lay down regarding the bus network tender?

2 What were the factual grounds of Concordia's complaint about discrimination?

3   What reasoning was adopted by the Competition Council?

4   What was the key question the Supreme Administrative Court wanted guidance about from the Court of Justice?

5   What did the Court of Justice say?

15.2 LEGISLATIVE EXCERPT: THE ENTERPRISE ACT 2002

15.2.1 Legal summary

The Enterprise Act 2002 is a UK Act of Parliament that made major changes to UK competition law with respect to mergers and also changed the law governing insolvency and bankruptcy. In particular, it aimed to make all competition decisions through independent bodies, prevent anti-competitive behaviour, create a strong deterrent effect, provide remedies for injured parties in respect of distortion of competition and raise the profile of competition policy in the UK.

15.2.2 Excerpt and exercises

Read the following extract from section 252 of the UK Enterprise Act 2002 (which amends the provisions of section 176 of the Insolvency Act 1986) and then do the exercises on it below.

252 Unsecured creditors

The following shall be inserted after section 176 of the Insolvency Act 1986 (winding up: preferential debt):

Property subject to floating charge

176A Share of assets for unsecured creditors

1   This section applies where a floating charge relates to property of a company:

    a   which has gone into liquidation,

    b   which is in administration,

    c   of which there is a (1) _____ liquidator, or

    d   of which there is a receiver.

2   The liquidator, administrator or receiver:

>   a   shall make a (2) _____ part of the company's net property available for the satisfaction of unsecured debts, and

>   b   shall not distribute that part to the proprietor of a floating charge except in so far as it exceeds the amount required for the satisfaction of unsecured debts.

3   Subsection (2) shall not apply to a company if:

>   a   the company's net property is less than the prescribed minimum, and

>   b   the liquidator, administrator or receiver thinks that the cost of making a distribution to unsecured creditors would be (3) _____ to the benefits.

4   Subsection (2) shall also not apply to a company if or in so far as it is (4) _____ by:

>   a   a voluntary arrangement in respect of the company, or

>   b   a compromise or arrangement agreed under section 425 of the Companies Act (compromise with creditors and members).

5   Subsection (2) shall also not apply to a company if:

>   a   the liquidator, administrator or receiver applies to the court for an order under this subsection on the (5) _____ that the cost of making a distribution to unsecured creditors would be disproportionate to the benefits, and

>   b   the court orders that subsection (2) shall not apply.

6   In subsections (2) and (3) a company's net property is the amount of its (6) _____ which would, but for this section, be available for satisfaction of claims of holders of (7) _____ secured by, or holders of, any floating charge created by the company.

7   An order under subsection (2) prescribing part of a company's net property may, in particular, provide for its calculation:

       a   as a percentage of the company's net property, or

       b   as an (8) _____ of different percentages of different parts of the company's net property.

8 An order under this section:

       a   must be made by statutory instrument, and

       b   shall be subject to (9) _____ pursuant to a resolution of either House of Parliament.

9 In this section:

- "floating charge" means a charge which is a floating charge on its creation and which is created after the first order under subsection (2)(a) comes into force, and

- "prescribed" means prescribed by order by the Secretary of State.

10 An order under this section may include (10) _____ or incidental provision.

15.2.2.1 Exercise 1: terminology choice

Fill the gaps in the text numbered (1) to (10) with the most appropriate word or phrase from the choices set out below in respect of each gap.

1   temporary, provisional, floating, part-time

2   stipulated, proscribed, prescribed, inscribed

3   disproportionate, unproportionate, unbalanced, irrelevant

4   removed, overruled, disapplied, displaced

5   reasoning, ground, basis, proviso

6   estate, holdings, assets, property

7   dentures, debentures, debutants, diasporas

8   aggregation, amount, aggregate, average

9   cancellation, revocation, termination, annulment

10 transitory, transient, transitional, transition

15.2.2.2 Exercise 2: multiple-choice comprehension

Consider the questions below. In each case, decide which of the four statements (a) to (d) given in respect of each question corresponds most closely to the meaning of the passage.

1 Section 176A applies:
  a where a floating charge relates to the property of a trading company.
  b to a floating charge held by a company over liquidated property.
  c to a floating charge relating to the property of a company in receivership (and certain other stipulated situations).
  d to all floating charges over the property of insolvent companies.

2 The liquidator is entitled to distribute:
  a part of a company's net property to the proprietor of a floating charge only if the unsecured debts can be settled from the remaining value of such property.
  b the company's property in order to settle its debts.
  c a stipulated amount from the company's net property to the proprietor of a floating charge.
  d the company's net property in order to satisfy unsecured debts as distinct from those secured by means of a floating charge.

3 Subsection 2 does not apply to a company in circumstances where:
  a the liquidator thinks that it would not be beneficial to make a distribution to unsecured creditors.
  b the liquidator applies to the court for an order stating that it is not required to make a distribution to unsecured creditors.
  c the legislation so provides.
  d a voluntary arrangement disapplies it.

4 For the purposes of subsections 2 and 3, a company's net property:
  a is the property available to debenture holders.
  b is the property available to holders of floating charges under the relevant section.
  c means the property that would be available to holders of debentures or floating charges were it not for the provisions of the relevant section.
  d excludes real estate.

5 A company's net property in respect of orders under subsection (2) may be calculated:
  a as an aggregate of different percentages used to assess the value of the company's property.
  b as a percentage of the net property held by the company, or in one other specified manner.
  c in fractional terms.
  d as provided for in the relevant statutory enactments.

15.2.2.3 Exercise 3: drafting exercise

Draft replies to the following questions by reference to the excerpt from the Enterprise Act 2002 set out above. In each case, the aim is to explain the provisions of the Act in plain English – do not simply reproduce the language used in the Act unless this is unavoidable.

1 What does this section cover?

2 What provision does the liquidator need to make for the settlement of unsecured debts?

3 In what situations is the liquidator not required to make the provision for the settlement of unsecured debts the Act prescribes?

4 What does 'net property' constitute?

15.3 INDEPENDENT CONTRACTOR AGREEMENT

The contract below is used in a situation in which a company uses a contractor to provide certain services. This arrangement is often an attractive alternative to that of employing a person to provide these services, since it is usually cheaper, involves fewer formalities and is more flexible.

In order to save space, the contract below is fairly short and the schedules have been omitted. It might be a useful exercise to consider what boilerplate clauses could usefully be added to it.

Consider the contract and then do the exercises based on it.

15.3.1 Independent contractor agreement and exercises

This AGREEMENT is made and entered into this _____ day of _____ 20__

BETWEEN

(1)   Pan-Oceanic Shrimp Ltd (hereinafter referred to as 'the Company') of 4 Quail Road, Bournemouth, Dorset, UK.

and

(2)   Stephen Lyons (hereinafter referred to as 'the Contractor') of 15A Drax Avenue, Christchurch, Dorset, UK.

1   INDEPENDENT CONTRACTOR

Subject to the terms and conditions of this Agreement, the Company hereby (1) _____ the Contractor as an independent contractor to perform the services set forth herein, and the Contractor hereby accepts such engagement. The Contractor is and shall remain an independent contractor in his relationship to the Company, and this agreement shall not (2) _____ the Contractor an employee, partner, agent of or joint venturer with the Company for any purpose. The Company shall not be responsible for (3)_____ taxes with respect to the Contractor's compensation hereunder, and the Contractor shall not be (4) _____ for paid vacation, unemployment insurance benefits, health insurance, health or disability benefits, sick leave, retirement benefits, workers' compensation, employee benefits of any kind or any other benefits (a) _____ the Company.

2   EXCLUSIVITY

The Contractor shall provide services to the Company from the date of this agreement on an (5) _____ basis in the (6) _____ defined in clause 3 below. The Contractor shall devote his best efforts and attention to the performance of his duties under this Agreement, and shall not engage in any other business duties, activities or employment without the prior (7) _____ or written consent of the Company.

3   SERVICES TO BE PROVIDED

The Contractor shall provide the services specified in Schedule I hereto. He shall report directly to the External Services Manager and to any other party (8) _____ by the External Services Manager in connection with the performance of the duties under this Agreement and shall fulfil any other duties reasonably requested by the Company and agreed to by the Contractor.

4   TERM

This engagement shall commence upon (9) _____ of this Agreement and shall continue in full force and effect until 31 December 2020. The Agreement may only be extended thereafter by (10) _____ agreement, unless terminated earlier by operation of and in accordance with this Agreement.

5   COMPENSATION

As full compensation for the services rendered (11) _____ this Agreement, the Company shall pay the Contractor at the rate and on the terms specified in Schedule II hereto.

6   **INVOICING**

Payment by the Company to the Contractor in respect of the services provided by the Contractor shall be made against (12) _____ invoices presented in writing and delivered by post by the Contractor to the Company, with a payment period of 28 days.

7   **EXPENSES**

a.   All (13) _____ and expenses incurred by the Contractor in the course of carrying out work on the Company's instructions must be approved in advance by the Company and shall be separately remunerated on presentation of an invoice, receipt or other documentary evidence of the expenditure in such form as is sufficient for accountancy purposes.

b.   No reimbursement need be made by the Company to the Contractor in respect of disbursements or expenses in respect of which the Company has not granted prior approval or in respect of which no sufficient documentary evidence is produced by the Contractor.

c.   Notwithstanding the (14) _____, expenses for the time spent by Contractor in travelling to and from Company facilities shall not be reimbursable.

8   **WRITTEN REPORTS**

The Company may request that project plans, progress reports and a final results report be provided by Contractor on a monthly basis. A final results report shall be due at the conclusion of the project and shall be submitted to the Company in a confidential written report at such time. The results report shall be in such form and setting forth such information and data as is reasonably requested by the Company.

9   **TRADE SECRETS AND CONFIDENTIALITY**

(1)   The Company and the Contractor acknowledge to one another that as a result of this business relationship, the Contractor will be in possession of confidential customer information, trade secrets, technical data and know-how relating to the products, processes, methods, equipment and business practices of the Company and its clients (the 'Confidential Information'). Such Confidential Information includes, but is not limited to, technical and business information relating to the Company's products, research and development, strategies and methods which are not standard industry practices, specifications, proposals, reports, analyses, finances, client details, marketing, production and future business plans, business and personal data relating to clients, affiliates and to Contractors of the Company.

(2)   The Contractor agrees that he shall maintain in confidence and shall not disclose or use, at any time during or after the term of this Agreement without the prior written consent of the Company, any Confidential Information whether or not it is in written or permanent form.

(3)   Upon termination of this Agreement or upon request by the Company at any time before or after such termination, the Contractor shall deliver to the Company all written and tangible material in the Contractor's possession incorporating the Confidential Information or otherwise relating to the Company's business.

(4)   These obligations with respect to the Confidential Information extend to information belonging to clients and suppliers of the Company, or persons or entities which licence confidential information or technology rights to the Company, who may have disclosed such information to the Contractor as the result of the Contractor's business relationship with the Company.

10   INVENTIONS

Any and all inventions, discoveries, developments and innovations conceived by the Contractor during this engagement relative to the duties under this Agreement shall be the exclusive property of the Company; and the Contractor hereby assigns all right, title, and interest in the same to the Company. Any and all inventions, discoveries, developments and innovations conceived by the Contractor prior to the term of this Agreement and utilised by him in rendering duties to the Company are hereby licensed to the Company for use in its operations and for an infinite duration. This licence is non-exclusive and may be assigned without the Contractor's prior written approval by the Company to a wholly owned subsidiary of the Company.

11   CONFLICT OF INTEREST

The Contractor affirms that he is free to enter into this Agreement, and that this engagement does not violate the terms of any agreement between the Contractor and any third party. Further, the Contractor, in rendering his duties, shall not utilise any invention, discovery, development, improvement, innovation or trade secret in which he does not have a (15) _____ interest. During the term of this agreement, the Contractor shall devote such time, energy and ability to the performance of the duties and obligations stipulated hereunder as is necessary to perform such duties and obligations in a timely and productive manner.

AS WITNESS the parties have executed this Agreement effective as of the date of the Consultant's acceptance below.

Bournemouth, UK on the _____ day of _____ 20__

By: _____   By: _____

Elizabeth Mason   Stephen Lyons

Director   Contractor

[Schedule I]

[Schedule II]

15.3.1.1 Exercise 1: terminology

Fill the gaps in the text numbered (1) to (15) with the most appropriate of the four terms offered in each case.

1 engages, employs, takes on, hires

2 appoint, make, render, establish

3 paying, calculating, assessing, withholding

4 entitled, eligible, qualified, barred

5 ad hoc, inclusive, exclusive, non-exclusive

6 business areas, commercial arenas, trade areas, business domains

7 express, unwritten, spoken, verbal

8 appointed, designated, specified, identified

9 execution, implementation, commencing, initiation

10 specific, verbal, mutual, reciprocal

11 as a result of, via, following from, pursuant to

12 written, authorised, itemised, listed

13 costs, disbursements, fees, charges

14 aforementioned, above-mentioned, above, foregoing

15 proprietary, stakeholder, ownership, recognised

15.3.1.2 Exercise 2: true or false

Are the statements below true or false?

1 The agreement makes it clear that the company will not take responsibility for ensuring that the funds are available for the contractor's tax liability arising from the work done for the company to be satisfied. (true/false)

2 The contractor is under no circumstances entitled to work for others during the currency of this agreement. (true/false)

3 The contractor must ask the company's permission before incurring expenses, including the cost of travelling to the company's premises, otherwise these will not be reimbursed. (true/false)

4 Progress reports need not necessarily be submitted by the contractor on a monthly basis. (true/false)

5 Any invention made by the Contractor during the term of the agreement is automatically the property of the company. (true/false)

15.1.1.3 Exercise 3: email drafting

Imagine you are the lawyer for Stephen Lyons. He has sent you an email, in which he writes:

Dear X

As discussed, I'm sending over the contract that Pan-Oceanic Shrimp want me to sign. It generally looks okay, but just to be on the safe side please run your eye over it and let me know the answers to the following questions:

1 What is the point of the first para. of the contract? It looks like a load of waffle.
2 What expenses can I have reimbursed, and how does it work?
3 About the confidentiality clause – I get the general point that I have to keep the company's confidential information confidential, but what other information is covered by this rule?
4 Innovations made during the contract – it looks like if I come up with some new innovation, the company owns it. Are there any exceptions to this?

Cheers,

Steve

Reply to Steve's email, giving answers to the points he raises.

15.4 CORRESPONDENCE

15.4.1 Overview

The letters below are from solicitors to clients who wish to form limited companies for certain purposes. The first letter is well drafted and may be used as an example. However, the second letter has been deliberately drafted badly – your job is to improve it.

In the UK, the office of the Registrar of Companies is known as Companies House. It contains a register of all UK private and public companies, and their directors, shareholders and balance sheets. It is a legal requirement that companies provide all this information, which is available for public inspection. A new company cannot validly exist until it has been registered at Companies House.

15.4.2 First letter

The letter below is from a solicitor to a client who wishes to form a limited company with a colleague. The company will be used to run a small gardening and landscaping business. The letter summarises the instructions the solicitor has been given by the client during the initial interview, advises on relevant issues and indicates the steps that need to be taken to process the matter.

As noted above, this is a well-drafted letter.

Tarby & Co Solicitors
3 Barland Way
Oxford

2 March 2018

Our ref. HJW/GRO.1–1

Your ref.

Joanne Goodman

12 Audsley Road

Oxford

Dear Joanne

Greenscape Ltd

Thank you for coming in to see me yesterday when we discussed the formation of a limited company under the name Greenscape and you instructed me to assist in forming the company.

I have now carried out a search at Companies House and confirm that the name Greenscape is not currently registered. This means that you are free to use that name.

We discussed the particulars of the company, which will be as follows:

1 The objects of the company shall be gardening and landscaping services.
2 The authorised share capital will consist of 1,000 £1 shares.
3 Initially 100 shares will be issued: 51 to you and 49 to Amanda Shorter.
4 You and Ms Shorter will be the company directors. You will need in due course to decide who is to act as company secretary.
5 The registered office will be 12 Audsley Road.

The next step is for me to draw up the memorandum and articles of association, then transfer the company to you, issue the shares and appoint directors and a company secretary.

We also discussed the question of the shareholders' agreement. Briefly, this is an agreement between the shareholders (in this case, you and Ms Shorter) about how the company should be run. It is worth having mainly because it can be used to protect your individual interests in the company in ways which cannot be achieved through the articles of association. We should consider this issue in more detail once the company is registered.

I enclose this firm's client care letter in duplicate. Kindly sign, date and return the spare copy.

Yours sincerely

Howard Williamson

Enc

(1) Client care letter in duplicate

15.4.2.1 First letter: exercise

Write short answers to the following questions.

1 What has the solicitor done to find out whether the name Greenscape is currently registered?

2 What documents will the solicitor now draw up?

3 How much of the share capital will be issued to begin with?

4 Who will the shareholders be?

5 Why is a shareholders' agreement desirable?

15.4.3 Second letter

This letter has been drafted badly. It is excessively informal, confusing, repetitive and badly structured. Consider it and then complete the exercise below.

Rangle & Co
10 Ark Street
London

5 January 2018
Benjamin Ward
127 Dranglet Drive
Reading

Hi Benny

It was really greeat to see you when you came in for a chat on Tuesday about putting up a firm. We think the way you truste us is awesome and totally justified, because we're pro's and never kiss and tell. Like I said before, probably private limited is the way to go for the type and size of business you're talking about.

I mean, basiclly the way it's done is, like, not that difficult. Anyways you told me to go right on ahead and get the companey made. I'd better let you know we got the one grand in dogh you payed upfront.

So this is where the rubber hits the road. I started out this morning by taking a peeke into the good ol official records and found the name you wanted for the biz – 'Esoteric Guitar Widgets for Droning Shoegaze Bands' – is avalble just now (no surprise there, huh?). So you can use that name.

Basically you said the whole pint of the biz is to sell guitar widgets direct to punters off the street or by mail order. We went over the actual nitty gritty of how the legals are done in this area and agreed there wood be 100 one pound shares. Bill Ardley will have 49 and you will have 51. This one pound share thing is not sposed to be about what the cmpany is actually worth – it's more for calculating the size of your bag of shares against Bills. The points that you have a bigger bag, see, which puts you in a stronger position than Bill. Also, you are both going to be head honchos and will officially work out your home address, 127 Dranglet. Hope your landlord is OK about that – you better take a look at the paperwork. Is all that stuff right?

What I'm going to do next, Benny, is bang out the co docs for ya – the memo and arts I talked about. I'll also take care of registration.

We went into having this crazy old thing called a shareholders' agreement. That's where you and Bill agree big stuff about the biz – not just the daytoday stuff but a lot of what ifs? too. Like, for instance, what happens if there's a disagremet between you about how the co is run, what happens if one of you wants to sell up and get out, what happens if one of you kicks the bucket. The big scary stuff. Just taking care of your interests. Anyway we can talk about this more once the co's registered. I'll tell you when that is done.

Call me if there's anything you need to know. Otherwise I'll be in touch once registration's done.

Ciao!

15.4.3.1 Second letter: exercise

Redraft the letter in appropriate formal English. Pay attention, in particular, to the following issues:

1 Dead wood: does the letter contain useless words and phrases that can simply be cut out?

2 Terminology: is the terminology used appropriate for the context? Are there more precise legal terms that can be used? Is terminology used consistently?

3 Phrasing: is the phrasing used appropriate for the context? Consider whether more formal phrases should be used.

4 Tone: is the tone of the letter suitable (see notes above)?

5 Conventions: have the conventions relating to the beginning and ending of the letter been followed?

6 Organisation/structure: could the topics covered in the letter be placed in a more logical and reader-friendly order?

7 Grammar and spelling.

Part 2

SPOKEN ENGLISH

Aspects of spoken English

SPOKEN AND WRITTEN ENGLISH COMPARED

Compared to written English, spoken English is both more and less clear.

When reading a piece of written English, all the information in the communication is in the text. It is usually presented in a finished state and contains full, grammatically complete sentences. Some care will have been taken to structure and present the document effectively. The document exists in a permanent form and can be read at leisure as many times as necessary.

By contrast, when speaking English with another person the meaning of the dialogue only emerges gradually. The conversation is likely to be filled with unfinished sentences, interruptions, repetitions, pauses and meaningless phrases and words (such as 'er', 'um', 'you know?' and 'if you see what I mean'). The course of the dialogue is unpredictable and infinitely flexible.

However, when speaking English with another person you receive all kinds of clues, which cannot be found in written English, as to what the other person is really thinking or feeling. These include:

- body language;
- tone of voice;
- vocal emphasis (sometimes called stress).

When you are involved in a conversation with another person you instinctively read the meaning of these clues. Conversation also allows you to use a range of techniques that can only be used to a limited extent in writing. These include:

- humour;
- implying;
- euphemisms;
- rhetorical questions;
- open questions;
- narrow and closed questions;
- simple or conditional forms;
- choice of terminology;
- diplomatic language;
- metaphors and similes.

These issues are discussed in detail in section 16.5.

BODY LANGUAGE

Body language refers to the way in which people show their feelings by body movements or positions. While it is relatively easy to control your speech, controlling your body language is remarkably difficult. For this reason, it is well worth paying attention to the body language of the people you are talking to – it will tell you a lot about their reactions to what you are saying. Perhaps most significantly, a careful reading of someone's body language will tell you whether what they feel or think differs from what they say they feel or think.

It is worth bearing in mind that the culture from which a person comes will have some effect on the way they use body language. To take an obvious example, an Italian negotiator is much more likely than a Finnish negotiator to use expansive arm and hand gestures.

In addition, certain aspects of body language have defined meanings in particular cultures. For example, in Pakistan extending a clenched fist towards someone represents an obscene insult. If an American executive leans back in his chair and links his fingers behind his head while speaking to you this is probably a bad sign. It means that he has decided that he does not need to demonstrate eagerness or attention towards you.

Some examples of body language, together with their possible meanings, are given below.

Arms crossed. This usually represents defensiveness, arrogance, dislike or disagreement.

Eyebrows raised. Raised eyebrows generally mean uncertainty, disbelief, surprise or exasperation.

Fist clenched. A clenched fist usually accompanies an aroused emotional state (e.g. anger or fear). In a business meeting a clenched fist often denotes anxiety or unstated disagreement.

Hands behind head. This usually reflects negative thoughts or feelings. It can be taken as a sign of uncertainty, conflict, disagreement, frustration or anger.

Hands on hips. This usually indicates a preparedness to take action (e.g. to take charge of the organisation of an event). It may also be used to signal a threat against others, or defensiveness against a perceived threat.

Head tilted back. When someone has their head tilted back and is looking at you down their nose, this is a clear sign that they feel themselves to be superior to you.

Head tilted to one side. This can mean different things according to the situation in which it is used. It often indicates friendliness and rapport (for example in the course of negotiations). It may also be a gesture of submissiveness (when showing respect to a superior). It can also be used to show coyness (when flirting).

Looking down. This usually accompanies feelings of defeat, guilt, shame or submission. It may indicate that the person is lying.

Palm down. A gesture made in which the hand is extended with the palm tilted down is usually a sign of confidence, assertiveness or dominance.

Palm up. A gesture made in which the hands are extended with the palm tilted up is usually a sign of friendliness, permissiveness or humility. It represents non-aggressiveness and vulnerability. A gesture in which both hands are extended together with the palms up can simply mean, 'I don't know'.

Shoulder shrug. A shrugged shoulder is usually a sign of uncertainty and submissiveness, or sometimes dismissiveness. It can simply mean, 'I don't know'.

Steeple. The steeple involves the placing together of the fingertips of both hands whilst speaking or listening. It is generally used to show that you are listening thoughtfully or thinking deeply.

Stroking chin. This gesture usually indicates that you are considering a point.

TONE OF VOICE
16.3

A lot can be learned about someone's attitude or mood by the tone in which they speak.

This of course does not register in written English. Attitude or mood in written English can usually only be ascertained from specific statements, and even then it is hard to differentiate between genuine expressions of attitude and conventional formal expressions. For example, the phrase 'we are pleased to send you the documents you requested' tells you nothing about whether the writer is really pleased.

The English written in legal contexts is usually neutral as to the feelings of the writer. For example, the words 'we cannot agree to that proposal' seen in writing simply tell you that the proposal cannot be accepted. It gives you no clue as to why the proposal cannot be accepted. In speech, the words 'we cannot agree to that proposal' could be spoken in a variety of different tones, each of which would tell you something different about the attitude of the speaker. For example:

- Bored tone: the whole discussion is of little importance to the speaker.

- Angry tone: the speaker is insulted by the proposal.

- Dismissive tone: the proposal is not worth considering.

- Thoughtful tone: the proposal is worth considering but ultimately not acceptable. The stress in this version of the sentence might well be upon the word *that*, implying that although the speaker cannot agree to the particular proposal made, he or she might agree to a different proposal.

- Conciliatory tone: the speaker does not want to antagonise the person who has made the proposal.

- Condescending tone: the speaker believes that the person making the proposal is inferior or lacks credibility.

- Incredulous tone: the speaker is amazed that such a proposal has been made.

- Embarrassed tone: the speaker has to reject the proposal but is not comfortable with the fact that this has to be done.

16.4 EMPHASIS

One of the interesting aspects of spoken English is that the meaning of a statement that would seem perfectly clear when written down can be altered dramatically if the speaker places emphasis on a particular word or particular words in the statement. When speaking to someone in English you should pay attention both to the emphasis the other person places on particular words and to your own emphasis, otherwise misunderstandings can easily arise.

This point can be illustrated with this simple sentence:

The contract must be signed today.

This sentence could mean (emphasis in italics):

1 '***The*** contract must be signed today.'
   It is a particular contract that must be signed today.

2 'The ***contract*** must be signed today.'
   It is the contract that must be signed, and not something else.

3 'The contract ***must*** be signed today.'
   There is an obligation that the contract be signed.

4 'The contract must be *signed* today.'
The important thing is that the contract be signed (not drafted, agreed etc.).

5 'The contract must be signed *today*.'
The important thing is that the signing of the contract happens today.

6 'The contract must be signed today' (with upward inflection of voice).
Must the contract be signed today?

TECHNIQUES

16.5

There is always more than one way of approaching a discussion and there is always more than one way of saying something in English. The methods you choose will depend upon the subject you are discussing, with whom you are discussing it and what you want to achieve. Here are certain well-known techniques that may prove useful when conducting interviews and negotiations with other lawyers and clients.

Humour

16.5.1

Humour can be very useful, particularly when making a presentation. It breaks the ice and establishes a warmer atmosphere. If a speaker can make an audience laugh, the audience will like the speaker more. Consequently, the audience will be more open to the speaker's ideas and therefore easier to persuade.

In a negotiation situation, the use of humour can be used to reduce the degree of opposition and mistrust between the parties negotiating against each other. The establishment of a warmer atmosphere will increase cooperation between the negotiators, making it more likely that mutually acceptable terms will be reached.

Implying

16.5.2

Implying means to suggest rather than to state directly. It can be a helpful tactic during negotiations, when you wish to choose language that will allow the discussions to continue so that positions can be explored.

For example, you might wish to state your position on a subject but imply that if certain concessions were made by your opponent you might be prepared to take a different view. In this situation it would be more helpful to say:

£150,000 is the most we can offer based on our current understanding of your position.

rather than:

We're not offering more than £150,000.

The first sentence states a position but implies that if certain unspecified concessions were to be made by the opponent, a better price might be offered. It provides an impetus for negotiations to continue. The second sentence states a position that the opponent can either accept or reject, but it provides no impetus for further negotiation.

16.5.3   Rhetorical questions

Rhetorical questions are questions asked in order to highlight an issue or argument rather than to obtain an answer. For example:

Who would deny that a person who has suffered injury as a result of the negligence of others should be entitled to damages?

Rhetorical questions should not be overused, but in moderation can be an effective way to illustrate a point.

16.5.4   Open questions

Open questions are those that can be answered in a variety of ways, where the response is left open to the person to whom you are speaking. They are a useful form of questioning in the early stages of an interview, when you wish to obtain information from the client, or in the early stages of a negotiation, when you wish to explore your opponent's position.

Most conversations taking place in a legal context involve a gradual move from an open-ended, exploratory questioning style towards a more closed, focused style.

For example, when negotiating with another lawyer you might start with open-ended questions, such as 'What's your position on…?'. This style is likely to be accompanied by the use of conditional verb forms; for example, when airing certain possible solutions at an early stage. You might say, for example, 'one possibility **might** be…'. At the same time, you are likely to use neutral language. For example, you are likely to say, 'I'm **not sure** that is acceptable'.

16.5.5   Narrow and closed questions

Narrow questions seek specific information and only require short answers. For example:

What's your best offer?

Closed questions are those that can only be answered with a yes or a no. For example:

Did you accept that offer?

Leading questions are a particular kind of closed question that contain their own answer. For example:

You sold a batch of this product to Clamp Ltd at a unit price of EUR 150 last month, didn't you?

These kinds of questions are useful in client interviews when you require specific information or admissions of specific facts from the client. They are also useful when trying to bring negotiations to a close.

Simple or conditional forms   16.5.6

Simple forms are best suited to asking questions to which you require direct and factual answers ('What's your best price?') or when giving a final response to a question ('We can't accept that proposal.').

The main drawback to using simple forms is that they do not usually help the dialogue to flow. They are therefore employed to best effect when closing a negotiation or interview (as in 'We can't accept that proposal.') or when seeking to obtain an unequivocal response (as in 'What's your best price?'), but are not helpful in the early stages when options are being explored. When suggesting a compromise or formulating a hypothesis, for example, conditional forms are indispensable:

We might agree to…if you were prepared to…
Would you be able to indicate the likely price range when we've outlined our key requirements?

The use of **might** indicates to the other party that there is still room for discussion but does not commit you to any particular course of action. The negotiations can continue.

Conditional forms can also be used in a general way to soften the impact of what is being said. For example, in some situations it would be better to say, 'the right solution might be to…' (which seems respectful and humble) rather than to say, 'the right solution is to…' (which seems arrogant and presumptuous, albeit decisive).

Choice of terminology   16.5.7

English contains a large number of synonyms. Consequently, you are likely to have a wide choice of different words all meaning roughly the same thing at your disposal in any given situation. You should pay close attention to your choice of words – they are not all neutral, but laden with values and connotations. For example, consider this list of words, all of which refer to making a living:

- calling
- career
- profession
- employment
- job
- work
- occupation
- vocation

While all of these words basically refer to the same thing, they have different connotations. Words like **calling** and **vocation** imply an elevated sense of a person's ultimate role in life, whereas **job** implies little more than work done in return for money. **Employment** is the most neutral term in the list.

16.5.8   Diplomatic language

When dealing with difficult or sensitive subjects – or difficult or sensitive people – it is sensible to choose your words carefully. The following suggestions indicate how to soften the way in which you express yourself.

- Using **would**, **could** or **might** to make what you say sound more tentative. For example, you might say, 'this could be a problem' instead of 'this is a problem' in order to leave open the possibility that it may be possible to find a solution to the problem.

- Presenting your view as a question, not a statement. For example, you might say, 'how about offering them EUR 900,000?' instead of 'we'll offer them EUR 900,000' in order to leave the matter open for further discussion.

- Using an introductory phrase to prepare the listener for your message. For example, 'Here's one possibility. Suppose we…' or 'We'd like to make an offer to settle this case. This is what we were thinking…'.

- Adding **I'm afraid** to make clear that you recognise the unhelpfulness of your response. For example, 'that's the most we can offer, I'm afraid'.

- Using words that qualify or restrict what you say to make your position more flexible (**a bit difficult**, **a slight problem**). For example, you might say, 'We have a slight problem with that proposal. We don't like clause seven.' This leaves greater room for flexibility than saying, 'We can't accept clause seven.'

- Using 'not' with a positive word instead of the obvious negative word. For example, **not very convenient** usually means 'I don't agree'.

- Using a comparative (**better**, **more convenient**) to soften your message. For example, 'It would be better if you could agree to…' instead of 'This proposal is not acceptable. We want…'.

- Using a continuous form (**I was wondering**) instead of a simple form (**I wondered**) to make a suggestion more flexible. For example, 'we were wondering if you'd like to make a proposal at this point'.

Metaphors and similes

16.5.9

A metaphor is a figure of speech in which a word or phrase is used to stand for something else (e.g. **food for thought**).

A simile is a figure of speech in which one thing is compared to another of a different kind, using the words **as** or **like** (**like a rolling stone**, **as safe as houses**).

Both of these techniques can be useful ways of illustrating a point. A good example is Winston Churchill's phrase **the iron curtain**, used to great effect to create a mental picture of the divide created by the USSR's influence in eastern Europe. However, metaphors and similes must be carefully handled. Clichéd expressions should be avoided. The figure of speech being used must be relevant to the matter being discussed.

CONFERENCE CALLS AND SKYPE

16.6

Many meetings and interviews are not held face to face nowadays but via video conferencing facilities such as Skype, Zoom, Microsoft Teams and various others. At the time of writing (July 2020) this technology has entered into even more regular usage due to the COVID-19 pandemic and it seems likely that this trend will continue. While video conferencing can replicate most of the features of a face-to-face meeting (including document-sharing), it is not quite the same. Limitations in picture quality may make body language and facial expressions harder to interpret. Limitations in sound quality may make it hard to distinguish small changes in tone of voice and intonation.

Therefore, when speaking to colleagues or clients via a video call, it is worth taking a slightly different approach to that you might take in a face-to-face meeting. The following tips can be offered.

- Familiarise yourself with the options and settings offered by the technology being used. In many cases, audio and picture settings can be adjusted to achieve optimal performance for the type of meeting you are attending.

- Ensure that you are close enough to the microphone to be heard clearly, but not so close that your voice becomes distorted. If you use video conferencing facilities for business purposes on a regular basis it may be worth investing in a USB headset with a microphone to ensure better sound quality.

- Speak slightly more slowly and clearly than you might do in a face-to-face meeting in order to overcome the limitations of the technology.

- Check that the person you are talking to has a clear view of your face. This will help them understand both what you are saying and the way in which you intend it to be understood. However, in order to achieve this, you should take account of the fact that the other person is looking at you from the camera, not from the screen. This means that you need to look into the camera instead of at the screen to give the impression of eye contact, and also ensure that the camera is at eye level so that the other person is not looking at you at a strange angle. Avoid placing your face too close to the screen as this can create a disconcerting visual effect.

- Keep your language relatively simple. In particular, avoid fine nuances of meaning, irony and styles of speech whose correct interpretation depends heavily on observing body language or facial expression, or on detecting small variations in tone of voice or intonation.

- If making a video call from home, ensure that you are not going to be interrupted; that background noise (children, pets, lawnmowers, the heavy metal fan next door) is minimised; and that both the room from which you are making the call and you yourself look presentable. In this context it is worth ensuring that the room you are using is adequately lit but that the camera on your laptop is not picking up glare from bright light. This may be a problem, for instance, if you are sitting with your back to the window and sunlight is streaming in.

Meeting, greeting and getting down to business

The notes contained in this chapter are relevant to the opening phases of business meetings or negotiations.

THE OPENING PHASE

Key considerations

The opening phase of any discussion is often critical, as the skill (or otherwise) with which it is handled often sets the tone for the negotiations that follow and therefore has a bearing on their success or otherwise.

The aim, essentially, is to establish a basis for communication with people whom you do not know at all or do not know well. By starting discussions with some neutral topic the people involved can get to know each other, trust each other and find their common ground. It is an important phase in any meeting with strangers. If it goes well, a solid basis for discussing matters of importance will have been laid down.

It should be acknowledged, of course, that the duration of this phase varies from culture to culture. When opening discussions with Germans or Finns, for example, it can be kept short – but even then, you don't just launch straight in. With native English speakers, it may be a little longer. In Asian cultures the process may be prolonged due to the emphasis placed on establishing an atmosphere of social harmony.

Useful phrases

In the meeting and greeting stages, the following phrases may be useful:

Conventional greeting:

Hello. How are you?
Nice to meet you.
I'm Giles Dangerfield, managing partner here, and this is my colleague Jane Arthurs, our finance director.

Weather:

The weather's been great recently, hasn't it?

OR

Terrible weather we've been having recently.

The other person's journey to your office:

Did you have a good journey here?

OR

I hope you managed to find us alright?

Show the other person around your office, commenting on key features and introducing key people:

This is my office/This is where I tend to lurk.
I'd like you to meet Daniel Jones, our finance director.

If arriving at someone else's office, praise the location and facilities:

Great location you have here – right in the centre of town!

OR

What a fantastic view over the city!

(If the view from the window is over the back of a waterlogged car park or piece of waste ground, maintain a tactful silence on this topic.)

Offer refreshments to your guest (tea, coffee, water, orange juice etc.):

Can I get you a cup of tea or coffee? Or would you prefer a cold drink? Try one of these. It's a local speciality.

17.2   ESTABLISHING A BASIS FOR COMMUNICATION

17.2.1   Key considerations

In the second stage, the genuine art of communication comes more into play. One of the key techniques here is to try to find out what the other person is interested in and let them talk about it. All you need then do is demonstrate a genuine appreciation of those things.

While excessive talkativeness may be viewed with suspicion in certain cultures, the feeling that someone is really interested in you and your thoughts and opinions is almost always a positive one. Remember that:

- Nobody enjoys listening to someone talking about something that doesn't interest them; but

- Everyone enjoys being given the chance to talk about something that interests them, particularly when they have an appreciative audience.

Consequently, the more you can discover about the other person's interests and views prior to your meeting, the better. By building up something of a mental picture of the person you will be speaking to, you are likely to find it easier to talk to them about things that interest them. You will then find some common ground more quickly and this will significantly assist your negotiations with that person.

You should also pay attention to any clues given by the person's appearance. For example, if someone walks into the office, puts down their set of golf clubs in a corner and removes their Ferrari cap, it is pretty likely that golf and motor sport will be successful topics of conversation. Admittedly this is an extreme example, but it is amazing the amount of information you can deduce about a person from a fairly cursory glance at their general appearance and deportment.

When talking to another person, also consider their body language. Do they appear relaxed? Ill at ease? Tired? Tense? Bored? Aggressive? Adjust your approach accordingly.

Also consider the non-verbal signs you are sending to that other person. Are you presenting yourself as a normal, sociable and friendly person? Try to smile as much as possible: smiles (except the kind used by Jack Nicholson and Sir Anthony Hopkins) are reassuring.

Topics and suggested phrases   17.2.2

What topics can be discussed in small-talk situations?

In the absence of such helpful clues as described above (the golf clubs and the Ferrari cap), try to engage the other person as soon as it appears convenient to do so on any neutral but reasonably interesting and relevant topic that suggests itself. Avoid any topic that might be taboo for the other person, or anything that might lead to violent disagreement (religion and politics are difficult subjects in this respect). Also think carefully about what the choice of topic conveys to the other person about you personally. Safe neutral subjects include the following:

- Current events, so long as they are not of a politically sensitive nature.

- The place where the other person comes from: 'Ah, I know Budapest – a wonderful city'.

- Sport: 'Did you see the Formula 1 race at the weekend? Great to see Hamilton get another win!'

- Personal interests. At least, up to a point. The key considerations here are:

    1. Only to mention interests likely to help the conversation along and promote social harmony. Therefore, 'I enjoy a round of golf myself – do you play?' is fine; but 'I enjoy killing large wild animals, such as foxes and badgers, and then stuffing them – what do you think about that?' might lead to social discomfort.

    2. Don't go into excessive detail. Keep it light and general in order to give yourself time to gauge the other person's response and leave room for an escape route if it is clear they are not interested.

- Family, particularly if you know the other person slightly: 'How's John getting on? And the children? Wonderful!' (However, avoid asking overly direct or specific questions about such matters.)

- What they did at the weekend: 'Were you able to get out in the sunshine at all over the weekend?'

- What they are going to do at the weekend coming up: 'Have you got anything planned for the weekend?'

It is important to remember that when conducting small talk, it's usually best to make your questions relatively indirect and unspecific. In that way they'll sound less pointed and threatening, and the other person will be able to give a diplomatic but uninformative reply without loss of face or dignity. So, don't say, for example:

Tell me what you are going to do over the weekend.

which doesn't allow the other person to avoid the question without appearing evasive.

Try instead:

Do you have anything special planned for the weekend?

which allows them to say 'not really' if they don't feel like telling you what they'll be doing.

17.3   GETTING DOWN TO BUSINESS

The point will come when you sense that it is time to bring the general conversation to an end and get down to business. There are various ways in which you can signal that this process is beginning. Here are some suggestions:

- Adjourn to the room in which the negotiation is going to take place. You might say at this point something like *'**Right, ladies and gentlemen. Since time is getting on, might I suggest we make our way to the conference room now?**'*

- Stand up and make a short introduction. *'**Okay, I think we're all here now, so perhaps now might be a good time as any to get started. Perhaps I could begin by introducing everyone…**'*

- Outline the parameters of the meeting. *'**Okay, we're all gathered together here to discuss the terms of settlement in this case. I'd anticipate that we might expect to be here until about four this afternoon, breaking for lunch between one and two and I'd hope to see/the key areas we need to discuss appear to be as follows…**'*

- Suggest an agenda and introduce a speaker. *'**Okay, there are maybe five or six key areas we need to cover this afternoon. I'd suggest we start with the option Danchester Ltd are seeking. Richard, perhaps you could fill us in on the background to that matter.**'*

18 Interviewing and advising

18.1 ## OVERVIEW

The essence of an interview between a lawyer and a client is an exchange of information and views. The client wants advice from the lawyer. The lawyer needs information from the client in order to be able to give that advice.

The lawyer and the client must then jointly decide what should be done to progress the case, and what each of them must do to contribute to this process. In addition, the lawyer must ensure that the client has been informed of and understands certain vital points. These naturally include:

- How much the client will have to pay for the lawyer's services.

- What the lawyer can and cannot do for the client.

- What further information the lawyer needs from the client and why this information is needed.

- What steps the lawyer will take on the client's behalf.

- The timeframe within which these steps will be taken.

- The prospects of success in the client's case (and the strengths and weaknesses of the client's case).

There may be other vital factors according to the type of case being handled and the client's own expectations. Establishing a clear understanding with the client is crucial – if the client has not clearly understood these important issues, there is a strong likelihood that he or she may become frustrated or angry at a later stage if the case does not proceed according to his or her expectations. These expectations may of course be wildly unrealistic – it is the lawyer's role to 'manage the client's expectations'.

18.2 ## PREPARATION

It is crucial to prepare thoroughly for all interviews with clients. Here are some tips:

- Determine the purpose of the meeting. When dealing with the first interview with a new client, it is helpful to instruct staff who book client interviews to obtain as much information from the client as possible about the nature of the legal issue on which they want your advice. If possible, handle the first enquiry from the prospective client yourself.

- Consider the most appropriate structure for the meeting.

- Plan an agenda.

- If the client has been referred from a colleague, speak to that colleague about the work being carried out for the client.

- If dealing with a corporate client, carry out some research into the client's company.

- If dealing with an old client of the firm, retrieve the old files for the client and refresh your memory about the cases the firm has handled for the client.

- Prepare the physical setting – clear your desk to avoid that omnipresent law firm panic/chaos look. A physical setting that is informal, friendly and private will help make the client feel relaxed and comfortable. If you need access to your computer during the meeting, have it started and readily accessible.

- Avoid interruptions – particularly avoid having to take phone calls mid-interview.

- Be prepared to offer the client refreshments – coffee, tea, water etc.

- If the client has special needs (e.g. has a disability or requires an interpreter), ensure the appropriate arrangements are made beforehand.

Certain types of case lend themselves to the use of checklists and factsheets. Using these will help ensure that you obtain the most important facts in respect of the client's case during the first interview. If it can be kept short, such checklists can be referred to and completed in the client's presence during the course of the interview. Lengthy form-filling exercises should be avoided where possible, however, as the client may start to feel that you are more interested in filling in your form than in discussing their concerns. Likewise, some care should be taken about the making of notes – while it is important to obtain all the relevant facts, the client will find it off-putting if you spend all your time staring down at your notebook or laptop screen. Try to maintain eye contact with the client and do not allow your note taking to impede the flow of conversation.

CONDUCT OF THE INTERVIEW   18.3

Overview   18.3.1

The purpose of the interview is for the lawyer and client to work together to identify the client's interests and achieve the client's aims. The lawyer should know the topic of the interview in advance. This will allow him or her to determine what is relevant and to structure the interview so that all the relevant information is obtained.

However, the structure of the interview should not be too rigid. The lawyer must ensure that a natural flow of conversation occurs, involving a genuine exchange of views. The interview should move naturally from one topic to the next. It should feel comfortable and positive: the art of interviewing clients lies largely in the ability to guide the conversation smoothly so that all the relevant points are covered without this appearing too obvious to the client. In particular, the lawyer should avoid asking too many highly specific questions, as doing so may give the client the feeling that they are being interrogated and cause them to give limited and evasive answers.

18.3.2   Listening

Listening is different from hearing and is actually quite difficult. Hearing is the process of receiving information. Listening is the mental processing of what you have heard. You need to pay attention not only to what is said but also to what is left unsaid, and to the body language that accompanies what is said.

The average rate of speech is between 125 and 175 words per minute, and the average rate at which information is processed is between 400 and 800 words per minute. The listener should therefore be able to assimilate thoughts, organise them and respond to the speaker, and have time to spare to deal with other unrelated mental processes.

18.3.3   Feedback

Feedback falls into two parts. First, it may be used with the intention of allowing the lawyer to summarise what he or she has been told by the client and clarify it with the client. The lawyer might say, 'So let's see if I've got this right. You told me that …', or 'OK, we've identified about five or so issues that we need to look at a bit more'. This process allows the lawyer to investigate further the matters being summarised and invite the client to expand upon or clarify certain issues.

Second, feedback may be used to encourage the client to communicate with the lawyer, for example when the client seems to lack confidence about the relevance of an issue ('I'm not sure if this is relevant, but…'). Giving positive feedback at this stage ('Please tell me what's on your mind. I'm here to listen and help as much as I can.') enables the lawyer to obtain fuller information from the client than might otherwise be possible.

It is also important to give continuous feedback to the client in the form of short phrases that tell the client you are listening carefully. You should encourage the client to speak by using phrases and words like 'I see', 'that's interesting', 'go on', 'right', 'yes' etc. Even meaningless encouraging noises ('mmm', 'uh huh', etc.) can be helpful in this context. They signal to the client that you are still actively listening to what they are saying.

Body language

It is important to demonstrate interest in the client and in what the client is telling you. Pay attention to your body language in this regard. The skills needed can be summed up by the acronym SOLER:

S – Face the client **Squarely**, adopting a posture that indicates involvement.

O – Adopt an **Open** posture, one that suggests you are receptive to the client.

L – **Lean** slightly forward; not aggressively, but enough to show that you are interested in the client.

E – Maintain **Eye** contact, but do not stare. Use your eyes to show interest but vary your eye contact in response to the flow of the questioning.

R – Stay **Relaxed**. Do not fidget and try to be natural in your expressions.

See 16.2 for further discussion of body language.

Identifying the client's aims

What does the client really want? The answer may be simple – the client may have told you at the outset. Sometimes, however, it is necessary to dig a little deeper. What are the client's underlying concerns? What would he or she regard as a satisfactory result? Is the client in dispute with another business with which the client has an ongoing relationship? Is the health of the long-term relationship of more value than short-term compensation of a specific breach?

It may also become clear in the course of your discussions that the client has other problems of which he or she may be unaware or may not have identified as problems. You will need to point these matters out in an appropriate way and either advise the client upon them or arrange for the client to be referred to one of your colleagues on the matter.

Perceived irrelevance

A common problem in interviews is that the client may become confused or frustrated because he or she cannot see the connection between the questions you are asking and the issue on which he or she has sought your advice. The client is unlikely to be a lawyer and will not think like a lawyer and may therefore perceive your questions as irrelevant.

This problem highlights the importance of lawyer–client communication. The only way to tackle the issue is to explain carefully to the client why the question is relevant to the issue on which your advice has been sought. This issue is discussed in full in section 19.9.

18.4   LANGUAGE

18.4.1   Jargon

The first point to be made on this issue is that lawyers should try to minimise the use of jargon when speaking to clients. Jargon has its place within the legal community – it is a shared language full of familiar terms and common expressions – but it is likely to mystify and alienate the client. So, try to speak plainly, using everyday terms. Find alternatives for jargon terms where possible.

For example, do not say, 'We will effect postal service upon the defendant company'. Say instead:

We'll send the documents to Acme Ltd by post.

We must now consider what language can be used at different stages of the interviewing process.

18.4.2   Opening

During the opening phase of a client interview, you may wish to use some of the small-talk techniques mentioned in Chapter 17.

After you've got the client into the meeting room, offered them a chair and some suitable refreshments, and indicated the breathtakingly panoramic view from the window, you'll want to open the discussion. You could say simply:

Right. How can I help you?

Or, if you already know what issue the client wants to discuss, you might say:

I understand that you'd like some advice on your employment situation. Perhaps we could start by going over some of the background details.

At this stage, you might also indicate to the client how you suggest the meeting might be structured and seek their agreement on this. You might say, for example:

Okay, perhaps we should start by going over the details of this matter. After that we can discuss what might be done and then we can think about the way forward. Would that be okay with you?

And you might warn the client that you'll be making notes:

Do you mind if I make a few notes as we're talking?

It's important to advise the client as to what kind of fees they'll be letting themselves in for at an early stage. You might say:

I should mention at this point how this firm's charging system works. We charge by the hour and my hourly rate is 300 euros.

OR

I should start by giving you an idea of what sort of fees are likely to be involved in this case. A realistic estimate for carrying out this kind of work would be 15,000 euros.

Listening and questioning   18.4.3

Once the interview proper is underway, you will need to listen carefully to what the client has to say and ask appropriate questions to obtain the information you need in order to provide advice to them. To obtain information from the client, you could say, for example:

Perhaps you could tell me a bit about what happened during your meeting with the managing director.

OR

Maybe you could give me some background information about that.

When you need to obtain more information about a particular issue, you might say:

Tell me more about that.

OR

What happened next?

It's also a good idea to check periodically throughout the client's account of the case that you have a full understanding of what they are telling you. This involves summarising and checking for understanding. You might say, for instance:

Okay, let me see if I've got this right. You told me that the managing director actually said, quote unquote, 'I'll make damn sure you never work in this business again'. It's important to be clear about this – is that actually what he said?

OR

Okay, we've identified about three or four issues that we need to focus on. These are the fees payable to the key service providers, the question of confidentiality in respect of know-how and the exclusivity or otherwise of the agency agreements. Is that how you see it?

Equally, you may sometimes need to clarify your own remarks to the client. For instance, you might say:

Perhaps I should make that clearer. The term 'waiver' basically means a variation of the original agreement so that duties set out in it may no longer need to be carried out in the same way or at all.

OR

Perhaps we should just go over that issue again.

At times, you might want the client to stick to the point instead of wandering off onto different issues. There are various linguistic strategies you can use to achieve this. For instance, you might say:

That's an interesting point. However, I'm not sure it's strictly relevant to the issues we need to discuss at this moment. Could we focus on the issue of confidentiality just for the moment and come back to this other issue in a minute?

Conversely, you might need to get the client to move from one point to the next. You might say:

Okay, I think we've dealt with that issue. Let's move on now to the question of exclusivity.

OR

Let's leave this point for a moment and move on to the question of exclusivity.

18.4.4   Advising

After you have all the necessary information you need from the client, you will want to proceed to advising them on the case. It may be best to start by identifying the client's aims. You might say, for instance:

What would be an ideal outcome for you?

OR

Perhaps you could let me know what your priorities are in this matter.

You might also want to give some structure to the way in which you advise the client. For example:

Okay, we've been over the key issues in this matter. I think it would be helpful now to look at what your legal and non-legal options might be. I'll give you a quick rundown of the applicable law and how it relates to your case. Then we can discuss what we should do to move things forward.

Then you might provide the client with a quick rundown of the applicable law:

The legal position is as follows…

OR

This question is governed by the provisions of the Sales of Goods Act.

After you've done that, it will probably be time to outline the client's options. You could signpost this by saying, for instance:

You have maybe three options here. The first is to go to court. The second is to seek a negotiated agreement through mediation, and the third is to do nothing for the moment and see how things develop. Now there are pros and cons for each of these, and it would make sense to run through them before you make any kind of decision on the matter.

OR

The best thing to do, from a legal point of view, would be to terminate the contract immediately and sue for damages. However, we should also consider the non-legal factors, such as the difficulty of finding an alternative supplier given the current state of the market.

It may be necessary to point out certain legal issues that the client has overlooked, perhaps with a view to referring the client to one of your colleagues for advice. For example, you might say:

Incidentally, you should also consider the tax consequences of taking that kind of step. I'm not a specialist in this area, but my colleague Stephanie Willis is a very experienced tax specialist and would be happy to advise you. Would you like me to arrange an appointment for you to come in and go through the tax side of things with her?

Concluding

When concluding the first interview with a new client, you will of course want to obtain confirmation as to whether you will be retained to handle the case. You might say:

I'd be more than happy to handle this case for you. Perhaps you could let me know how you'd like to proceed?

Then you will need to agree what follow-up action is to be taken. For example, you could say:

What I'll do now is draft a letter to Granton Ltd, asking for payment of the outstanding sums by 24 August. That should go out to them before the end of the week. Does that timeframe sound OK to you?

OR

Here's what we need to do. I'll start by getting a letter out to Granton Ltd seeking payment of the outstanding sums by 24 August. Then, if that doesn't produce a result, we'll need to think about issuing court proceedings. I'll keep you informed.

In some cases, you may need the client to provide further information or documentation before you can take any action on the case. So, in order to stress that you can't move until the client has done his or her part, you might say:

As soon as I've heard from you with the employment records mentioned earlier, I'll be able to start work on the case.

When you're satisfied that everything has been covered that needs to be covered, you might say:

Okay, I think that covers everything we need to discuss today, unless there's anything else you'd like to discuss before we wrap things up?

Finally, you'll want to see the client out courteously. So, you might say:

Thanks for coming in to see us today. Don't hesitate to phone or send me an email if you have any questions you'd like to ask or need any information on anything. If I'm out, my colleague Emma Stapleton would be glad to help you.

18.5 CHECKLIST

This checklist is designed to help you to prepare for and structure a client interview.

Preparation

- Purpose of meeting?
- Structure?
- Agenda?
- Ongoing work for client? Which lawyer is handling it?
- Client company researched?
- Previous files retrieved?
- Any special needs of client?

Opening

- Greet client, offer refreshments, preliminary small talk.

- Obtain client's account, concerns and goals.

- Explain preliminary matters including fees, retainer, what can and can't be done for the client, and the nature and proposed structure of the interview.

Listening and questioning

- Listen actively to the client's account and show understanding of it.

- Use appropriate questioning techniques (open, closed and leading questions) where necessary to:
  - Prompt;
  - Clarify;
  - Prevent deviation;
  - Probe.

- Pay attention to body language – remember SOLER.

- Identify aims of client.

- Take notes discreetly (use checklist if appropriate).

- Give feedback.

Summarising

- Summarise the client's account, concerns and goals.

- Identify the relevant facts.

- Identify deficiencies in the available facts.

- Avoid giving premature legal advice.

- Seek further information from client.

Advising

- Give a brief introduction to the advising process.
- Give a brief outline of the relevant law.
- Apply the law to the client's problem.
- Outline the available legal and non-legal options.
- Discuss the available options with the client and help him or her reach a decision if appropriate.

Concluding

- Confirm whether lawyer is to be retained.
- Describe clearly follow-up action to be taken by lawyer.
- Describe clearly follow-up action to be taken by client.
- Give clear timeframes for action and future meetings.
- Confirm the follow-up procedures with the client.
- Conclude interview appropriately.

Throughout

- Establish and maintain rapport with client.
- Use appropriate language.
- Maintain professional courtesy.
- Move smoothly between interview stages.
- Deal appropriately with any issues of professional conduct or ethics.

Dealing with difficult people
Ten-point guide

Most legal professionals, at some time or another, have to deal with difficult people – or with otherwise perfectly pleasant and rational people who for some unknown reason become highly emotional and completely irrational in the presence of a legal adviser.

What strategies does the English language provide for dealing with such situations? This chapter contains a ten-point guide outlining the types of approach that may assist in taming an enraged client, colleague or partner – and the language that can be used to support these approaches.

EMPATHISE

Your client is upset. Therefore, you have to indicate that you understand their concerns. If you fail to do so, the conversation will not progress. In particular, you should show you are actively listening to what they are saying. To a great extent, this can be achieved by body language – lean forward slightly, face the client, maintain eye contact, nod occasionally and use expressions that simply show you are listening: ***mmm hmm***, ***yes***, ***I see***, ***OK***, ***go on***, ***right*** etc.

In addition, it is helpful to summarise and reflect what the client is saying. This reinforces the feeling that you are interested in their concerns. Certain phrases can be used in this respect:

- *Tell me more about that.*

- *And naturally you felt annoyed when they said they weren't going to pay you.*

- *Let's see if I've got this right. To summarise, you said that you sent a reminder letter on 16 July and when you got no response you made a personal visit to Mr Brown's office on 5 August.*

- *Do you mind if we just go over this again? I'd like to make sure I've got it right.*

AVOID DEFENSIVENESS

When attacked, the natural reaction is to defend ourselves. However, this is exactly the wrong way to deal with an angry client.

Never say things like, ***Well, it's not my fault*** or ***I didn't get the message*** or ***Our IT systems went down***. Even if these things are true, raising them will only make the situation more difficult, as the client will think that you are trying to avoid responsibility for the problem that has arisen.

At the same time, it is obviously unwise, if it's not precisely clear where the fault lay, to use language that amounts to an admission of liability, such as ***I'm sorry we messed things up for you***.

The best approach is to find a way of apologising without necessarily admitting fault. For example:

I'm really sorry that you feel we let you down…

Once you have established these parameters – that you're sorry that the client is upset, on the one hand; but that you don't admit any liability for the actual problem, on the other – then you can go ahead and pacify the client further. Note that it may be wise, however, to keep things reasonably vague rather than making specific promises that you may not be able to keep:

…and, of course, we'll do whatever we can to sort matters out for you.

19.3 SEEK MORE INFORMATION

It is important to be careful here. When someone is angry, a tactless question can sometimes send them over the edge. On the other hand, unless you get the information you need, you will not be able to make much progress with the problem they have.

One useful tip here is to try to use tentative or conditional language. For example:

- *Perhaps you could tell me a little more about what happened when you got to Mr Brown's office.*

- *Maybe you could give me a little more information about exactly what happened when he said that to you.*

- *Just coming on to this question of the broken vase…*

- *Is there any way in which we might perhaps find a compromise here?*

19.4 ANGER MANAGEMENT

Sometimes you may find yourselves dealing with someone who is apparently rational but evidently seething with anger inside. The anger may betray itself in one or all of the following ways:

- artificially calm voice, which may have a clipped or over-enunciated quality ('I...am...not...angry...I...am...just...very...disappointed');

- tense facial expression: clenched teeth, unblinking eyes, immobile mouth;

- fidgety body language: drumming of fingers on table, hands on hips, clenching of fist etc;

- curt and dismissive language: (*LAWYER: This is my assistant, Terry Fisher. CLIENT: Yeah, whatever*);

- over-rigid body language: very upright posture, holding onto edge of table etc.

This is a dangerous situation: they are keeping tight control on their anger, but it may explode at any time. You need to think of strategies to avoid this happening.

One way forward is to encourage the client to talk about their feelings. For example:

Look Bill, I appreciate you're giving me the chance to explain, but before I get to that, can I say it's obvious that you are very unhappy with the service you have had and I want to say how sorry I am that you feel that way.

This approach may well result in some criticism of you by the client – but this will be much more manageable than the explosion you will get if you simply ignore the fact that the client is unhappy. Remember that once the client has completely lost his or her temper, there is not much you can do except wait for it to blow over.

Another line that can be tried is:

Bill, you're obviously very upset about this, which I understand, and if it makes you feel better to stand here and shout at me I'm happy to do that, but maybe it would make more sense to talk again this afternoon.

This might seem a bit defeatist – but rage is a tiring emotion, difficult to sustain over a long period, so in a little while you are likely to have a much calmer client.

DON'T BE JUDGEMENTAL

19.5

Sometimes it may be entirely clear to you that the client's problems have been caused by his or her own actions – or at least worsened by them.

In such situations, it's best to try to avoid making comments of the **Well, it's your own damn fault** type, or shaking your head sadly but wisely and telling the client that **If only you'd done as I advised you to do in the first place none of this would have happened**.

It's more than likely that the client will be acutely aware of any fault on his or her part, angry with him or herself – but looking for someone else to take it out on. This is where you come in.

One technique that can be used here is that used by Kinsey in his pioneering study of sexuality, which was conducted in conservative 1940s America. He used to ask things like: **When did you have your first homosexual experience?** – in other words, a technique of questioning that takes the behaviour in question for granted, implying no condemnation of it, leaving the other person free to confirm the interviewer's expectations.

Shifted into the legal arena, this simply means avoiding any element of criticism (which is in any case not the lawyer's role). For example, don't say:

So, you smashed a priceless Ming vase. What on earth did you do that for?

Try instead:

So, you smashed a vase. Okay. It happens. Perhaps you could tell me a little about the events that led up to that.

19.6 AVOID UNREALISTIC PROMISES

Never agree to do something that you cannot realistically guarantee to achieve ('we can definitely win this case for you'). It will only lead to making the client even angrier when you disappoint them a little further down the line.

At the same time, there are linguistic strategies you can use to cushion a client's disappointment at the news that you cannot achieve what they want you to do. Try to explain why that is and try to empathise with the client as you do it.

For example, don't fold your arms and say:

No appeal is possible.

Instead try leaning forward, making eye contact and saying:

Susan, I'd love to be able to tell you we could appeal, and if we could I'd file it now and fight with all our resources to put this decision right – but, being honest, I can't. And the reasons I say that are as follows…

19.7 USE HUMAN LANGUAGE

One fairly common characteristic of lawyers who find themselves being criticised by clients is to take refuge in the use of legal jargon at the expense of plain language. For instance:

It's perfectly clear that your longstanding acquiescence in the continuing breach by the counterparty serves to abrogate your rights of rescission by reason of implied waiver or estoppel arising on the basis of the doctrine of laches.

Don't do this! Ensure that you use clear and straightforward language at all times. If you have to use jargon, explain why you have to use it and what it means. So – our example above can be 'translated' as follows:

The problem we've got here, Bill, is that the court will almost certainly take the view you've let them get away for this for so long that in effect the position has changed, meaning it's legally no longer possible to use it as a reason to terminate the contract.

SET A REALISTIC TIMETABLE FOR ACTION   **19.8**

The client will want to know that his or her problem is going to be dealt with. A good way of handling this issue is to set out in detail the steps that need to be taken, and when each step will occur.

Okay, there are three or four things we need to do here. The first of those is to gather the relevant evidence. That will take about a week, and the main information we need to get hold of is an estimate of the cost of replacement of the Ming vase…

DEAL WITH PERCEIVED IRRELEVANCE   **19.9**

One common cause of client frustration is that he or she cannot see the link between the questions you are asking and the problem he or she consulted you about in the first place. They become confused and start to feel that you have not understood the problem; as a result, tension grows.

The best way of dealing with this is to identify those aspects of your questioning that are likely not to appear relevant to the client, and then to prepare the client for the fact that they will not appear relevant.

Okay, Sarah. I'm going to ask you one or two questions now about some of the other personnel in your office, the roles they are filling at present and the treatment they are receiving from the company's management. This might not seem strictly relevant to your case, but it is in fact very important. The reason I say that is that in order to establish whether discrimination has occurred in your case, the tribunal will need to compare your situation to some extent with that of your colleagues.

19.10 AVOID ECHOING THE CLIENT

As noted above, an important aspect of empathy is to reflect on what the client has said. However, it is all too easy to fall into the habit of simply echoing or repeating what the client has just said, without really reflecting on it.

You felt annoyed when that happened, did you? Uh huh. Okay. Right. Yeah.

Try to avoid this – it is annoying, sounds mechanical and gives the impression you are just going through the motions and not really thinking about the issues that lie behind the words used by the client. At worst it can even sound sarcastic, but it's all too easy to fall into if you are not really concentrating.

Court advocacy

This chapter looks at the typical stages of a court hearing and the linguistic requirements of those stages. Court advocacy calls for the exercise of specialist and multifaceted skills, and the way in which those skills are exercised will vary according to the type of court (civil, criminal, national, international etc.) in which the case is being heard, the legal jurisdiction under which that court operates, and the nature of the case. Consequently, this chapter does not aim at comprehensive coverage of the topic but provides a short overview.

EXAMINATION-IN-CHIEF   20.1

Overview   20.1.1

The aim of the examination-in-chief is to get the witness to tell the court his or her version of events. In practice the witness statement exchanged prior to the trial will often stand as the witness' evidence-in-chief. The lawyer will then simply seek explanatory comments from the witness where necessary.

Where a witness does give evidence-in-chief in full before the court, the lawyer should take the witness through all the evidence that he or she wishes to obtain from that witness. Vital facts should not be omitted: if you fail to elicit sufficient relevant detail it may be impossible to establish your case. However, it is important not to overwhelm the court with unnecessary detail.

Leading questions are not allowed during the examination-in-chief. These are questions that contain their own answers. Often, but not always, they are questions to which the only answer is 'yes' or 'no'. For example, the question, 'Did you last see him at 10.00 a.m.?' is a leading question. It should be rephrased as, 'When did you last see him?'.

Guidelines for the advocate   20.1.2

At the beginning of the examination-in-chief, you should ask the witness to introduce himself or herself to the court by providing details of his/her name, address and, if relevant to the case, employment details. Then you should refer the witness to the dispute being tried and to the point at which his or her evidence begins. You should then take the witness through the evidence in a logical way. It is usually best to approach the evidence in a chronological order, although the structure chosen will also depend on what elements of the narrative need to be emphasised, which may call for occasional departure from a strictly chronological approach and increased focus on certain details at the expense of others.

However, it is important to avoid repetition: when one aspect of your case has been incontestably established there is no need to prove it all over again.

Generally, open questions beginning with **what**, **where**, **who**, **when**, **how** and **why** offer the best means way of obtaining information in the examination-in-chief.

If you think the cross-examination is likely to reveal unhelpful information, consider whether it might be better to introduce it in evidence during your examination-in-chief.

20.2 CROSS-EXAMINATION

20.2.1 Overview

Examination-in-chief is followed by cross-examination. The purpose of cross-examination is to challenge the version of events given during examination-in-chief.

There is no rule preventing the asking of leading questions in cross-examination. In fact, it is best to control the witness when conducting a cross-examination. One of the best ways of doing this is to limit your questions exclusively to leading questions, or to questions to which the witness can reply only with yes or no or other one-word answers. For example, 'you drank four pints of beer in the hour before the crash, didn't you?'

You may challenge a witness either on specific parts of his or her evidence or by challenging his or her credibility more generally; for example, by demonstrating to the court that the witness is biased, or untrustworthy.

The cross-examining lawyer must put his or her own client's case to the witness in cross-examination, where that witness is in a position to comment on it.

20.2.2 Guidelines for the advocate

Do not conduct a cross-examination that does nothing more than allow the witness to repeat his or her evidence given during the examination-in-chief.

Only cross-examine the witness if there is something to be gained by doing so. Work out want you want to achieve, organise your points by subject and go through them. Cross-examination need not cover all the ground covered in the examination-in-chief – only ask a question if there is something to be gained from the expected answer. Be cautious about asking a question to which you do not know what the answer is likely to be.

Cross-examination need not be conducted in an aggressive manner. You will probably get more out of a witness by setting him or her at ease than by creating a confrontational relationship by hostile questioning. In many cases the combination of an apparently soft style with very direct questions will produce better results than direct questions accompanied by an aggressive style – it is the tone of voice, more than the nature of the question, that alerts the witness to your intentions.

RE-EXAMINATION

20.3

Finally, the examining advocate has the opportunity to re-examine the witness on any matters that arose during the cross-examination. The purpose of the re-examination is to give the examining advocate an opportunity to salvage evidence shaken in cross-examination and restore the witness' credibility. No new evidence may be admitted in re-examination without the leave of the judge.

The rule against leading questions applies to re-examination as it does to examination-in-chief.

GENERAL POINTS

20.4

Your questions should be short, simple and easy to understand, for a number of reasons:

- It is essential for your audience to understand your question to enable them to understand the answer.

- On an examination-in-chief, the insecurities and anxieties of the witness on whose evidence you are relying will only be increased if he or she does not understand the question.

- On a cross-examination, a complex or argumentative question provides an opportunity for the witness to evade the point.

NB Avoid asking about more than one thing per question!

Listen to the witness' answers. In an examination-in-chief, if you do not get the necessary evidence before the court, you may not have an opportunity to do it later. In both examination-in-chiefs and cross-examinations, you are entitled to answers from the witness for your questions and you should make sure you get them.

You should be polite to the witness and allow him or her to finish answers to your questions (resist the temptation to try to cut your witness off if it looks like he or she is not giving quite the answer you wanted!).

You should cross-examine on facts, not assertions. For example, saying, 'You are dishonest' provides the witness with the opportunity for denial. Saying, 'You have six convictions for offences of dishonesty, don't you?' gives scope for a yes or no answer only.

20.5   STRUCTURE OF A CIVIL TRIAL

A civil trial in the English courts follows this basic structure:

1 The claimant's lawyer will make an opening speech to the court. This speech should:

    a State the nature of the case before the court;

    b State the issues that will need to be decided;

    c Summarise the facts that you will seek to establish during the trial.

2 The claimant's lawyer will then call the claimant's first witness and conduct an examination-in-chief.

3 The defendant's lawyer will then have the opportunity to cross-examine this witness.

4 The claimant's lawyer may then conduct a re-examination of the witness if appropriate.

5 The claimant's lawyer will then call any further witnesses and the process will be repeated.

6 Once all the claimant's witnesses have been heard, the defendant's witnesses will be called one by one to give evidence in the same way as indicated in steps (2) to (4) above.

7 The claimant's lawyer will give a closing speech to the court. This speech should summarise the argument that underpins the whole case, which you hope will persuade the judge to decide the case in your favour. The suggested structure for this speech is as follows:

    a Introduction;

    b Issues;

    c Narrative;

    d Argument;

    e Confirmation and refutation;

    f Result.

8 The defendant's lawyer will give a closing speech to the court. This will follow a similar structure to that presented by the claimant's lawyer but will present an alternative theory of the case designed to persuade the judge not to decide in favour of the claimant.

9 The judge will pass judgment and make an order.

The burden of proof in a civil case is for the claimant to prove his or her case on the balance of probability. This may be contrasted with the criminal law burden of proof which is for the prosecution to prove the case beyond reasonable doubt.

MODES OF ADDRESS IN COURT

20.6

The table below sets out the names of some of the personnel who appear in court and how these persons are traditionally addressed. Note that the scope of this table is limited to the English courts. The terms 'Your Honor' or 'Judge' are, however, widely used in the US in respect of judges.

Title	Mode of address in court
High Court judge	My Lord/My Lady, Your Lordship/Your Ladyship
Judge (except High Court)	Your Honour
Magistrates (when addressing several collectively)	Your Worships
Magistrate (when addressing a single magistrate)	Your Worship OR Sir/Madam
District Judge, Master	Sir/Madam
Chair of Tribunal	Sir/Madam
Barrister	My learned friend (when addressed by another barrister or solicitor – when addressed by a judge the title Mr/Ms/Miss/Mrs is likely to be used, followed by the barrister's surname) OR Counsel for the [Prosecution/Claimant/Defendant]
Solicitor	My friend (when addressed by another solicitor or barrister – when addressed by a judge the title Mr/Ms/Miss/Mrs is likely to be used, followed by the solicitor's surname)
Claimant or Defendant in person	If addressed directly, the claimant or defendant is referred to either as claimant or defendant OR by his or her title and surname (e.g. Mr Smith, Ms Jones)

21 Negotiation

NEGOTIATION STYLES AND STRATEGIES

Negotiation style refers to the personal behaviour the negotiator adopts to carry out the strategy they have chosen. Three main styles of negotiation have been identified, and these are usually referred to as cooperative, adversarial and problem-solving.

Negotiation strategy refers to the specific goals to be achieved and the pattern of conduct that should improve the chances of achieving those goals.

Research has found that all effective negotiators have a number of features in common – they prepare on the facts, prepare on the law, take satisfaction in using their legal skills, are effective advocates and are self-controlled.

The main features of the three main styles of negotiation are set out in the table below.

Cooperative	Adversarial	Problem-solving
Participants are friends	Participants are opponents	Participants are problem-solvers
The aim is agreement	The aim is victory	The aim is a wise outcome reached efficiently and amicably
Make concessions to cultivate the relationship	Demand concessions as a condition of the relationship	Separate the people from the problem
Be soft on the people and the problem	Be hard on the people and the problem	Be soft on the people, hard on the problem
Trust others	Distrust others	Proceed independent of trust
Change your position easily	Stick to your position	Focus on interests, not positions
Make offers	Make threats	Explore interests
Reveal your bottom line	Mislead as to your bottom line	Avoid having a bottom line

Accept one-sided losses to reach agreement	Demand one-sided gains as the price of agreement	Invent options for mutual gain
Search for the single answer: the one *they* will accept	Search for the single answer: the one *you* will accept	Develop multiple options to choose from; decide later
Insist on agreement	Insist on your position	Insist on objective criteria
Try to avoid a contest of will	Try to win a contest of will	Try to reach a result based on standards independent of will
Yield to pressure	Apply pressure	Reason and be open to reason; yield to principle, not pressure

Adversarial/cooperative

21.1.1

Adversarial and cooperative styles of negotiation can be regarded as different forms of positional bargaining. In effect, both styles draw on the principle that the negotiators are opponents. The difference between them is the degree to which the cooperative negotiator is prepared to work with the other side in resolving the differences between them.

By contrast, the stereotypical adversarial negotiator is a tough and aggressive advocate whose aim is victory by defeating the opponent, in much the same manner as he or she might do in court.

Problem-solving

21.1.2

The problem-solving style can be characterised as a form of principled bargaining. Problem-solving negotiators 'separate the people from the problem' and seek to negotiate in a non-confrontational and non-judgemental way, by applying standards of fairness and reasonableness.

Fisher and Ury summarise the essentials of this approach in their book, *Getting to YES: Negotiating Agreement Without Giving In* (1991):

In most instances to ask a negotiator, 'who's winning' is as inappropriate as to ask who's winning a marriage. If you ask that question about your marriage, you have already lost the most important negotiation – the one about what kind of game to play, about the way you deal with each other and your shared and differing interests.

(p. 148)

21.1.3   Negotiation strategies compared

The different negotiation strategies are compared in the table below.

Competitive/adversarial	Problem-solving
The negotiator	**The negotiator**
Tries to maximise resource gains for own client	Tries to maximise returns for own client including any joint gains available
Makes high opening demands and is slow to concede	Focuses on common interests of parties
Uses threats, confrontation, argument	Tries to understand the merits as objectively as possible
Manipulates people and the process	Uses non-confrontational debating techniques
Is not open to persuasion on substance	Is open to persuasion on substance
Is oriented to qualitative and competitive goals	Is oriented to qualitative goals: fair, wise, durable agreement
Negotiator's assumptions	**Negotiator's assumptions**
Motivation is competitive/antagonistic	Common interests valued
Limited resources	Limited resources with unlimited variation and personal preferences
Independent choices: tomorrow's decision unaffected materially by today's	Interdependence recognised
Goal	**Goal**
Win as much as you can and especially more than the other side	Mutually agreeable solution that is fair and efficient for all parties
Weaknesses	**Weaknesses**
Strong bias towards confrontation, encouraging the use of coercion and emotional pressure as persuasive means; hard on relationships, breeding mistrust, feelings of separateness, frustration and anger, resulting in more frequent breakdowns in negotiations; distorting communications, producing misinformation and misjudgements	Strong bias towards cooperation, creating internal pressures to compromise and accommodate

Guards against responsiveness and openness to opponent, thereby restricting possibility of joint gains	Avoids strategies that are confrontational because they risk impasse, which is viewed as failure
Encourages breakdown by creating many opportunities for impasse	Focuses on being sensitive to other's perceived interests; increases vulnerability to deception and manipulation by a competitive opponent. Increases possibility that settlement may be more favourable to other side than may be fair
Increases difficulty in predicting responses of opponent because reliance is on manipulation and confrontation	Increases difficulty in establishing definite aspiration level and bottom lines because of reliance on qualitative goals
Contributes to overestimation of return possible through all alternatives (court, arbitration) because it does not focus on a relatively objective analysis of substantive merits as standard for resolution	Requires substantial skill and knowledge of process to do well
	Requires strong confidence in own assessment powers regarding interest/needs of other side and other's payoff schedule

DIFFERENCES IN NEGOTIATION LANGUAGE BETWEEN THE US AND THE UK

21.2

In Chapter 9 we saw that there are certain differences between American and British English. These are relatively minor in comparison to the differences that exist in the mentality and cultural values of the two countries – with the caveat that this is a sweeping generalisation and one must also take into account differences in individual personalities and approaches.

The table below contains a brief summary of how these differences affect the way American and British people use English in negotiations. Note that the US and the UK are selected here purely on the basis that they are the most prominent English-speaking countries. Differences also exist in the way in which other English-speaking countries, such as Australia, New Zealand, Canada, South Africa and Ireland (where English is the second official language) use the language in negotiations.

British	American
Formal and reserved on first meeting (informal later on)	Informal and friendly from the start (but initial friendliness may be purely social habit)
Prefer to use indirect language ('I'm not quite with you on that')	Prefer to use direct language ('That's bullshit')
Tend to use understatement ('I'm afraid that might be a bit difficult')	Tend to exaggerate ('Are you kidding me? This is the best deal you'll ever get!')
Extensive use of irony	Straight-talking. May misunderstand irony
Rarely disagree openly (but will qualify agreement or use non-committal terms to indicate lack of enthusiasm about a proposal)	Will disagree openly if necessary
Use humour as a tactic in itself (to break tension, speed up discussion, criticise someone or introduce a new idea)	Use humour to break the ice
Insular but may have some cultural awareness	Insular, may be culturally naïve
Use vagueness as a tactic (to confuse or delay)	Dislike tactics to delay negotiations but use vagueness to confuse
Dislike making a decision during the first meeting	Will press for a decision on main points during the first meeting (and work out details later)
Generally (but not always) interested in long-term relationships rather than making a quick buck	Interested in getting the deal
Patient	Impatient ('time is money')
May not reveal bottom line (may be plotting against you)	Likely to place cards on the table and work towards a deal by exchange of offer and counteroffer
Do not usually respond well to hard-sell tactics	Require and expect hard sell
Often use woolly, old-fashioned phrasing (may be trying to trick you into underestimating their abilities)	Enthusiastic use of latest business jargon

Apparent formality may conceal more individualistic tendencies	Apparent informality and friendliness may conceal deeply conservative beliefs
Appear to 'muddle through' without clear aims (but known for lateral thinking)	Have a plan and pursue it aggressively, persistently and consistently
May resort to sarcasm when angry ('That's a fantastic idea! You must be a genius!')	May resort to threats when angry, particularly a threat to end the negotiations there and then if progress is not being made ('I can see I'm wasting my time here')

American business and legal people have the reputation of being the world's toughest, most aggressive negotiators. However, they are relatively consistent and rarely renege once a deal has been struck. They also tend to be relatively uninformed about the culture of other countries. This means you have one important advantage over them: you know a lot more about them than they know about you. This can be exploited by at times negotiating on the American wavelength and at other times shifting to the cultural norms of your own country.

British negotiators often like to present themselves as diplomatic amateurs. They often appear to 'muddle through' negotiations without any clear idea of what they wish to achieve. However, do not underestimate the British love of plotting (evidenced by the fact that one of Britain's national heroes, Guy Fawkes, was a man who tried to blow up Parliament). Furthermore, the woolly exterior may in fact conceal a considerable capacity for ruthlessness when needed. However, like American negotiators, they rarely renege once a deal has been struck. The apparent disorganisation and understatedness of some British negotiators are often viewed as a weak point by Americans and they may instinctively increase the aggressiveness of their approach when confronted with this style in order to 'break' their counterpart.

THE QUALITIES OF A GOOD NEGOTIATOR

21.3

Negotiation is the process of bargaining to reach a deal – but what does it actually involve? Does it mean being as tough as possible in order to get everything you want at that particular moment, or does it mean reaching a compromise that will preserve and even enhance a working relationship that will continue in the future?

The answer clearly depends on the kind of relationship you have, or want to have, with your opponent in the future. A good working relationship, like a good marriage, will probably involve neither of the parties getting everything they want, and both parties having to make concessions to the other.

So, what are the qualities that make a good negotiator? As a negotiator, you'll find yourself in different settings, and dealing with different issues. However, there are three key skills that all negotiators need to develop:

1 an awareness of the need to live together after the talking has ended and life goes back to normal;

2 an anticipation of how people will be feeling and are likely to react;

3 the ability to conduct an ongoing 'risk assessment' as the negotiations progress.

In addition, it is often said that a good negotiator is one who:

- listens to what the other party is saying and observes their body language carefully;

- is able to assess changes in power between the parties;

- has the ability to persuade;

- is assertive where necessary (note that being assertive is not the same as being aggressive);

- has total commitment to the client's case;

- is patient and remains cool under pressure;

- maintains self-control;

- knows the value to the client of each item to be negotiated – and, if possible, to the other side;

- is flexible, able to think laterally, and has imagination;

- avoids cornering the opponent unnecessarily and avoids impasse;

- knows when to conclude – and when to push on;

- is realistic, rational and reasonable;

- is capable of self-evaluation;

- is able to put himself or herself in the other side's shoes – but doesn't stay there too long.

PREPARATION: FIVE-STEP PLAN

Preparation for negotiation is of crucial importance. The process of carrying out such preparation can be divided into five key steps, as follows:

Step 1: Research facts and law

Without a sound grasp of the facts and the applicable law, effective negotiation is impossible. Before the negotiation you should do the following:

- Review the case file.

- Consider the history and development of the case and identify the relevant facts.

- Identify the legal issues for each set of facts.

- Review agreements similar to those that will be the subject of the negotiation.

- Review the position of your opponents. How do they view the facts, what interpretations of the law favour their standpoint, what strengths and weaknesses are there in their case? You then need to prepare a balance sheet matching the strengths and weaknesses in each side's case.

Step 2: Establish the client's aims and agree strategy

You need to explore the full range of options that might be available to you, discuss these with your client and then develop specific objectives for achieving these in the context of a particular negotiation.

The client needs to be advised that sticking at a certain point could lead to deadlock. A client who intends to adopt a cooperative strategy also needs to be warned that this could provide an opportunity for exploitation by the other side.

Step 3: Identify the client's best alternative to a negotiated agreement (BATNA)

Negotiation is one of several means that might be used to achieve your client's aims. The best test of any proposed joint agreement is whether it offers better value than any other solution outside of an agreement.

You should always seek to identify your client's best alternative to a negotiated agreement (BATNA). Your client's BATNA is the standard against which any proposed agreement is measured. Developing a BATNA protects your client from accepting terms that are too unfavourable and from rejecting terms that it would be in the client's best interests to accept. It provides a realistic measure against which you can measure all offers.

Alternatives to an agreement might involve:

- Agreement with another party.
- Unilateral action.
- Mediation or arbitration.
- Going to court.

Working out a BATNA should give you a feel for what may be acceptable and what is not. To arrive at your BATNA you should construct a list of actions that your client might take if no agreement is reached, then select the option that seems best. You should then measure all proposed settlements against this alternative option.

21.4.4 Step 4: Decide what information you need to obtain

Information is continually exchanged during negotiations, and as this process occurs each party learns more and more about its opponent.

You should identify the following in advance of the meeting:

- the information you need from the negotiation;
- the information the other side is likely to protect;
- any information you want to give to the other side.

21.4.5 Step 5: Plan the agenda

An agenda should identify and illustrate the issues in dispute. It should distinguish three different dimensions of the negotiation:

- Content: the range of topics to be settled.
- Procedures: the manner in which the negotiation will take place, the control of the meetings, the matters to be discussed, the preliminaries, the timing of the different phases of the meeting.
- Personal interaction: the manner in which the individuals involved in negotiating interact with each other.

THE NEGOTIATION PROCESS

Negotiation stages

Most negotiators have three basic positions in mind when carrying out negotiations. These are:

- The ideal position – what they would like to achieve in an ideal world.

- The realistic position – what they realistically expect to be possible.

- The fallback position. What is the lowest offer the negotiator will accept? What other options does he or she have if the negotiation does not work out (i.e. the BATNA)?

How does the process of negotiation work in practice? It is possible to break it down into five typical stages.

1 Preparation. This is crucial. The more you know about the subject-matter being negotiated and the other party's interest, as well as your own, the quicker you will be able to adapt to new negotiating positions. In this way, you will be able to remain in control of the process throughout. This area is discussed in detail below.

2 Opening moves. Your opening moves will largely involve investigating the issues and exploring the positions of both parties. You will need to express your views as well as actively listen to the views of others. It's also worth drawing attention to any flaws in the other party's position at this stage.

3 Offers. This is the stage where the most active negotiation occurs. As you receive and make offers, you may find yourself having to re-evaluate your position or re-package your ideas. You need to read the signals the other party is giving off quickly and accurately. Don't be afraid to be creative.

4 Narrowing differences. Once the basic positions of each party have been established, and offers have been made, the process of narrowing the differences between the parties can begin. At this point you will need to consider the priority of the positions you have taken. What issues are you prepared to compromise on, and which are you not? What compromises do you require from the other party? What is the bottom line?

5 Concluding. As well as reaching – and recording – an agreement, this is a time to evaluate how the process has worked. One matter that is often overlooked at this stage is to set a date to review what has been agreed.

21.5.2   **Conduct of the negotiation**

The way in which the process of negotiation is handled will depend on the negotiation strategy each party is using.

A problem-solving negotiator will aim to identify mutual needs and produce solutions that satisfy both parties. He or she will seek to expand the options available to each party in a win/win negotiation.

An adversarial negotiator will try to maximise the gain to his or her client in a win/lose situation. He or she will seek the best for the client by denying options to the other side, and will only make concessions if absolutely necessary. The adversarial style can lead to deadlock and adversarial negotiators may have to switch to a more cooperative style towards the end of the negotiation.

21.5.2.1   **Opening**

Problem-solving negotiator. A problem-solving negotiator will aim to create an atmosphere that is cordial and collaborative but business-like. He or she will start with some neutral non-business topic and will avoid sitting opposite the opponent – this can set up a face-to-face confrontation from the start. A problem-solver is likely to have prepared an outline agenda and may start by seeking agreement with the other side about the procedure to be followed.

Adversarial negotiator. An adversarial negotiator is likely to keep the opening phases of the negotiation short and try to use it to project power and establish a psychologically dominant position. The negotiator will engage in initial ice-breaking to establish a basis for communication but will be brisk and business-like. He or she will then move swiftly on to business, without discussing the procedures to be followed.

21.5.2.2   **Exploring positions**

Problem-solving negotiator. A problem-solving negotiator will wish to tackle each of the issues across a broad front. This leads to a process in which the overall pattern is cleared and some progress is made on some of the issues. Then the discussion moves on to consider each aspect of the broad pattern. Finally, the parties move into more detailed discussion of the issues. The object of structuring the discussion is to facilitate agreement.

In a problem-solving situation each party will make a brief opening statement that should present their view of the overall negotiation, identify the party's interest, specify how each party can contribute to achieving a solution for mutual gain and stress those areas in which agreement has already been reached. The parties will then try to identify issues for mutual gain.

Adversarial negotiator. An adversarial negotiator will consider whether to start with the most difficult issues or the least difficult issues.

A cooperative negotiator might wish to start with the least difficult issues, since this is likely to lead to success for both parties in the early stages, thus creating a good working relationship. The negotiator may then be able to gain concessions on bigger and more difficult issues.

A competitive negotiator may wish to start with big and difficult issues. In this way he or she issues a challenge to the opponent and destroys the expectation that the early stages of the negotiation will be marked by civility and trust.

Persuading and making offers

21.5.2.3

Problem-solving negotiator. A problem-solving negotiator may wish to generate solutions by making hypothetical suggestions instead of concrete offers. He or she may introduce a proposal, on a 'what if?' basis, and invite the other side to develop it further. Neither side is obliged to make any commitment or oppose the idea. A more relaxed discussion can then follow, with adjustments to the original idea arising as a result of the joint discussion.

The problem-solving negotiator will try to make it as easy as possible for the other side to shift their position and agree on a compromise. This is achieved by stressing the benefits that a proposed solution offers the other party.

Adversarial negotiator. An adversarial negotiator is more likely to make a concrete offer. He or she is likely to make it at an early stage – by making the first offer, the adversarial negotiator seizes the agenda and clarifies the issues at stake. The offer should be made as soon as the negotiator has assessed the other side's strengths, weaknesses and bargaining positions.

All offers should be justified. By articulating a justification, commitment to that position is conveyed. The other side are forced to confront the justification.

When making an offer, the adversarial negotiator will start with a high opening position. There is a high correlation between the amount of the negotiator's original demand and the ultimate payoff. But the offer should be reasonable – if it is unreasonable, the other side may conclude that the parties are so far apart that it is not worth negotiating further.

The initial proposals must be made firmly. The offer should be specific so as to create commitment. The sum proposed should be exact – not 'around about' or 'in the region of'.

The offer should also be justified. The negotiator should express commitment to his or her offer to show that it is not negotiable.

21.5.2.4   Narrowing differences

Problem-solving negotiator. Problem-solvers will take care to ensure that the creative possibilities of any hypothetical or concrete proposals are fully explored before taking any decision. They will ask themselves questions like:

- Can a proposal actually achieve a wider benefit than first seems possible?

- Can a new condition be introduced to compensate for the disadvantage of any concession that may be made?

- Can agreement on an apparently minor issue create a useful precedent for use at some later stage?

- Can the negotiation and its outcome be used to create or improve a mutually beneficial relationship with the other party?

Adversarial negotiator. When trying to achieve agreement the adversarial negotiator is likely to use certain tactics designed to force the opponent to accept his or her offer. For example, the negotiator may seek to 'educate' the other side by expressing anger, using threats and presenting arguments. He or she may also seek to enhance his or her own power by releasing information that suggests there is no clear alternative to settlement.

As each party learns more about the other's position, the differences between them are likely to narrow. Eventually the adversarial negotiator may switch to a more cooperative style to avoid deadlock. This may lead to certain concessions being made, although an adversarial negotiator will seek to reach agreement whilst making as few concessions as possible. Concessions are only made in response to concessions from the other side.

21.5.2.5   Closing the negotiation

Once agreement has been reached it is essential to record all the elements of the agreement in a summary. You should check for clarification and confirm the details of the agreement in writing. Heads of agreement can be useful in this situation.

Where the parties cannot reach agreement on every detail, a draft agreement can be drawn up as a basis for agreement. The idea is that an initial draft is produced, which does not purport to be complete. It is acknowledged to have faults, but is to be used as a basis for further negotiation. Each party is encouraged to make suggestions for improvement. These suggestions are noted and agreed suggestions are incorporated into the text.

NEGOTIATION PLOYS

A ploy is defined in the Oxford English Dictionary as 'a cunning act performed to gain an advantage'. A number of standard ploys are often used in commercial negotiations. They are worth knowing about – you may not wish to use such tactics yourself, but you will certainly wish to know when your opponent is using a ploy against you. Here are some of the more common ploys:

The bogey

This is a buyer's ploy. The buyer assures the seller that he or she loves the product but has a very limited budget, so that in order for a sale to occur the seller must reduce the price.

The idea is to test the credibility of the seller's price. The seller might react positively by revealing information about costing, so that you can force the price downwards. It may also provoke the seller to look at your real needs.

'I am only a simple grocer'

The idea of this ploy is to make your opponent believe they are dealing with an inexperienced negotiator because he or she claims to be 'only a simple grocer'. They may then relax too much and commit indiscretions about their objectives, tactics and intentions. In fact, although you claim to be 'only a simple grocer' you are the managing director of the world's largest chain of grocery stores.

'I'm sorry, I've made a mistake'

This is an irritating and rather dishonest ploy used by sellers. You order some goods at $4.55 per item. The seller then calls you back claiming that he or she has made a mistake in the arithmetic of the order you placed. Instead of the products costing $4.55 each, they actually cost $4.95 each. The seller then claims that he or she cannot sell them at $4.55 because his or her boss will not authorise the sale.

If you believe the seller to be genuine, you agree to the higher price. If you do not, you cancel the order. Buyers usually submit to the ploy.

21.6.4   Minimum order ploy

This is a ploy used by the seller whereby the seller maximises the value of the order by placing restrictions or conditions on the order the buyer has placed. Examples include:

These are only sold in packs of 12.

If we represent you in the purchase of the building, we must also act as letting agents if you acquire it.

21.6.5   Over and under ploy

This ploy is a handy response to a demand made by your opponent. For example, your opponent might demand that you reduce your price by 5% if they pay your invoice within seven days. You could respond with an 'over and under': 'if you agree to a 5% premium for late payment'.

21.6.6   Quivering quill

This is a ploy used by buyers in which the buyer demands concessions at the very point of closing the deal – i.e. when the quill (an old-fashioned pen made from a feather) is quivering over the contract and about to sign it. At this point, the buyer suddenly demands, for example, 3% off the purchase price. When the seller expresses unwillingness to agree, the buyer threatens not to sign the contract. A typical result is that the seller is pressured into giving a 1.5% reduction on the purchase price.

21.6.7   Shock opening

This is a negotiation ploy designed to pressure the opponent. The other negotiator starts with a price that is much higher than you expected. You are shocked into silence. If – but only if – they back up their opening price with a credible reason for it, you have to review your expectations.

21.6.8   Tough guy/nice guy

Sometimes called 'good cop/bad cop', this is a ploy that sometimes works on intimidated negotiators. It is an act in which two negotiators working as a team adopt different negotiation styles: one is tough, uncompromising and adversarial while the other appears more friendly, cooperative and open to persuasion.

You prefer to deal with the apparently softer negotiator but he or she claims to be unable to act without the approval of the tougher colleague. He or she wants to help you but needs you to give concessions in return. You end up moving a lot closer to his or her position than you intended, but are comforted by the illusion that you have had to give way less than would have been the case if you had been dealing one-on-one with the 'tough guy'. You have been tricked – the act was a set-up to make you concede.

Waking up the dead

21.6.9

This is a risky ploy. It is used where you are dealing with a team of negotiators and are making little progress. The idea behind the ploy is to try to exploit any differences of opinion in the opposing team. You invite a member of the other team who has remained silent throughout to comment:

What do you think, Mr Linden?

Do you have any suggestions on how we might break this impasse, Ms Yardleyo?

You are taking a risk, as the other negotiators may resent your interference and react by hardening their position. The ploy is unlikely to succeed against a disciplined team.

What do you know?

21.6.10

This is a ploy used to try to obtain information.

The other negotiators open the discussion with the question, 'What do you know?'. If you tell them, you might end up revealing more about the state of your knowledge than would be wise at that stage of the negotiation. The best response is to say, 'Not much. Perhaps you could go over the issues for me?'

SUGGESTED LANGUAGE

21.7

Opening

21.7.1

Making introductions

21.7.1.1

Good morning. I am [__]and this is my colleague Mr/Miss/Ms/Mrs [__]

Ice-breaking

21.7.1.2

Is this your first visit to [__]?
I hope that you had no trouble finding our office?

It looks as if the weather is going to improve/get worse.
Would you like a cup of tea/coffee?
[if you know the other party slightly] How was your weekend?

OR

How is/how are [mention name of wife/husband/partner/children/colleague]?

21.7.1.3   Setting an agenda

Are we agreed that today's meeting should be used to cover the following…?

OR

We'd like to use this meeting to… [e.g. explore each other's position, exchange information]. Is that okay with you?

Possible response:

Yes, we'd like to exchange views, but I think we'd like to move towards an agreement on some of the issues.

Reply:

That's fine. I assumed this meeting would last for an hour. Shall we see if we can agree on a timetable?

21.7.1.4   Opening the discussion

Perhaps we could start with the issue of…

OR

There are three/several/a number of points I'd like to make…

OR

Perhaps you'd care to give us your thoughts on this matter.

21.7.2   Exploring positions

21.7.2.1   Investigating options

[opening the questioning process] How do you see this matter?

OR

Right, I think we are clear on how we both see the position. Let's look at the creative possibilities.

OR

Another way of looking at this question might be…

Moving to the next point

Okay, I think we've covered that point. Let's move on to the question of…

OR

Let's leave this point for a moment and move on to…

OR

We'll come back to this issue in a while, but let's move on to…

OR

Okay, we seem to be in agreement on that point. Let's move on to…

Asking for an opinion

What's your position/view on…?

OR

How do you see this issue?

Giving an opinion

[*tentative, subjective*] *I believe/think/feel that…*

OR

My view is…

OR

[*firm*] *It is clear that…*

Stating a position

[*firm*] *Our position on this issue is that…*

OR

[*neutral*] *We believe/think/take the view that/are of the opinion that…*

OR

[*indirect*] *We are approaching this question on the basis that…*

21.7.3   Persuading and making offers

21.7.3.1   Putting forward a legal analysis

[*tentative*] *Our analysis of the law relating to this matter is that…*

[*firm*] *The law is very clear on this issue. It says that…*

21.7.3.2   Making offers and concessions

We are prepared to make an offer in the following terms to settle this matter…

OR

We are prepared to concede on the question of…

21.7.3.3   Rejecting an offer

[*firm, unequivocal rejection*] *I'm afraid that's out of the question…*

OR

[*firm, but indicating willingness to consider revised offers without specifying what is expected*] *You're going to have to do better than that…*

OR

[*neutral*] *We're unable to accept that…*

21.7.3.4   Rejecting an offer and making a counteroffer

We can't accept that proposal in its current form. However, if you were prepared to compromise on the question of…

OR

We can't accept that. However, we would accept…

OR

We would be prepared to agree on…if you were prepared to agree on…

21.7.3.5   Defending an offer

That is the best offer we can make in the light of the facts as we understand them at the moment. We might be inclined to take a different view if new facts were to emerge that affected the position. Perhaps you could give us some more information on your situation?

Offering a compromise   **21.7.3.6**

[*committing oneself if certain conditions are met*] *We are prepared to...on condition that...*

OR

[*not committing oneself if certain conditions are met*] *We might agree to/take a more favourable view of* [*state subject-matter*] *if you accept that...*

Checking understanding   **21.7.3.7**

What's your view on that?

OR

Am I making myself clear?

OR

Are there any questions you want to ask about that?

OR

If I understand you correctly, you'd like to...

OR

Let me see if I'm following you. What you're saying is...

Bringing others into the discussion   **21.7.3.8**

[*formal*] *Allow me to give the floor to...*

[*informal*] *Perhaps I could bring in X at this point. X, what's your view on this?*
[*addressing a member of other side's negotiating team*] *What's your view on this, Mr/Miss/Ms/Mrs Y?*

Entering the discussion   **21.7.3.9**

Could/May I come in at this point?

OR

Let me just add that...

21.7.3.10   **Agreeing**

I think we're in agreement on that.

OR

Yes, we take the same view on that issue.

OR

We agree.

OR

Agreed.

21.7.3.11   **Agreeing partially**

I would tend to agree with you on that.

OR

I basically agree. However, I have the following reservations…

OR

I basically agree. However, have you taken into account the fact that…?

21.7.3.12   **Disagreeing tactfully**

I agree up to a point, but…

OR

There's some truth in what you say, but…

21.7.3.13   **Disagreeing**

[*very politely*] *I'm not quite with you on that, I'm afraid.*

[*politely*] *That's not a view I share, I'm afraid.*

OR

[*forcefully*] *With all due respect I entirely disagree.*

OR

[*dismissively*] *Oh, that's nonsense!*

Expressing outrage

[*polite*] *That suggestion entirely lacks merit/credibility.*

OR

[*forceful*] *That's an outrageous suggestion!*

OR

[*dismissive*] *That's absurd!*

OR

[*dismissive*] *Rubbish!/Ridiculous!/Nonsense!*

Accepting an offer

[*enthusiastically*] *We would be more than happy to accept that…*

OR

[*neutrally*] *Yes, I think we are prepared to accept that…*

OR

[*less enthusiastically*] *Yes, I think we could probably live with that…*

Refusing an offer

[*forcefully*] *No, I'm afraid that's totally unacceptable.*

OR

[*neutrally*] *No, we can't accept that offer.*

OR

[*regretfully*] *Unfortunately, we are unable to accept that.*

Playing for time

I'm afraid I'm not in a position to comment on that just yet.

OR

I'm afraid I don't have authority to accept that without checking with…

OR

I'll need to discuss that with…and get back to you.

OR

Perhaps I could suggest we take a short break?

OR

Could you just go over that proposal again? I want to make sure I've understood it properly.

OR

We'll have to think a bit more about that and get back to you.

21.7.3.18 **Interrupting**

If I might just interrupt you for a moment, I'd like to…

OR

I'm sorry, you've lost me there. You were saying…?

OR

Can I just stop you there a moment? I'd like to clarify…

21.7.3.19 **Stopping interruptions**

[forceful] Just hear me out on this.

OR

[polite] If I could just finish what I was saying…

21.7.3.20 **Deflecting an unwanted line of questioning**

What exactly are you getting at?

OR

Where is this line of thought leading to exactly?

OR

How is that relevant, exactly?

Narrowing differences

Summarising

To sum up then, there seems to be…

OR

The key issues are…

Correcting misunderstandings

Perhaps I should make that clearer by saying…

OR

Let me just repeat, in case there is any confusion, that…

OR

[responding to mistaken impression of other party] There seems to have been a misunderstanding/I'm not sure we're quite on the same page. What I meant was…

Asking for further information

Could you be a little more specific/precise?

OR

You mentioned something about…Perhaps you could just tell me a little more about…

OR

That sounds interesting. Perhaps you could give us a few more details.

Seeking clarification

Am I right in thinking that…?

OR

Could you just go over the…again? I'm not quite sure how it was supposed to work.

21.7.4.5   **Making recommendations, proposals and suggestions**

I recommend/suggest/propose that…

OR

Can I suggest something?

OR

[to break a deadlock] Okay, we seem to have reached an impasse. Perhaps I could suggest something?

21.7.4.6   **Sketching a hypothesis**

Let's suppose for a moment that…

OR

One way of looking at this matter would be…

OR

What if…

21.7.4.7   **Projecting false naivety**

Correct me if I'm wrong but…

OR

This is obviously not my field, but…

OR

I may be off point here, but isn't it the case that…

21.7.4.8   **Expressing support**

I'm in favour of…

OR

I like that idea. Tell me more about it.

OR

I can definitely see that working.

Expressing opposition

I can see many problems in adopting this.

OR

I'm not sure how realistic this proposal is.

OR

If this matter were to be tested in court, the court would never make such an order…

Closing

Persuading

[*mentioning certain factors to influence the other party*] *Have you taken into account…?*

OR

[*casting the issue in a new light*] *Look at it this way. Suppose that…*

OR

[*demonstrating empathy*] *If I were in your shoes/on your side of the table, I would be very interested in…*

Pressuring for a decision

[*threatening a deadline*] *We're going to have to ask you to make a quick decision. The deadline is…*

OR

We can't keep this offer open for longer than…There are other interested parties.

OR

[*stressing simplicity of matter*] *The issues are very simple. There's no reason why this can't be decided by…*

OR

[*keeping up the pressure*] *I'll phone you tomorrow morning to see what progress has been made.*

OR

[*threat*] *Either you accept this or…/If you don't accept our offer/request, we'll…*

21.7.5.3 Emphasising

I particularly want to emphasise/stress/highlight/underline the fact that…

OR

A point that we need particularly to bear in mind is…

OR

The fundamental point/issue is…

21.7.5.4 Reaching an agreement

Okay, we're in agreement that…

OR

We have agreed on the following…

21.7.5.5 Closing the negotiation

[*adjourning to another day*] *Okay, I think we've done as much as we can today. Let's adjourn to…*

OR

[*reaching deadlock*] *We seem to have reached deadlock today. Let's take some time out/a break.*

OR

[*agreement reached*] *We seem to be in agreement on all major points. Can we agree that a memorandum of understanding will be prepared by…for circulation on…*

21.7.5.6 Concluding

In conclusion, I'd like to say…

OR

I'd like to finish by saying…

Saying goodbye

Let me get your coat…

It's been a pleasure doing business with you. Have a safe journey home.

KILLER LINES FOR NEGOTIATIONS

There are certain make-or-break points in any negotiation. In such situations, your choice of words becomes critically important. Here are just five examples of these, and some tried and tested linguistic strategies for dealing with them. While some of these are set out under 21.7, they bear repetition in this context.

Avoiding impasse/sketching hypothesis

Sometimes the parties reach deadlock in a negotiation and seem unable to make progress. They have in effect exhausted the possibilities of the parameters within which they are working. One solution is to discard these parameters and invent new ones: i.e. to think creatively.

Here are some lines you can use to introduce a fresh perspective on the issues under discussion.

Right, I think we are clear on how we both see the position. Let's look at the creative possibilities.

OR

Another way of looking at this question might be to think in terms of a long-term lease rather than an outright sale.

OR

Let's suppose for a minute that we were prepared to consider a long-term lease rather than an outright sale. How might that change things?

OR

What if we looked at the possibility of a long-term lease?

Rejecting an offer but keeping the door open

Sometimes you need to reject the offer that has been made but are keen to indicate to the other party that you are willing to listen to further offers. In particular, you might want to indicate that a concession on one issue by the other party could be rewarded by a concession on another issue on your part.

[firm, but indicating willingness to consider revised offers without specifying what is expected] You're going to have to do better than that.

OR

We can't accept that proposal in its current form. However, we might be prepared to agree on/consider raising our offer to 25%, if you were prepared to move on the question of usage rights.

OR

[not committing oneself if certain conditions are met] We might agree to 25% if you accept that we retain usage rights.

OR

We might be inclined to take a different view if you were to move a little on the issue of usage rights.

21.8.3 Responding to the question 'is that your best offer?'

This question is a clear attempt to get a better deal without attempting to justify it. If you say yes, you are committed to defending that offer and the other party might walk away. If you say no, you are committing yourself to making an improved offer.

The following response is one way of getting yourself out of trouble:

That is the best offer we can make in the light of the facts as we understand them at the moment. We might be inclined to take a different view if new facts were to emerge that affected the position. Perhaps you could give us some more information on your situation?

It throws the ball back into the other party's court.

21.8.4 Playing for time

Sometimes you might find you need time to think over a proposal made by the other party, or the issues generally. There are a number of ways of dealing with this. One is to simply state, for example, 'We'll have to think a bit more about that and get back to you'. The following responses will also work.

I'm afraid I'm not in a position to comment on that just yet.

OR

I'm afraid I don't have authority to accept that without checking with our managing director.

OR

I'll need to discuss that with the project manager and get back to you.

OR

Perhaps we could take a short break?

OR

Could you just go over that proposal/issue again? I want to make sure I've understood it properly.

Pressuring for a decision

In order to finalise a negotiation, you may need to apply pressure to the other party to make a decision. Standard tactics in this area include the imposition of deadlines, intimating that other parties are interested in the offer and various other methods that more or less amount to mild forms of verbal harassment – see below.

[*threatening a deadline*] *We're going to have to ask you to make a quick decision. The deadline is…*

OR

We can't keep this offer open for longer than 14 days. There are other interested parties.

OR

[*stressing the simplicity of matter*] *The issues are very simple. I'd have thought there's no real reason why this can't be decided by the end of the week.*

OR

[*keeping up the pressure*] *I'll phone you tomorrow morning to see what progress has been made.*

OR

[*applying pressure by way of projecting empathy*] *If I were in your shoes, I would jump at an opportunity like this.*

CHECKLIST

Caution: This model should not be followed slavishly. Not all elements of the model are applicable to each type of negotiation.

NAME(S):

CASE:

NAME OF OPPONENT:

Relevant facts

- Summary of client instructions.
- Summary of facts relevant to each issue.
- Further information needed.
- What information you might reveal.

Interest

- Identify the client's interests that are achievable by negotiation.
- Consider the possible interests of the other side that are achievable by negotiation.
- Consider the extent to which both sides' interests can be achieved in the negotiation.

Client's aims

- Identify aims that are achievable by negotiation. Distinguish between those aims that must be achieved and those the client would ideally like to achieve.
- Identify areas of potential disagreement between the parties. Identify objective criteria for resolving conflicting interests.

Relevant law

- Give a brief summary of the relevant law and how it might be applied to the negotiation.
- Identify the client's BATNA.
- Consider the other side's possible BATNA.

Agenda

- Identify issues for negotiation and order them in priority.
- Draft an agenda for a meeting.

Negotiation strategy

- Choose a strategy to suit the negotiation and your opponent's likely tactics.

Professional conduct

- Pursue the negotiation in a professional manner.
- Pursue the negotiation in a courteous manner.

22 Chairing a formal meeting

22.1 **THE ROLE OF THE CHAIR**

It is likely that during the course of your working life you will be called upon fairly regularly to chair meetings. The nature of the role you play as the chair will vary slightly according to the degree of formality the meeting requires, what matters are being discussed and who is discussing them. However, in all cases the chair must:

- control and coordinate the meeting;
- ensure that all matters under discussion are properly presented;
- allow participants to comment on the matters being discussed;
- ensure that the meeting is not dominated by a single individual;
- move from one issue to the next;
- ensure that business is transacted efficiently;
- ensure that the necessary decisions are made;
- not allow the meeting to exceed the time allotted;
- see that all necessary minutes and records are kept.

22.2 **STRUCTURE AND LANGUAGE**

Most formal meetings commence with the reading of the minutes of the previous meeting and the presentation of the agenda for the current meeting. The matters set out on the agenda are then introduced and discussed by the participants. Towards the end of the meeting, motions are proposed and votes are taken on the matters proposed as motions. The participants then deal with any other business (often marked as 'AOB' on meeting agendas) that needs to be dealt with at that point, and the meeting is then closed.

A typical meeting structure is as follows:

1 the chair opens the meeting;

2 the minutes are read;

3 the agenda is introduced;

4 the first subject introduced;

5   the chair gives the floor to a participant;

6   another speaker takes the floor;

7   the chair keeps order;

8   the chair moves the discussion to a new point;

9   the chair directs the discussion;

10   participants propose new motions;

11   the chair moves to a vote;

12   voting occurs;

13   consensus reached;

14   any other business dealt with;

15   meeting closed.

The language of formal meetings, particularly the language used by the chair, can be rather stylised. The meeting itself is likely to follow a fairly fixed schedule. The suggestions set out in section 22.3 cover the kinds of language employed in formal meetings. Where relevant, alternatives are given for formal and less formal language. To a great extent, the language used during the meeting will depend on what is being discussed. Refer to section 21.7 for further language suggestions in this respect.

SUGGESTED LANGUAGE   22.3

Opening   22.3.1

[*very formal*] *Ladies and gentlemen, I declare the meeting open.*

[*less formal*] *Right, shall we get started?*

OR

Let's get down to business, shall we?

The minutes   22.3.2

[*very formal*] *May I read the minutes?*

OR

Would someone move that the minutes of the last meeting be accepted?

[*less formal*] *Has everyone seen the minutes?*

OR

Can we take the minutes as read?

22.3.3 The agenda

Has everyone received a copy of the agenda?

OR

Has everyone got the agenda in front of them?

[*introducing first item*] *The first item on the agenda today is…*

[*amending agenda*] *I would like to add an item to the agenda.*

22.3.4 The subject

The purpose of today's meeting is…

OR

The first problem we have to consider is…

OR

Perhaps we could first look at…

22.3.5 Giving the floor

[*very formal*] *I'd like to give the floor to Mr Lee.*

OR

Ms Sanchez, do you have any views on this/would you like to say something about this?

OR

Mr Steiner, I think you know something about this matter.

[*less formal*] *Have you got anything to say, Dieter?*

OR

What are your views on this, Maria?

22.3.6 Taking the floor

[*very formal*] *With the chair's permission, I'd like to take up the point about…*

[*less formal*] *Could I just make a point about…?*

OR

Could I say something here, please?

Finishing a point

Has anyone anything further they wish to add before we move on to the next item?

OR

Has anyone anything further to add?

Directing

[very formal] We seem to be losing sight of the main point. The question is…

OR

This isn't really relevant to our discussion. What we're trying to do is…

[less formal] Could we stick to the subject, please?

OR

Let's not get sidetracked. The issue under discussion is…

Keeping order

We can't all speak at once; Ms Sanchez, would you like to speak first?

OR

Ms Robertson, would you mind addressing your remarks to the chair, please?

OR

I shall have to call you to order, Mr Ramirez.

Moving to a new point

[very formal] Could we move on to item four on the agenda, please?

[less formal] Now, I'd like to turn to…

OR

Can we go on now to…

22.3.11 Postponing discussion

[*very formal*] *Well, ladies and gentlemen, with your approval, I propose to defer this matter until we have more information at our disposal.*

OR

If no one has any objections, I suggest that we leave this matter until our next meeting.

OR

Perhaps we could leave this for the time being. We can come back to it on another occasion…

[*less formal*] *Let's come back to this later on.*

OR

We can talk about this next time we meet.

22.3.12 Proposing the motion

[*very formal*] *With the chair's permission, I move that…*

OR

I would like to propose the motion that…

OR

Would anyone like to second the motion…?

[*less formal*] *I suggest/propose we…*

OR

I'm in favour of that.

OR

Is anyone else in favour of that?

22.3.13 Moving to a vote

[*very formal*] *Perhaps we should take a formal vote?*

OR

Can I ask for a show of hands?

OR

Let's put it to the vote.

OR

Could we take a vote on it?

OR

Can we move to a vote on this?

[less formal] Should we vote?

Voting   22.3.14

[very formal] In the event of a tie, I would like to remind you that I have a casting vote.

Those for the motion, please?
Those against?
Any abstentions?
The motion is carried unanimously.

OR

The motion has been rejected by six votes to five.
[less formal] If there's a tie, I have the deciding vote.
Who's in favour?
Who's against?
Abstentions?
Everyone was in favour.

OR

The motion was rejected.

Seeking consensus   22.3.15

Would everyone agree if…?

OR

I'd be interested to know if anyone has any objections, but shall we try…?

OR

Am I right in thinking that…?

22.3.16   Clarifying questions

Could you just go over the...again? I'm not quite sure how it was supposed to work.

OR

I'm afraid you've lost me there. Could you just go over that again?

OR

I don't understand the question, I'm afraid. How do you mean?

22.3.17   Consensus

[very formal] It seems that we have a consensus. Can I take it everyone's in favour?

[less formal] We're all agreed.

OR

I think we all agree on that.

22.3.18   Any other business

[very formal] Is there any other business?

[less formal] Any further points?

OR

Is there anything else to discuss?

22.3.19   Closing

[very formal] I declare the meeting closed. Thank you, ladies and gentlemen. That concludes our business for today. Thank you.

[less formal] Well, I think that covers everything.

OR

That's all for today. Thank you.

Making a presentation

PREPARATION

It has been said that the greatest speeches have two things in common:

- The speaker cared about the topic.
- The audience cared about the topic.

When considering your presentation, therefore, you should try to pick a topic that you care about and that the people you will be making the presentation to care about. You may not, of course, have the luxury of being able to pick any topic you wish to speak about. However, you should try to find those aspects of the given topic that interest you and that are likely to interest your audience.

Try to divide your speech into a few manageable sections (say two to five) that cover the main parts of your presentation and make it easy for the audience to follow you. These sections should be logically ordered and should support the main theme of the presentation.

When preparing, make notes but do not write everything down. Brief, clear notes will stop you getting lost but if you write everything down your style will become very boring and your presentation will be less flexible.

Dress appropriately. Do not turn up in jeans and a T-shirt if everyone in your audience is going to be wearing business suits.

Consider the following points when preparing your presentation:

- You should not talk too long. Mark Twain once remarked that few sinners are saved after the first 20 minutes of a sermon. If you go on too long, people will gradually switch off and will end up understanding less, not more, of what you have said.

- Are you going to use any visual aids? If so, what kind? Check that the room in which you will make the presentation has the facilities you will need. Prepare your materials and place them in the correct order for the presentation. Only use visual aids if they will actually help illustrate the points you want to make.

- What will you do if there is a power cut? Ensure that your presentation can be given even if your audio-visual props are not available.

- How big is the room in which you will give your presentation? Remember that you will need to project your voice effectively. Think about using a microphone if necessary.

- Think about the kind of audience you are going to address and tailor your speech to that audience's interests and needs.

- Don't be afraid of repetition – if you are going to tell the audience something you want them to remember, you are going to have to say it several times to get it into their heads.

- Use illustrations and examples where possible.

23.2 STRUCTURE

Your presentation should have a clear beginning, middle and end. An effective way of presenting an argument is to start by indicating the theme of your presentation and the points you are going to make in support of that theme. Then make those points. Then at the conclusion of your presentation, summarise the points you've made and explain how they support your theme. This technique is sometimes characterised as the 'tell them what you're going to say, say it and then tell them you've said it' approach. The main benefits of this approach are (1) clarity and (2) that it gives the opportunity to make each point at least three times in different ways, so that the audience is likely to remember at least the main points made.

23.2.1 Beginning

The introduction should be used to:

- Make an impact – you should try to say something immediately that will make the audience want to continue to listen to you (e.g. 'What I'm going to tell you today will fundamentally change the way this firm treats its clients').

- Contain a preview of what you're going to talk about (e.g. 'in my talk today I will explain what needs to be done in order to increase the firm's profits by 100% in the coming year').

- Show appreciation and respect to the audience (e.g. 'I'd like to thank X for inviting me to come here today. I must say I've been very impressed by how friendly and professional everyone here is').

23.2.2 Middle

In the middle of your speech you should present and develop your main points:

- The middle of your presentation should be divided into a few manageable sections, each including arguments, examples and supporting statistics. These should be presented logically so that each point you make leads naturally to the next point (see checklist).

- Use verbal tagging where possible. This is a technique in which you use a neat mental image that summarises your main points. Winston Churchill's use of the phrase 'iron curtain' is an excellent example of this technique. In a presentation on a particular area of the law, one might say something like:

  So, as you see, the present law is like a dam with holes in it. The law reforms the government is proposing will plug those holes.

End

The end of your presentation should be used to summarise the main points you have made:

- You should signal to the audience that you are coming to the end of your presentation. If anyone has fallen asleep, the words 'and finally' or 'in conclusion, I'd like to say' will wake them up.

- Summarise the points you have made. Show how they support the main theme of your presentation.

- End on a high note. Say something that the audience will remember – an insight based on the theme of your presentation ('Remember this. All this points to one thing. That is…') or a call to action ('This shows very clearly the need for us to…'). Never end weakly with words like, 'well, that's about it I suppose'.

- Invite questions from the floor. Deal with all questioners with respect and answer all questions fully, no matter how ridiculous they are.

CONTENT

The techniques you use to make and illustrate your points can be decisive as to whether you persuade or alienate your audience. Much will depend on the nature of your audience and subject. Here are some tips:

- Use terms that the audience can relate to and agree with. People like to hear stated in general terms what they already believe in a particular connection. They feel justified in their beliefs. A bond between the speaker and the audience is established. Relate your arguments to things that matter to the audience.

- Relate the points you make to the main theme of the presentation. The separate points should contribute to the whole.

- Use different kinds of arguments and different kinds of evidence to make your points – different people respond to different kinds of argument.

- Use quotations and statistics wisely. Only use them when they will genuinely support the points you are making. They should not be used as a substitute for argument.

- Use humour, but only if it can be introduced in a natural and relevant way. It is seldom essential. It must fit the context.

- Simple comparisons can be a good way to illustrate a point but make sure they will withstand attack. Do not compare things that are not comparable (e.g. 'if we can't trust X to be faithful to his wife, then how can we trust him with the management of the company?' is an irrelevant use of this device).

23.4 LANGUAGE

When giving a presentation, the language you use to make your arguments is at least as important as the arguments themselves. Here are a few tips:

- Use simple and clear language. The small words are easier to say and often more powerful than the long words ('I love you', 'it's a boy', 'she's dead').

- Consider the level of understanding of your audience. For example, when addressing non-lawyers do not use legal jargon. If you have to use jargon, be sure to explain it in layperson's terms. For example:

  This is what is known as a contractual waiver. A contractual waiver occurs when one party to a contract agrees with the other party not to insist on something specified in the original contract being done.

- Avoid using language that is sexist, racist or ageist, or that may be taken as indicative of any other unacceptable bias. In particular, do not use *he* when referring to a hypothetical person who could be either male or female. For example, do not say: 'if a lawyer wants to compete effectively in today's market he must understand information technology'. Say instead: 'the lawyer who wants to compete effectively in today's market must understand information technology'.

- Think carefully about how your choice of language colours what you are saying about an issue and what it says about your own attitudes. To use a well-known example, when referring to the same militant group, you might refer to *terrorists* or *freedom fighters*. The term you use will influence the audience's perception of your subject and of you personally.

WHAT TO AVOID

The following should be avoided:

Waffle. Waffle is talking in a vague or trivial way. Your audience will lose patience with you rapidly if you indulge in it. If you have nothing more to say, stop.

Truisms. A truism is something so obvious that it is not worth repeating ('war is a bad thing').

Misinformation. If you are unsure about the truth or accuracy of a statistic or other piece of information, avoid using it. Someone is bound to notice if you use it.

Assertion. Do not state that something is true without backing it up with evidence.

Contradictions. A presentation that contains inconsistencies can be easily dismissed as being poorly thought out. It is also vulnerable to attack. Obvious factual inconsistencies should be easy to remove. Where contradictions exist in the underlying principles on which your speech is based, the position is more complex. In such a situation, if the contradiction is really unavoidable, the best course is to soften the degree of contradiction or even point out and explain the contradiction.

Mumbling. Always speak clearly, project your voice and try to appear self-confident. If you appear to be doubtful about what you are saying, you can hardly expect to persuade your audience.

Unnecessary apologies. Don't apologise for what you are saying. Never say things like, 'I'm sorry if this is a bit boring, but...'. If even you – the speaker – find it boring, why should the audience bother to listen to what you are saying?

SUGGESTED LANGUAGE

Beginning

Introducing yourself

Good morning/afternoon/evening. I'm/my name is __. I'm going to speak to you today about...

23.6.1.2 **Establishing rapport**

It's very nice to see so many people here. I must say I've been impressed at how friendly and professional everyone here is…

OR

As all of us involved in the business of __ know, this question of…is one of the biggest challenges facing the business.

23.6.1.3 **Thanking people**

I'd like to thank X for inviting me here today.

OR

I'd like to thank X who's done a great job of getting us all here today/organising this event…

23.6.1.4 **Introducing theme of presentation**

In my talk today I'm going to show that…

OR

I'm going to talk today about the important new developments in…I know a lot of you will have heard something about them and will be thinking 'how does this affect me exactly?'

23.6.1.5 **Make people want to listen to what you have to say**

In my talk today I will explain what needs to be done in order to increase the firm's profits by 100% in the coming year.

23.6.1.6 **Giving a preview of the points you are going to make**

I'm going to make a couple of points/three/four/five points today. Briefly, these are…

23.6.2 **Middle**

23.6.2.1 **Introducing a point**

Now, the first point I'd like to make this evening is…

Introducing a controversial point

Many people blindly assume that X is the case. The truth of the matter is rather different. Let me explain why…

Moving from one point to another

And that brings me neatly to the next point I'd like to make, which is…

Introducing an example or statistic

Now, a great deal of research has been done into this matter, and X Institute – which, as you know, is the world's leading research body in this area – has recently produced a report, which most experts agree is definitive. I have a copy of it here. On page 12, the report states categorically that…

Verbal tagging

Now at the moment we're like a bunch of wasps banging our heads against the kitchen window, unable to figure out how to escape. But the point is that the window is open at the top, if we could only work out how to get there.

Reinforcing verbal tagging

I expect you remember those wasps I mentioned a few minutes ago, banging their heads against the window? Well, this new sales system we're introducing will open that window right up and let them fly out into the garden. And not just any garden either, but our garden.

End

Signalling conclusion

And finally…

OR

In conclusion I'd like to say…

OR

By way of summary…

23.6.3.2   Giving an insight

'So, what does all this mean?', I hear you asking. What it means is…

OR

The most important effect of all of this is…

23.6.3.3   Making a call to action

What we must now do is…

OR

We must take a number of steps. These are…

23.6.3.4   Inviting questions

I'm sure some of you would like to ask questions. I'd be happy to answer them.

OR

Any questions?

23.6.3.5   Acknowledging a question

That's an interesting point…

OR

That's a good question…

OR

I see what you mean.

23.7   TIPS FOR POWERPOINT PRESENTATIONS

The PowerPoint feature available from Microsoft is a very useful tool for making presentations, which allows the user to present information in an effective and memorable way.

However, it is important to remember that PowerPoint is a servant, not a master. It should *support* your talk, not replace it or entirely define it. The phrase 'death by PowerPoint', coined back in 2001,[1] highlights the very common problem of people giving dull and static business presentations entirely chained to the contents of a number of pre-prepared slides.

A good presentation is one in which the presenter speaks freely and directly addresses the audience.

That said, here are some tips on PowerPoint use. It is worth noting that many of the points relevant to presentations generally are also relevant to PowerPoint use – and vice versa.

Consider your target audience

23.7.1

As with any presentation, consider your target audience. In particular, think about the following issues when designing your PowerPoint slides:

- What do you need to tell them?

- What do they know already (i.e. what don't you need to tell them)?

- What are they expecting from you?

- What will be interesting to them and keep them focused on your presentation?

- What can you teach/brief/inform them about?

Design

23.7.2

Here are some general points to bear in mind when designing the individual slides from which your overall presentation is constructed. More specific issues, such as fonts and colours, are dealt with below.

- Keep the design simple so as not to distract the audience.

- Keep the design, use of colours, font size and face etc. consistent throughout the presentation.

- Don't copy and paste slides from different sources.

- Organise each slide by topic and clearly label each at the top so that the audience can see immediately what it is about.

Note

1 See Garber, Angela R., 'Death by Powerpoint' in *Small Business Computing*, 1 April 2001: www.smallbusinesscomputing.com/biztools/article.php/684871

- Align the text left or right, not centred. Centred text tends to look ragged and amateurish.

- Leave room for highlights, such as images or take-home messages (see sections 23.7.6 and 23.7.7 below).

23.7.3   Fonts

Here are some tips on the use of fonts.

- Pick an easy-to-read font face and size. Arial size 24 or upwards works well.

- Use a larger font (35 to 45 points) or different colour for the title.

- Use different font colours, sizes and styles (bold, underline) for impact.

- Avoid italicised fonts as they are difficult to read quickly.

- Be consistent in the use of font faces and sizes.

23.7.4   Colours

The main point to remember when using colours is to ensure that the mix of colours leaves the text legible to the audience. This is achieved by ensuring effective contrast and avoiding having an excessively garish mixture of colours on each slide.

Here are a few specific points.

- Colour contrast can be achieved by using a dark colour against a light background. Black text on a white background always works well but can be a little dull.

- Avoid using too many colours at a time.

- Avoid garish colour combinations (purple and yellow, green and orange and red and green are particularly headache-inducing) but ensure effective contrast throughout, so that the audience can easily read what appears on the projector.

- Use colours to highlight your message – don't let them obscure it.

23.7.5   Avoid clutter

Remember that your slides are supposed to support your talk and not replace it. If you simply read your slides and do it slowly and badly, the audience will get bored and stop listening.

The key points here are to resist the temptation to crowd your slides with text, and to make sure that each slide is visually appealing. In particular:

- Remember that the slides are a cue for your talk, not the whole of it.

- Restrict the amount of text: if possible, use keywords only, and no full sentences.

- No more than six to eight words per line is a good rule of thumb.

- For bullet points, try to keep to no more than six words per line and no more than six lines per slide.

Hook and take-home message

A 'hook' acts in the same way as a riff in a catchy song. It's something you say at the beginning of your talk that makes the audience want to hear more. A 'take-home message' is the summary that expresses the main point of your presentation or the conclusion that you want the audience to draw from it.

- Try to have an effective hook at the beginning and a take-home message at the end.

- The hook might be a question or a hypothesis. For instance, 'What would your reaction be if I were to suggest that this firm could double its profit in two years by taking five simple steps?'

- The take-home message might be your conclusion, a summary of your data or story.

- Make both highlights of the talk that stand out.

- Relate the take-home message logically and explicitly to the hook.

Images

There is an old saying that a picture is worth a thousand words. A good visual cue can help your audience understand your message. But images should only be used when they add something important.

- Use images sparingly.

- Use images to visualise and explain, not to decorate.

- Contextualise the images you use so that their significance can be understood. A caption or short explanatory text may be needed for this purpose.

23.7.8   ## Animations and media

Animations offer powerful means to visualise and explain complicated matters, although they may be quite expensive to produce and are perhaps not ideally suited to most legal matters. They can also be rather distracting for the audience.

- Use animations and media sparingly.
- Use animations to draw attention to a point or to clarify an issue.
- Avoid noisy animations.
- Keep them short, ideally less than one minute.

23.7.9   ## Practice

A knowledgeable, smoothly executed and enthusiastic talk will help you convince your audience and maintain their attention. All these elements are directly related to the level of practice and preparation the speaker has put into the talk beforehand. Here are a few pointers.

- Know your slides inside out.
- Master the technology so that you can give the presentation in a smooth and fluent way.
- Practise giving the presentation, preferably in the room in which you will actually give the presentation.
- Never read your slides when practising but talk freely.

23.7.10   ## Things to check and prepare

Here are some things to check and prepare in advance of the presentation, in order for everything to run smoothly.

- Check the spelling and grammar in the text on your slides.
- Check all colours on a projection screen before giving the presentation to ensure that they appear in the same way as on your monitor.
- If the content is complex, print out the slides as handouts so the audience can take notes. Find out beforehand how many people are expected to attend and then print out a few more copies than you expect to need.
- Position the monitor so you can speak from it without having to turn your back on the audience at any point.

- To test whether the font size is legible, stand back a couple of metres from the monitor and see if you can read the slide.

PRESENTATION CHECKLIST

Preparation

- Consider your audience. What are they interested in? What do they need to know? What is the best way of presenting it to them?

- Prepare the room in which the presentation is to be given. Is it big enough? Too big? If you are going to be presenting your talk in a room that is larger than necessary and suspect that certain audience members may try to lurk at the back if allowed to do so, it may be a good idea to arrange the seating in such a way that the participants can't position themselves too far away from you.

- Ensure that you will have all the equipment you need (e.g. flipchart, computer terminals, microphone, overhead projector, television/video).

- Consider what visual aids you will be using (e.g. PowerPoint presentation, slides, handout materials, videos). Make sure they will actually improve your speech and are not simply distractions.

- Place your materials in the order you need them to be in for the presentation.

Beginning

- Make an impact – say something that will make the audience want to listen to you.

- Give a preview of the argument you are going to present.

- Establish a relationship with the audience. Thank anyone who should be thanked. Use humour if appropriate.

Middle

- Divide speech into a few manageable points.

- Place them in a logical order. For example, when discussing a problem:

  ○ What's the problem?

  ○ What are we currently doing about it?

- ○   Why isn't this working?
- ○   What should we be doing about it?
- Demonstrate how each point contributes to the main theme of the presentation.
- Use verbal tagging.

End

- Indicate that you have reached the end part of your presentation ('and finally').
- Summarise the key points of your presentation.
- End with a clear, decisive statement.

Dealing with questions

- Show respect to the questioner, however stupid or aggressive the question.
- Always answer the question in sufficient detail.

Throughout

- Project your voice so that everyone can hear you.
- Maintain eye contact with your audience.
- Use visual aids to illustrate your points. Do not use them excessively.
- Try to avoid contradicting yourself.
- Do not waffle.
- Do not assert that something is true without backing it up with evidence.

Telephoning

CONSIDERATIONS

The telephone – at least in terms of using it for speaking – has declined in importance as a primary means of communication over the last 20 years. Furthermore, alongside email and social media messaging apps, videophone apps have recently come more to the fore in business life than used to be the case. That said, telephone calls have qualities of directness, immediacy and spontaneity that cannot easily be replicated by other means, and most lawyers continue to make and receive calls on a regular basis in working life.

There is nothing especially different about using English on the telephone from using any other language on the telephone. However, there are a number of common phrases that people tend to use when speaking on the telephone. Knowing what these are, what they mean and how they are used should help make communication easier.

One of the particular problems with telephoning (as opposed to videotelephony) is that you cannot see the person you are speaking to. You therefore do not have the benefit of the non-verbal clues given by body language that assist communication in face-to-face situations. This makes it especially important for both parties to speak clearly and use simple terms.

An additional consideration for lawyers is that what is said over the telephone is likely to be noted down (or even recorded automatically) and recorded in a case file by the person to whom you are speaking. You should do the same. It is therefore important that you do not accidentally reveal something about your client's case that should be kept confidential or say anything that might be misunderstood. If you are unsure, write a letter or email instead. Always make a note of the contents of all discussions with other lawyers over the telephone immediately after the call is made – in that way, if the other lawyer has misunderstood what you have said, you have the evidence to show that this is the case and put the matter straight.

SUGGESTED LANGUAGE

There are a number of phrases that are only used when telephoning. Some examples are contained in this dialogue, which, incidentally, assumes the use of company desk phones:

Receptionist: Hello, Smith Ltd. How can I help you?

Juan Ramirez: This is Juan Ramirez (from…). Could I speak to Clare Peters, please?/Could I have extension 736?

Receptionist: Certainly Mr Ramirez, hold on a minute, I'll put you through…

Clare Peters' office: Tim Brown speaking.

Juan Ramirez: Hello. This is Juan Ramirez calling. Is Clare in?

Tim Brown: I'm afraid she's out at the moment/in a meeting/with a client/not taking any calls/on holiday until Thursday/on a business trip [etc.]. Can I take a message?

Juan Ramirez: Yes, this is Juan Ramirez from… Could you ask Clare to call me as soon as she gets a chance? My number is +34 9 456 8965. I need to talk to her about the Statchem case, it's urgent.

Tim Brown: Could you repeat the number please?

Juan Ramirez: Yes, that's +34 9 456 8965 and my name is Juan Ramirez.

Tim Brown: Could you tell me how you spell 'Ramirez'?

Juan Ramirez: It's R-A-M-I-R-E-Z.

Tim Brown: Thank you Mr Ramirez. I'll make sure Clare gets this ASAP.

Juan Ramirez: Thanks, bye.

Tim Brown: Bye.

The language used during telephone calls is usually informal and differs in some respects to everyday English. Here are some typical language functions and suggested language.

24.2.1   Introducing yourself

This is Anna Lindgren.

OR

Anna Lindgren speaking.

OR

Anna Lindgren here.

24.2.2   Asking who is on the telephone

Excuse me, who is this?

OR

Can I ask who is calling, please?

OR

[when putting a call through to someone] Who shall I say is calling, please?

Asking for someone   24.2.3

[formal] May I speak to...?

OR

[very informal] I need to speak to...

OR

Is [X] in? [informal phrase meaning 'is [X] in the office?']

Connecting someone   24.2.4

Hold on a minute, I'll put you through. ['put through' is a phrasal verb meaning 'connect']

OR

Can you hold the line?

OR

Can you hold on a moment?

OR

I'm just connecting you now.

How to reply when someone is not available   24.2.5

I'm afraid __ is in a meeting at the moment/is with a client/is out of the office/is not available at the moment.

OR

[when the extension requested is being used] The line is busy.

Asking for someone else   24.2.6

Okay. Is __ there by any chance?

OR

I see. Perhaps I could speak to __ instead?

OR

Could I have extension 971 instead?

24.2.7   Offering to help when the requested person is unavailable

I'm afraid __ is not available/is out of the office/is in a meeting with a client. Can I help you?

24.2.8   Offering to connect the caller to someone else

Would you like to speak to __ he/she also deals with these issues?

OR

I'm sure __ could help you with this. Hold the line and I'll put you through.

24.2.9   Explaining why you're calling

I'm calling about…

OR

I wanted to speak to __ about…

OR

It's about the…

OR

I wanted to ask about…

Or

I need some advice on …

24.2.10   Taking a message

Can I take a message?

OR

Would you like to leave a message?

24.2.11   Leaving a message

Perhaps you could tell __ I called and ask him/her to call me back on [give number]. I'll be in the office until…

OR

Could you tell __ that I called? I'll try him/her again tomorrow.

Clarifying that your number has been noted correctly

24.2.12

Perhaps you could just read the number back to me?

Stressing importance

24.2.13

Please tell __ that this is an urgent matter and I need to hear from him/her…

OR

It's crucial that I hear from __ no later than…

Stating a deadline

24.2.14

I need to hear from __ by…because…

Concluding the call

24.2.15

Okay. Thanks for your help. Bye…

OR

Okay. Many thanks. Bye…

LEAVING A MESSAGE ON AN ANSWERING MACHINE

24.3

Occasionally, there will be no one available to answer the telephone and you will need to leave a message. Here is an outline that covers all the information the person being called might need.

Introduction

24.3.1

Hello, this is Suzanne Dubois.

OR

[*more formal*] *My name is Suzanne Dubois.*

OR

[*if you know the person well*] *Hi __, Suzanne here. How are you?*

24.3.2   State the time of day and the reason for calling

It's 11am on Tuesday 6 November. I'm phoning/calling/ringing to find out if…/to see if…/to let you know that…/to tell you that…

OR

[when replying to a previous telephone message] I got the message you left for me. Thanks for calling. You asked about…The answer is…

24.3.3   Make a request

Could you call/ring/phone me back?

OR

Would you mind calling/ringing/phoning me back?

24.3.4   Leave your telephone number

My number is…

OR

You can reach/call me at…

24.3.4.1   State a good time to call (if appropriate)

The best time to get hold of me is …

OR

I'll be on that number until…

OR

[indicating times to avoid] I'm in a meeting from 2 to 4 pm but you can get hold of me before or after that.

24.3.5   End message

Thanks a lot, bye.

OR

I'll talk to you later, bye.

MAKING PEOPLE SPEAK MORE SLOWLY

Native English speakers, especially businesspeople, tend to speak very quickly on the telephone. They may also use slang and jargon that you may not be familiar with. These factors can cause difficulties for non-native speakers of English.

Here are some tactics you can use to make people speak more slowly on the telephone:

- Immediately ask the person to speak more slowly.

- When taking note of a name or important information, repeat each piece of information as the person speaks. By repeating each important piece of information or each number or letter as they spell or give you a telephone number, you automatically slow the speaker down.

- If you have not understood, do not be afraid to say so. Ask the person to repeat until you have understood.

- If the person does not slow down, begin speaking your own language! A sentence or two of another language spoken quickly will remind the person how lucky they are that they do not need to speak a foreign language to communicate. Used carefully, this exercise in humbling the other speaker can be very effective.

Glossaries

EASILY CONFUSED WORDS

Many words in English sound and look alike but have different meanings. It is important to be aware of the more common of these false pairs – the consequences of confusing them could be disastrous. If in doubt, consult a good dictionary.

The following is a non-exhaustive list of the most common examples.

Advice is a noun that means guidance or recommendation about future action (e.g. 'friends always ask his advice').
Advise is a verb that chiefly means to recommend a course of action (e.g. 'we advised him to go home').

Affect is a verb that means to make a difference to (e.g. 'the pay cuts will affect everyone').
Effect is used both as a noun meaning a result (e.g. 'the substance has a pain-reducing effect') and as a verb meaning to bring about (a result), (e.g. 'he effected a cost-cutting exercise').

Anonymous is an adjective that refers to a name that is not known or not made known (e.g. 'he wrote anonymously in the newspaper') or that means having no outstanding or individual features (e.g. 'the building looked rather anonymous').
Unanimous is an adjective meaning to be fully in agreement (e.g. 'the decision was made unanimously').

Ante means 'before' (e.g. 'ante-meridiem').
Anti means 'against' (e.g. 'anti-nuclear').

Appraise means to assess something (e.g. 'we appraised the services offered by the company').
Apprise is to inform somebody about something (e.g. 'he apprised me of the news').

Assent means approval or agreement (e.g. 'her proposal received the assent of all present').
Ascent means an instance of going up something (e.g. 'the first ascent of the Matterhorn').

Aural refers to something that relates to the ear or sense of hearing.
Oral means spoken rather than written.

Biannual refers to something that occurs twice a year (e.g. 'a biannual review').
Biennial refers to something that occurs every two years (e.g. 'a biennial review').

Born means to exist as a result of birth (e.g. 'she was born on 15 February 2001').
Borne is the past participle of 'bear' (e.g. 'the costs were borne by the losing party in the case').

Canvas is a type of material.
Canvass means to seek political support before an election or to seek people's opinions on something (e.g. 'I canvassed her opinion on the matter').

Chance means (1) the possibility of something happening (e.g. 'there is a chance that it might rain today'), (2) an opportunity (e.g. 'your chances are excellent') and (3) the way in which things happen without any obvious plan or cause (e.g. 'we met entirely by chance').
Change means (1) to make or become different (e.g. 'we'll change this provision of the contract'), (2) to exchange a sum of money for the same sum in a different currency (e.g. 'she changed her dollars into euros') and (3) to move from one thing to another (e.g. 'he changed jobs often').

Compliment means to politely congratulate or praise (e.g. 'he complimented her on her appearance').
Complement means to add in a way that improves (e.g. 'she selected a green sweater to complement her blonde hair').

Council means an assembly of people meeting regularly to advise on, discuss or organise something (e.g. 'the town council held a meeting on 15 February').
Counsel means (1) advice (e.g. 'he received wise counsel from his lawyer') or (2) a barrister conducting a case (e.g. 'the applicant's counsel addressed the court').

Credible means convincing or believable (e.g. 'the evidence was credible').
Creditable means deserving recognition and praise (e.g. 'Louise's performance in the examination was creditable').

Curb means a check or restraint (e.g. 'curbs on public spending').
Kerb means the edge of a pavement (sidewalk) (e.g. 'the car's tyres scraped along the side of the kerb').

Defuse means to remove the fuse from an explosive device (e.g. 'the bomb squad defused the device').
Diffuse means spread over a wide area (e.g. 'the crowd gradually diffused').

Dependant is a noun that refers to a person who relies on another for financial support (e.g. 'she has three dependants').
Dependent is an adjective meaning (1) relying on someone or something for support (e.g. 'we are dependent on the services offered by that firm'), (2)

determined or influenced by (e.g. 'our decision is dependent on the outcome of the arbitration') or (3) unable to do without (e.g. 'my colleague is dependent on strong coffee').

Discreet means careful and judicious (e.g. 'she gave discreet advice').
Discrete means separate, distinct (e.g. 'that is a discrete issue').

Disinterested means impartial (e.g. 'a lawyer is under an obligation to give disinterested advice').
Uninterested means not interested (e.g. 'a person uninterested in fame').

Draft means (1) to prepare a preliminary version of a text, (2) a preliminary version of a text, (3) a written order requesting a bank to pay a specified sum and (3) US compulsory recruitment for military service.
Draught means (1) a current of cool air indoors, (2) an act of drinking or breathing in and (3) (of beer) served from a cask.

Elicit is a verb meaning to draw out a response or reaction (e.g. 'my questioning elicited no response from him').
Illicit is an adjective meaning forbidden or unlawful (e.g. 'he was caught trying to smuggle illicit substances into the country').

Eligible means satisfying the conditions to do or receive something (e.g. 'you are eligible to enter this competition').
Illegible means not clear enough to be read (e.g. 'your handwriting is illegible').

Equable means calm and even-tempered (e.g. 'she remained equable at all times').
Equitable means fair and just (e.g. 'this is an equitable system').

Flare means (1) a sudden brief burst of flame or light, (2) a device producing a very bright flame as a signal or marker, (3) a gradual widening towards the hem of a garment or (4) trousers of which the legs widen from the knees.
Flair means (1) natural ability or talent (e.g. 'she showed great flair for litigation') or (2) stylishness.

Flaunt means to display something ostentatiously (e.g. 'he flaunted his newly acquired wealth').
Flout means to disobey a rule or law (e.g. 'she flouted the speeding restrictions').

Hoard means a store of something valuable, or the act of storing it (e.g. 'he hoarded money beneath his bed').
Horde is a disparaging term for a large number of people (e.g. 'there were hordes of people at the airport during the morning of the public holiday').

Insidious means proceeding in a gradual and harmful way (e.g. 'that is an insidious practice').
Invidious means unacceptable, unfair and likely to arouse resentment or anger in others (e.g. 'she was placed in an invidious position').

Lapse means to become invalid (e.g. 'this offer lapses on 23 November 2021').
Elapse refers to time going past (e.g. 'a period of six months has elapsed since the last review').

Loose means not fixed in place or tied up (e.g. 'a loose tooth').
Lose means to no longer have or become unable to find (e.g. 'it is a mistake to lose your textbook').

Omit means to leave something out (e.g. 'paragraph three should be omitted').
Emit means to discharge something (e.g. 'the factory emitted smoke').

Pedal means a foot-operated lever (e.g. 'the bicycle has two pedals') or the act of pedalling (e.g. 'she pedalled the bicycle up a hill').
Peddle is a verb meaning to sell goods and has a somewhat negative connotation (e.g. 'he peddled fake remedies').

Perquisite means a special right or privilege enjoyed as a result of one's position and is often abbreviated as 'perk' (e.g. 'the perks of the job').
Prerequisite is a thing that must exist or happen before something else must exist or happen – in other words, a precondition (e.g. 'a law degree is a prerequisite for this position').

Pour is what is done with liquids (e.g. 'she poured milk into her coffee cup').
Pore is to read text attentively (e.g. 'she pored over her notes on contract law the night before the exam').

Practice is a noun meaning the action of doing something rather than the theories about it (e.g. 'in principle that idea is feasible but putting it into practice would be problematic'). Practice is also the spelling for the verb in American English.
Practise is the British English spelling of the verb (e.g. 'I need to practise my French').

Prescribe means to recommend the use of a medicine or treatment or to state officially that something should be done (e.g. 'the doctor prescribed a course of treatment').
Proscribe means to forbid or condemn something (e.g. 'the statute proscribes the use of dangerous chemicals').

Prosecute means to bring an action in a criminal court against someone (e.g. 'thieves will be prosecuted').
Persecute means to subject someone to hostility and ill-treatment, especially because of their race or political or religious beliefs (e.g. 'he was persecuted by the authorities because of his political beliefs').

Principal is usually an adjective meaning main or most important (e.g. 'the country's principal exports').

Principle is a noun that usually means a truth or general law used as the basis for something (e.g. 'the general principles of law').

Stationary is an adjective meaning not moving or changing (e.g. 'the car was stationary at the traffic lights').

Stationery is a noun meaning paper and other writing materials (e.g. 'the paper is kept in the stationery cupboard').

Story means a tale or account of something (e.g. 'we listened to his story with interest').

Storey means the floor of a building (e.g. 'the office was on the 10th storey of the building').

Tortious means having the nature of a tort, wrongful (e.g. 'he committed a tortious act and is therefore likely to be sued').

Tortuous means (1) full of twists and turns (e.g. 'a tortuous route'), or (2) excessively complex (e.g. 'a tortuous case').

Unexceptional means not out of the ordinary (e.g. 'his performance in the examination was unexceptional').

Unexceptionable means not able to be objected to but not particularly new or exciting (e.g. 'the hotel breakfast was unexceptionable').

Whose means belonging to or associated with which person, or of whom or which (e.g. 'whose is this?' or 'she's a woman whose views I respect').

Who's is short for either who is or who has (e.g. 'he has a daughter who's the managing partner of an international law firm' or 'who's arranged the conference?').

ABBREVIATIONS

Here is a list of some common legally relevant abbreviations and their definitions.

ABC	activity-based costing
ACH	automated clearing house
ADR	American depositary receipt
AGM	annual general meeting
a.k.a.	also known as ('John Smith a.k.a. King of Style')
AMEX	American Stock Exchange
AOB	any other business (often used in meeting agendas)
APR	annualised percentage rate (of interest)
ATM	automated teller machine (cash dispenser)
B2B	business-to-business
B2C	business-to-consumer
CAPM	capital asset pricing model

cc	carbon copy (used to show that a copy of a letter has also been sent to another person or persons, and also reflected in most email programs)
CCA	current cost accounting
CD	certificate of deposit
CEO	chief executive officer
c.f.	compare(d) with
CFO	chief financial officer
CGT	capital gains tax
c.i.f.	cost, insurance, freight contract
CJEU	Court of Justice of the European Union
COA	court of appeal
c.o.d.	cash on delivery
COO	chief operating officer
COSA	cost of sales adjustment
CPA	certified public accountant (US); critical path analysis
CPP	current purchasing power (accounting)
CRC	current replacement cost
CVP	cost-volume-profit analysis
DCF	discounted cash flow
ECHR	European Convention on Human Rights
ECHR/ECtHR	European Court of Human Rights
ECJ	European Court of Justice (see also CJEU)
EBIT	earnings before interest and tax
EBITDA	earnings before interest, tax, depreciation and amortisation
EDP	electronic data processing
EFT	electronic funds transfer
EFTPOS	electronic funds transfer at point of sale
EMS	European Monetary System
EMU	economic and monetary union
enc	enclosed
EPS	earnings per share
ESOP	employee stock or share ownership plan
EU	European Union
EV	economic value
EVA	economic value added
FASB	Financial Accounting Standards Board (US)
FBI	Federal Bureau of Investigation
FDI	foreign direct investment
FIFO	first in, first out (used for valuing stock/inventory)
f.o.b.	free on-board contract
forex	foreign exchange
FRN	floating rate note
GAAP	generally accepted accounting principles (US)

GAAS	generally accepted audited standards
GATT	General Agreement on Trade and Tariffs
GBH	grievous bodily harm
GM	genetically modified
GmbH	German business vehicle equivalent to the common law limited company (Ltd)
GMT	Greenwich Mean Time
GNP	gross national product
HR	human resources
ID	identification
i.e.	id est ('that is to say')
Inc	incorporated (USA)
IOU	I owe you
IPO	initial public offering
IRR	internal rate of return
IRS	Internal Revenue Service (US)
IT	information technology
LAN	local area network
LIBOR	London Interbank Offered Rate
LIFFE	London International Financial Futures Exchange
LIFO	last in, first out (used for valuing stock/inventory value, popular in the US)
Ltd	limited company (UK)
M&A	mergers and acquisitions
MBI	management buy-in
MBO	management buy-out
MCT	mainstream corporate tax
MD	managing director
MEP	member of the European Parliament
MLR	minimum lending rate
NAFTA	North American Free Trade Agreement
NATO	North Atlantic Treaty Organization
NASDAQ	National Association of Securities Dealers Automated Quotations System (US)
NBV	net book value
NDA	non-disclosure agreement
NPV	net present value; no par value
NRV	net realisable value
Nymex	New York Mercantile Exchange
NYSE	New York Stock Exchange
OTC	over the counter
PA	personal assistant
PC	(1) personal computer, (2) politically correct, (3) police constable

P&L a/c	profit and loss account (known as the income statement in the US)
P/E	price/earnings (ratio)
PIN	personal identification number
plc	public limited company (UK)
PPP	purchasing power parity
PPS	post postscript
PO	post office
PR	public relations
PS	postscript
PSBR	public sector borrowing rate
PTO	please turn over
QC	Queen's Counsel
ROA	return on assets
ROCE	return on capital employed
ROE	return on equity
ROI	return on investment
RONA	return on net assets
ROOA	return on operating assets
ROTA	return on total assets
S&L	Savings and Loan Association (US)
SDR	special drawing rate (at the IMF)
SEAQ	Stock Exchange Automated Quotations (UK)
SEC	Securities and Exchange Commission (US)
SET	secure electronic transaction
SIB	Securities and Investments Board (UK)
SITC	standard international trade classification
SME	small- and medium-sized enterprises
SRO	self-regulating organisation
STRGL	statement of total recognised gains and losses
T-bill	Treasury bill
TQM	total quality management
TSR	total shareholder return
UK	United Kingdom
UN	United Nations
USA	United States of America
USP	unique selling proposition
VAT	value-added tax
WDV	written-down value
WIP	work-in-progress
WTO	World Trade Organization
XBRL	extensible business reporting language
ZBB	zero-based budgeting

COMMONLY HYPHENATED WORDS AND TERMS

Here are some examples of commonly hyphenated words and terms. Note that this is a highly selective list intended for illustrative purposes only.

above-mentioned
after-effects
all-items index
all-out
all-purpose
all-round
bid-offer
blue-collar staff
broad-based
broker-dealer
by-product
carry-over effect
case-by-case approach
cash-flow crisis
clear-cut
coin-operated machine
cost-effective
cost-of-living index
cross-border transaction
cut-off times
debt-to-GDP ratio
deep-seated
deficit-debt adjustments
dollar-based
dollar-denominated paper
double-counting
end-of-year figures
end-user
end-year
energy-saving investment
Euro-currency
euro-denominated assets
far-reaching
fast-changing
fine-tuning
first-rate
fixed-term deposits
flow-of-funds survey

foreign-owned subsidiaries
free-of-charge
full-time basis
half-way
half-yearly
high-inflation countries
high-risk financial assets
hire-purchase
index-linked securities
inflation-adjusted data
in-house
jump-start
kick-start
know-how
labour-intensive
labour-saving
lay-offs
liquidity-absorbing
loss-making
loss-sharing arrangement
low-cost items
low-income workers
machine-readable
man-hour
market-maker
market-related rates
medium-sized
mid-2010
mid-month
middle-income earners
month-end
most-favoured nation status
multi-million-dollar deal
multi-purpose
night-time
non-interest-bearing deposit
non-paper
non-profit-making
non-resident
non-smoker
non-seasonally adjusted
off-balance-sheet items
off-budget

old-fashioned
one-off effect
one-sided
over-the-counter transaction
part-time working
phase-in
phase-out
policy-maker
price-fixing behaviour
profit-taking
proof-reading
ready-made
real-time processing
risk-averse
risk-based
risk-reducing benefits
second-hand source
second-mortgage loans
setting-up
short-lived
short-time working
single-handed
single-purpose
small and medium-sized enterprises (SMEs)
socio-economic
standard-setter
start-of-day period
supply-side effects
tax-exempt transfer
tax-free
terms-of-trade loss
third-generation mobile phone licences
three-day week
three-month period
time-consuming
time-lag
time-limit
two-tier system
up-to-date
upward-revised figures
US-led recovery
valuation-adjusted figures
wage-push

wage-setters
well-nigh
white-collar workers
window-dressing
write-down
write-off
work-life balance
year-end

PHRASAL VERBS USED IN LEGAL ENGLISH

The following is a non-exhaustive list of phrasal verbs used in legal English together with examples of usage.

Abide by means to accept a decision, a law or an agreement and obey it. For example, 'the parties must abide by the terms of the agreement'.

Accede to means to agree to or allow something that someone has asked for, after you have opposed it for a while. For example, 'the company eventually acceded to repeated requests for a price reduction'.

Account for means: (1) To explain how or why something happened. For example, 'how do you account for the fact that the goods were delivered late?'. (2) To be a particular part of something. For example, 'computer sales account for 50% of the company's profits'. (3) To keep a record of how the money in your care will be or has been spent. For example, 'every cent in the fund has been accounted for'. (4) To consider particular facts or circumstances when you are making a decision about something. For example, 'the costs of possible litigation were accounted for when calculating the amount of money to be set aside'.

Account to means to make a payment to someone together with an itemised breakdown showing how the payment is calculated. For example, 'the lawyer accounted to her client in respect of the damages received as a result of the litigation'.

Adhere to means to act in the way that a particular law, rule, agreement or set of instructions says that you should. For example, 'the parties have adhered strictly to the terms of the agreement'.

Amount to means (1) To add up to something or result in a final total of something. For example, 'the overall costs amounted to well over EUR 50,000'. (2) To be equal to or the same as something. For example, 'what they did amounted to a breach of contract'.

Arise from means to result from something or to become clear due to it. For example, 'several matters arose from the meeting'.

Appertain to (or 'pertain to') means to belong to something or be connected with something. For example, 'the duties appertaining to this position'.

Break down means (1) To separate into different parts to make something easier to discuss, analyse or deal with. For example, 'the figures break down as follows'. (2) To fail. For example, 'negotiations between the parties have broken down'.

Break off means (1) To stop speaking or to stop doing something before you have finished. For example, 'we had to break off the meeting'. (2) To separate something from something else using force, or for something to become separated in this way. For example, 'the handle of the cup just broke off'.

Break up means (1) The splitting up of a company or an organisation into smaller parts. For example, 'the company was broken up into smaller concerns'. (2) The splitting up of a group of people. For example, 'the conference broke up into discussion groups'.

Bring forward means to change to an earlier time. For example, 'the meeting was brought forward from Thursday to Tuesday'.

Bring up means: (1) To refer to something. For example, 'he brought up the question of fees'. (2) To care for a child until he or she is grown up. For example, 'she was brought up by her grandparents'.

Call in means (1) To request the return of something. For example, 'the bank has decided to call in the loan'. (2) To visit a place or person for a short time. For example, 'he called in at the office before going to court this morning'. (3) To telephone your office. For example, 'do you mind if I use your phone? I just want to call in and tell my assistant I'm running late'.

Carry on means to continue something. For example, 'the company carries on business as a garden furniture retailer'.

Carry out means to do something that you said you would do or that you have been asked to do. For example, 'the lawyer carried out his client's instructions carefully'.

Change over means to stop using one system or thing and start using another. For example, 'The Greeks have changed over to the euro'.

Charge with means (1) To formally accuse someone of a crime in a court. For example, 'He was charged with murder'. (2) To be given responsibility for some role or task. For example, 'the lawyer was charged with the task of conducting the defence'.

Consist in means to have something as its main or only feature. For example, 'the strength of this firm consists in its experienced litigation department'.

Consist of means to be formed from the people or things mentioned. For example, 'the team consists of a number of specialists in different areas'.

Cover up means to try hard to stop people finding out about a mistake, a crime or the true state of affairs. For example, 'the company attempted to cover up its trading losses by falsifying its accounts'.

Deal in means to do business; to make money by buying and selling a particular product or kind of goods. For example, 'the company deals in computer hardware'.

Deal on means to do deals in a particular forum or venue. For example, 'John deals on the London Stock Exchange'.

Deal out means to distribute (usually cards in a card game. For example, 'she dealt out the cards').

Deal with means (1) To do business regularly with a person or organisation. For example, 'we only deal with reputable suppliers'. (2) To talk to a person or organisation in order to reach an agreement or settle a dispute. For example, 'I like to deal with people I know I can trust'. (3) To solve a problem or carry out a task. For example, 'my lawyers dealt with the company sale very efficiently'. (4) To be about something. For example, 'this article deals with the issues raised by contractual waivers'. (5) To look after, talk to or control people in an appropriate way. For example, 'we sometimes have to deal with very difficult people in this job'. (6) To take appropriate action in a particular situation. For example, 'could you deal with this complaint?'.

Depart from means to behave in a way that is different from what is usual or expected. For example, 'we have departed from usual practice due to the exceptional circumstances of the case'.

Dispose of means (1) To get rid of or sell something that is not required. For example, 'the company disposed of many of its assets'. (2) To successfully deal with or finish with a problem. For example, 'there remains only the question of funding to dispose of'.

Do with means to need or want something. For example, 'I could do with a holiday'.

Draw up means (1) To make or write something that needs careful planning. For example, 'my lawyers will draw up the contract'. (2) To bring something nearer to something else. For example, 'she drew up another chair in order to participate more easily in the discussion'. (3) To come to a stop. For example, 'the car drew up outside the office'.

Draw upon/on means to use something that you have or that is available to help you do something. For example, 'the company will draw upon its reserves of capital to finance the deal'.

Engage in means to be involved in something, to take part in something or to be busy doing something. For example, 'this company is engaged in the manufacture of steel tubes'.

Enlarge on/upon means to say or write more about something you have mentioned. For example, 'Would you care to enlarge on that point?'.

Enter into means (1) To begin or become involved in a formal agreement. For example, 'the parties entered into an agreement relating to a share sale'. (2) To begin to discuss or deal with something. For example, 'the company agreed to enter into negotiations'.

Entitle to means to give a right to have or do something. For example, 'the parties are entitled to assign the benefit of the agreement on giving notice in writing'.

Equate to means to be equal or equivalent to something. For example, 'it is unclear whether her qualifications equate to any that can be gained in this country'.

Factor in means to include a particular fact or situation when you are calculating something or thinking about or planning something. For example, 'you must factor in labour costs when calculating the cost of the repairs'.

File away means to put papers, documents etc. away in a place where you can find them easily. For example, 'I filed the papers away in the drawer'.

Gear to means to make or change something so that it is suitable for a particular need or an appropriate level or standard. For example, 'it is vital that we gear our service to our clients' needs'.

Gear up means to be prepared, ready and able to do something or to become or make ready and able to do something. For example, 'the firm must gear itself up to be able to cope with these large corporate transactions'.

Go along with means to agree with something or to accept it, especially when you do not really want to. For example, 'we were not very keen on the proposal but went along with it in the absence of anything better'.

Hand down means (1) To give or leave something to a younger person or to pass from one generation to another as an inheritance. For example, 'this house has been handed down from generation to generation'. (2) To announce an official decision (particularly of a court of law). For example, 'the judge handed down a sentence'.

Hand over means (1) To give somebody else your position of power or authority or to give somebody else the responsibility for dealing with a particular situation. For example, 'he handed over the position to his deputy when he retired'. (2) To give someone else a turn to speak when you have finished talking. For example, 'I'd like to hand over now to our guest speaker'.

Limit to means to make something exist or happen only in a particular place, within a particular group or for a particular purpose. For example, 'limited to industrial use'.

Object to means to say that you disagree with, disapprove of or oppose something. For example, 'we object to further changes being made to the agreement'.

Opt for means to choose something or make a decision about something. For example, 'many clients now opt for this service'.

Opt in means to choose to take part in something. For example, 'all staff members have the chance to opt into a pension plan offered by the company'.

Opt out means to choose not to take part in something. For example, 'very few staff members have opted out of the company pension plan'.

Pass off means (1) To pretend that something or somebody is something that they are not. For example, 'the company tried to pass off their copied product as the real thing'. (2) If an event passes off in a particular way, it takes place and is finished in that way. For example, 'the meeting passed off without any trouble'.

Pass up means to decide not to take advantage of an opportunity, offer etc. For example, 'the company passed up the opportunity to submit a tender for the project'.

Pencil in means to write someone's name for an appointment, or the details of an arrangement, although you know that this might have to be changed later. For example, 'I've pencilled in 5 June for the meeting'.

Point out means (1) To show somebody which person or thing you are referring to. For example, 'I'll point out the court building when we arrive'. (2) To mention something in order to give somebody information about it or make them notice it. For example, 'I pointed out one or two typing errors in the document'.

Press for means to make repeated and urgent requests for something. For example, 'let's press for a final agreement today'.

Press on means to continue moving forward quickly or to continue to do a task in a determined way. For example, 'the company pressed on with its plans to expand into new markets'.

Proceed against means to start a court case against somebody. For example, 'my client is entitled to proceed against the manufacturer and the retailer'.

Proceed from means to be caused by or be the result of something. For example, 'the dispute proceeded from a misunderstanding between the parties'.

Provide against means to make plans in order to deal with or prevent a bad or unpleasant situation. For example, 'the insurance policy provides against loss of income'.

Provide for means (1) To make plans or arrangements to deal with something that may happen in the future. For example, 'the contract provides for assignment under certain circumstances'. (2) To give somebody the things that they need to live. For example, 'the family has three children to provide for'.

Put across means to communicate your ideas, feeling etc. to somebody clearly and successfully. For example, 'he put across his thoughts clearly and forcefully to the audience'.

Put back means (1) To return something to its usual place. For example, 'he put the papers back in the file'. (2) To move something to a later time or date. For example, 'the meeting has been put back to 11 July'. (3) To cause something to be delayed. For example, 'the strike has put back our deliveries by a fortnight'.

Put down means (1) To pay part of the cost of something. For example, 'I had to put down a deposit on the purchase of the property'. (2) To criticise somebody and make them feel stupid, especially in front of other people. For example, 'she's always putting other people down'. (3) To place something on the floor or on a surface. For example, 'put your paper down a minute and come and give me a hand with this'. (4) To write something down or make notes about something. For example, 'I've put down a few ideas that we can discuss during our meeting'. (5) To kill an animal because it is old or sick. For example, 'we had to have the horse put down because it was badly injured in an accident'.

Put forward means (1) To suggest an idea or plan so that it can be discussed. For example, 'an idea put forward during the meeting'. (2) To suggest somebody as a candidate for a job or position. For example, 'three people put themselves forward as candidates'. (3) To move something to an earlier time or date. For example, 'the meeting's been put forward a few hours'.

Put in means (1) To contribute money to something or pay money into a bank. For example, 'he put in EUR 20,000 of his own money into the business'. (2) To contribute time or effort to something. For example, 'she put in a lot of hours on that case'. (3) To make an official request or claim. For example, 'I've put in a request for a pay rise'. (4) To include something in a letter or document. For example, 'you should put in a paragraph explaining the indemnity provisions to the client'.

Put off means to cancel or delay something. For example, 'we'll have to put off discussion of that issue until our next meeting'.

Rake in means to earn or make a lot of money. For example, 'as a corporate lawyer in London, Henry's really raking in the cash'.

Reckon on means to rely on something happening. For example, 'we reckon on making a profit of EUR 200,000'.

Reckon up means to add figures or numbers together. For example, 'the total comes to EUR 200 if I've reckoned it up correctly'.

Refer to means (1) To mention or talk about somebody or something. For example, 'please refer to paragraph 7'. (2) To describe or be connected to something. For example, 'paragraph 7 refers to the question of indemnities'. (3) To look at something for information. For example, 'I'll refer to the textbook to see if paragraph 7 will be valid'. (4) To send somebody or something to a different place or person to get help, advice or a decision. For example, 'the case was referred to arbitration'.

Report to: if you report to someone in a company or organisation, that person is responsible for your work and tells you what to do. For example, 'I report directly to the senior partner of the firm'.

Resort to means to make use of something, especially something bad or unpleasant, as a way of achieving something, often because no other course of action is possible. For example, 'he resorted to threats in order to obtain their agreement'.

Rest on means (1) To depend on something. For example, 'our chances of winning this contract rest solely on price'. (2) To be based on something. For example, 'her argument seemed to rest on an incorrect assumption'.

Rest with means to be someone's responsibility. For example, 'the final decision rests with the client'.

Result in means to have a particular effect. For example, 'the presentation of the new evidence resulted in us winning the case'.

Revert to means (1) (of land or property) To return legally to the owner. For example, 'after his death the house reverted to the original owner'. (2) To go back to a previous condition or activity. For example, 'we reverted to our old methods'. (3) To start talking or thinking again about a subject being considered earlier. For example, 'to revert to the question of delivery of the goods'.

Rough out means to draw or write the main parts of something without including all the details. For example, 'I've roughed out the basis of the deal on the back of an envelope'.

Rule in if somebody rules something in, they decide that it is possible or that it can or should happen or be included. For example, 'the judge ruled in the disputed evidence'.

Rule out (1) If somebody rules somebody out, this means that they decide it is not possible for that person to do something or to have done something. For example, 'I think we can rule out Linden as a possible candidate'. (2) If somebody rules something out, this means that it is not possible or that it cannot or should not happen. For example, 'I think we can rule out trying to set up an office in Shanghai at this stage'.

Run to means (1) to go to someone for help, protection or advice. For example, 'he ran to his lawyer to sue for compensation after the accident'. (2) To reach a certain amount or size, particularly a large one. For example, 'the legal fees ran to hundreds of thousands of dollars'.

Scrape by/along means to manage to live with difficulty (on a small income). For example, 'due to the recession, a lot of people are only scraping by at the moment'.

Serve upon/on means to give or send somebody an official document, especially one that orders them to appear at court. For example, 'the court served a summons upon the company'.

Set down means (1) To place an object down on a surface. For example, 'he set the tray down on the table'. (2) To write something down on paper in order to record it. For example, 'I have set down my thoughts on this question in the paper you have in front of you'. (3) To give something as a rule or guideline. For example, 'this firm must set down clear guidelines about what procedures to follow if a client makes a complaint'.

Set forth means to state something clearly or make something known. For example, 'the position is set forth in paragraph seven of the contract'.

Set up means (1) To make something ready for use. For example, 'we set up the conference room before the meeting'. (2) To provide someone with the money they need to start a business or buy a home etc. For example, 'his uncle helped set him up in business'. (3) To create something or start a business. For example, 'setting up a business is not easy'. (4) To trick someone, especially by making them appear to be guilty of something they have not done. For example, 'the police set me up'. (5) To make someone feel healthier, stronger, more active etc. For example, 'a cup of coffee in the morning helps set me up for the day'. (6) To arrange or organise something. For example, 'we set up a meeting for 10am tomorrow'.

Settle up means to pay the money you owe. For example, 'we need to settle up with them for the hire of the machinery'.

Sift through means to carefully examine a large amount of something in order to find something important or decide what is useful and what is not. For example, 'we sifted through the evidence looking for weaknesses in their case'.

Skim through means to read something very quickly in order to get a general impression or find a particular point. For example, 'the lawyer skimmed quickly through the report'.

Speak for means to state the wishes or views of someone or to act as a representative for someone. For example, 'I speak for everyone when I say that this conference has been very useful and interesting'.

Speak out means to say what you think clearly and publicly, often criticising or opposing others in a way that needs courage. For example, 'she spoke out against the harsh treatment they had suffered'.

Square with means to agree with another fact, account or situation. For example, 'what you are telling me now does not square with the account of the matter you gave to the police last week'.

Strike off means to remove someone's name from the list of members of a profession so that they can no longer work in that profession. For example, 'the attorney was struck off after being convicted of a criminal offence'.

Strike out means (1) The removal by a judge or the court of a case before that court. For example, 'the judge ordered that the case be struck out as an abuse of process'. (2) To remove something from a text by drawing a line through it. For example, 'You should strike out all unnecessary words in the text'. (3) To start being independent and do something new. For example, 'he left the firm and set up his own business'. (4) To aim a violent blow at somebody. For example, 'he struck out with his fist'.

Subject to means (1) dependent on. For example, 'we agree subject to several conditions'. (2) To make somebody or something experience or be affected by something, usually something unpleasant or rigorous. For example, 'the products are subjected to rigorous tests'.

Subscribe to means to agree with an opinion, theory etc. For example, 'I don't subscribe to that point of view, I'm afraid'.

Substitute for means to take the place of somebody or something else. For example, 'there is no substitute for good legal advice'.

Sue for means to formally ask for something in a court of law. For example, 'the company sued for damages'.

Sum up means (1) To give the main points of something in a few words. For example, 'to sum up, there are three main points to remember'. (2) The summing-up is the speech made by a judge to the jury near the end of a trial, giving the main points of the evidence and the arguments in the case.

Take over means (1) To gain control of a company by buying its shares (hence *takeover*). For example, 'the company was taken over last year'. (2) To affect so strongly that one is unable to think about or do anything else. For example, 'my job is starting to take over my life'.

Tamper with means to do something to something without permission. For example, 'the agreement expressly prohibits any tampering with the machinery'.

Testify to means to show or be evidence that something is true. For example, 'this contract testifies to Johan's drafting skills'.

Trade down means (1) To sell something large or expensive and buy something smaller and less expensive. For example, 'she sold her Rolls Royce and traded down to a Toyota Corolla'. (2) To spend less money on things than you used to. For example, 'people are trading down and buying cheaper products'.

Trade in means to give something that you have used to somebody you are buying something new from as part of your payment. For example, 'we traded in our car for a lorry'.

Trade off means to balance two things or situations that are opposed to each other. For example, 'we agreed to trade off sharing information against a price reduction'.

Turn down means (1) To reject or refuse something. For example, 'we turned down their offer'. (2) To adjust the controls of something in order to reduce the amount of heat, noise etc. For example, 'the heating should be turned down now that the weather is warmer'.

Turn on means (1) To switch on or to arouse sexually. (2) To revolve around (an issue). For example, 'the interpretation of this clause turns on the meaning of the phrase "a reasonable time period"'.

Turn out means (1) To produce something. For example, 'the company turns out 100 new cars per day'. (2) To produce an unexpected result. For example, 'the cake turned out surprisingly well despite containing peculiar ingredients'. (3) The revelation of something surprising. For example, 'the little old lady who lived down the road turned out to be a spy'.

Weigh up means to think carefully about the different factors involved in an issue before making a decision. For example, 'we weighed up their arguments carefully before responding'.

Wind down means (1) To bring a business or an activity gradually to an end over a period of time. For example, 'the company is winding down its research programme'. (2) To relax after a period of stress or excitement. For example, 'it took me an hour or two to wind down after a stressful day at work'. (3) If a machine winds down, it goes slowly for a while and then stops. For example, 'the clock has wound right down'. (4) To make the window of a car open and go downwards by turning a handle or pressing a button. For example, 'she wound down the window and asked a passer-by for directions'.

Wind up means (1) To bring a company to an end and distribute its assets to its creditors. For example, 'the company was wound up last year'. (2) To bring something to an end (e.g. a speech, a meeting or a discussion). For example, 'let's wind up the discussion now'. (3) To deliberately make someone angry or annoyed. For example, 'are you trying to wind me up?'. (4) To close a car window and make it go upwards by turning a handle or pressing a button. For example, 'wind up the window, Pete, it's getting cold in here'. (5) To make something mechanical work by turning a handle several times. For example, 'I tried to amuse the cat by winding up the toy mouse and letting it run across the floor'.

Work around means to find a way of doing something in spite of situations, rules etc. that could prevent you doing it. For example, 'we can't get rid of this problem so we'll just have to work around it'.

Work on means (1) To be busy with a particular activity or project. For example, 'I'm working on a new case today'. (2) To practise or work hard in order to improve. For example, 'I'm working on my public speaking'. (3) To consider that something is true when planning or evaluating a matter. For example, 'I am working on the assumption that the defendant will not pay the amount claimed'.

Work out means (1) To happen or develop in a particular way, especially a successful way. For example, 'the plan worked out well'. (2) To calculate. For example, 'I'll work the sums out later'. (3) To understand something. For example, 'I can't work out what their bottom line is in this negotiation'. (4) To organise, plan or resolve something in a satisfactory way. For example, 'they worked out their difficulties'. (5) To continue to work at your job until the end of the period of time mentioned. For example, 'they made him work out his notice' (i.e. the period of time that is officially fixed before you can leave your job). (6) To train the body by physical exercise. For example, 'I work out three times per week'.

Wrap up means (1) To complete something in a satisfactory way. For example, 'let's try to wrap things up by 5pm'. (2) To be so involved in a person or activity that you do not notice what is happening around you. For example, 'he was so wrapped up in watching the match that he didn't notice me leave'. (3) To cover something in a layer of paper or other material, either to protect it or because you are going to give it as a gift. For example, 'we wrapped up the presents'. (4) To put on warm clothes. For example, 'wrap up warm – it's freezing outside'.

Write off means (1) To cancel a debt and accept that it will never be paid. For example, 'we wrote off EUR 10,000 in unpaid debts last year'. (2) To consider that somebody or something is a failure or not important. For example, 'I think we can write off any hope that this project will succeed'. (3) To damage a vehicle so severely that it is not worth spending money on to repair. For example, 'that's the second car she's written off this year'. (4) To write to a company or organisation, asking them to send you something. For example, 'I wrote off for their new catalogue'.

Yield up means (1) To reveal something that has been hidden. For example, 'a thorough investigation of the state of the company yielded up a few interesting facts'. (2) To allow somebody to take something that you own and feel is very important for you. For example, 'he was forced to yield up some precious antiques to his creditors'.

OBSCURE WORDS USED IN BUSINESS CONTRACTS

Here are some relatively obscure words that are often found in business contracts based on British and American drafting standards.

Where the word in question is generally used to mean one thing in legal English and another in ordinary English, only the legal usage meaning is given.

Abet means to encourage or help someone to do something wrong. For example, 'the perpetrators were aided and abetted by the company representative'.

Abstain means to refrain from doing something. For example, 'members have the right to abstain from voting'.

Accrue means to acquire or gain. For example, 'it is anticipated that benefits will accrue to the company as a result of the cooperation agreement'.

Acquiescence means consent that is implied from conduct. For example, 'the other party signalled their acquiescence by refraining from taking steps to protest'.

Adjudicate means to make a formal judgment on an undecided matter. For example, 'the court adjudicated on the case'.

Ambiguity means of uncertain or inexact meaning. For example, 'this clause is ambiguous and should accordingly be redrafted'.

Annex means a relevant document attached to a contract or other legal document for ease of reference.

Annual means every year.

Annul means to declare a contract to be no longer valid.

Arbitrator means an independent person who is appointed by agreement between parties to a contract or by a court to hear and decide a dispute. The process is known as arbitration.

Assent means to agree or concur. For example, 'the company is prepared to assent to that proposal'.

Assign means (1) A person or organisation to which something is transferred (e.g. the benefit of a contract). For example, 'the company and its successors and assigns'. (2) To make an assignment. For example, 'Neither party may assign any rights under the contract without the other party's express permission in writing'.

Barred means prevented or forbidden. For example, 'the proposed claim is statute-barred'.

Binding means legally enforceable. For example, 'this clause binds both parties'.

Clause means a provision in a contract.

Consent means agreement or compliance with a course of action or proposal. For example, 'no assignment shall be valid unless both parties have given their consent in writing prior to the proposed assignment being made'.

Consignment means a delivery of goods. For example, 'the first consignment must be delivered by 13 April 2018'.

Construction means interpretation. For example, 'on proper construction of this clause, it appears to mean that assignment is not permitted under the contract'.

Construe means interpret. For example, 'paragraph 16 shall be construed in the light of the provisions of paragraph 17'.

Convene means to call, summon or assemble. For example, 'the parties convened in the meeting room'.

Correspond means (1) To communicate by exchanging letters. For example, 'I have corresponded with the company's lawyers'. (2) Comparable or equivalent to another thing. For example, 'the corresponding obligations set out in this agreement'.

Correspondence means letters, memoranda, notes and other written messages. For example, 'there has been considerable correspondence between the parties'.

Counterpart means (1) A document that exactly corresponds to the original. For example, 'a counterpart of this agreement shall be prepared'. (2) A person fulfilling a similar role in another organisation. For example, 'I will telephone my counterpart to ask about her client's position in relation to the case'.

Covenant means an agreement or a term in an agreement. For example, 'the covenants contained in the lease agreement'.

Deadlock means a situation in which no progress can be made. For example, 'the negotiations have reached deadlock'.

Default means failure to fulfil an obligation, particularly one that involves performance by a particular date. For example, 'the company has defaulted on its repayment schedule'.

Delegation means (1) The grant of authority to a person to act on behalf of one or more others for agreed purposes. For example, 'the parties are entitled to delegate authority to sub-contractors'. (2) A body of delegates. For example, 'the company sent a delegation to an international conference'.

Derogation means to deviate from something. For example, 'the company derogated from the agreement'.

Designate means to officially give a particular name or status to someone. For example, 'John is our designated fire officer'.

Determine means to decide or resolve. For example, 'this issue shall be determined by means of the procedures that the company has established for that purpose'.

Discharge means (1) To release from an obligation. For example, 'the parties shall be discharged from all liability once all the terms of the contract have been performed in full'. (2) To emit or send out a substance. For example, 'the factory was found to be discharging noxious liquid into the ocean'.

Disclose means to make known, reveal. For example, 'the company disclosed certain information to the distributor'.

Dispose means to sell or transfer [property]. For example, 'the company had to dispose of some of its assets in order to pay its debts'.

Elect means (1) To decide, opt. For example, 'the parties may elect to refer the matter to arbitration if the dispute cannot be resolved by other means'. (2) To select by means of a vote. For example, 'the representatives were elected by secret ballot'.

Enforce means to compel, impose or put into effect. Hence **enforceable** (capable of being enforced). For example, 'the terms of the contract can be enforced if necessary'.

Entice means to attract by offering something pleasant or beneficial. For example, 'the company tried to entice their rival's employees to come and work for them'.

Essence means something intrinsic or essential. The essence of a contract means the essential conditions without which the contract would not have been agreed. For example, 'time is of the essence in this contract'.

Execution means the signature of a contract. For example, 'the parties executed the contract'.

Exclusive means restricted to certain parties. Hence non-exclusive: not restricted to certain parties. For example, 'Bondark Ltd holds exclusive distribution rights in respect of the product in the defined territory'.

Facilitate means to make easy or make easier. For example, 'implementation of the contract was facilitated by the assistance given by expert advisers'.

Fit means suitable for a particular role or position. For example, 'the judge took the view that Mr Jones was not fit to run a public company'.

Fixture means an item, usually a piece of equipment or furniture, which is fixed into position.

Forbearance means the act of refraining from enforcing a debt. For example, 'the suppliers' forbearance in extending credit to the company meant that the company was able to continue trading'.

Forthwith means immediately, without delay. For example, 'the goods must be returned forthwith'.

Gratuitous means given freely without anything being given in return. For example, 'he made a gratuitous promise to give her the property'.

Implement means to carry out, perform or put into effect. For example, 'the provisions of paragraph 12 of the contract have now been implemented'.

Induce means to persuade or influence someone to do something. For example, 'the parties were induced to enter into the contract'.

Instrument means a legal document, usually one which directs that certain actions be taken (e.g. a contract).

Invalid means not legally enforceable or legally binding. For example, 'this is an invalid clause'.

Irrevocable means not able to be revoked, i.e. not able to be changed, reversed or recovered. For example, 'the parties made an irrevocable commitment'.

Issue means (1) To print, publish or distribute. For example, 'the company issued shares'. (2) A person's descendants.

Know-how means practical knowledge or skill.

Lockout means a situation in which an employer refuses to allow employees to enter their place of work until they agree to certain conditions.

Material means relevant, important, essential. For example, 'breach of a material term of the contract can give the innocent party the right to rescind the contract'.

Mutual means (1) experienced or done by two or more people equally; (2) (of two or more people) having the same specified relationship to each other; (3) shared by two or more people; and (4) joint. For example, 'no assignment may take place without the parties' mutual agreement in writing'.

Nevertheless means despite. For example, 'nevertheless, the contract remains invalid'.

Notice means information or warning addressed to a party that something is going to happen or has happened; a notification. For example, 'any notice required to be served under this contract must be served in accordance with paragraph 18'.

Notwithstanding means despite. For example, 'the parties went ahead with the deal notwithstanding Statchem's financial problems'.

Null means invalid, having no legal force. For example, 'the contract is null [and void]'.

Omission means a failure to do something that one was supposed to do. For example, 'an omission may render the contract void'.

Onerous means involving much effort and difficulty. For example, 'the duties laid upon the company are onerous'.

Pass means to transfer to or inherit. For example, 'the property passed to his successors'.

Provenance means the origin or early history of something. For example, 'the provenance of this document is uncertain'.

Provision means a term or clause of a contract. For example, 'the contract contains provisions dealing with termination'.

Provisional means made for present purposes and may be changed later. For example, 'a provisional agreement'.

Purport means falsely claims to be. For example, 'a purported assignment is one made without the prior written agreement of both parties'.

Reasonable means (1) fair and sensible; (2) appropriate in a particular situation; (3) fairly good; and (4) not too expensive.

Rebut means oppose by contrary evidence, disprove or contradict something. For example, 'this presumption can be rebutted on the production of evidence to the contrary'.

Reciprocal means given or done in return or affecting two parties to a contract equally. For example, 'the contract contains reciprocal obligations regarding payment'.

Recognise means to accept as legally valid. For example, 'the court refused to recognise the judgment made in the foreign court'.

Redemption means the return or payment of property offered as security for a debt. The redemption date is the date upon which this occurs. For example, 'redemption of the mortgage will take place when the last instalment is paid upon it'.

Redress means a legal remedy or relief. For example, 'the innocent party has the right to seek redress'.

Remedy means any method available in law to enforce, protect or recover rights, usually available by seeking a court order. For example, 'the primary remedy is to claim damages'.

Render means deliver, provide, present for inspection. For example, 'the company agrees to render the goods for inspection'.

Revoke means to cancel, annul or withdraw. For example, 'we revoked the order we had placed'.

Severance means the removal of one part of the contract from the rest of the contract without affecting the validity of the rest of the contract. For example, 'the severance clause seeks to ensure that the contract will not be rendered wholly invalid if one part of it is deleted'.

Solicit means to ask for or try to obtain something (e.g. business) from someone. For example, 'the employee is prohibited from seeking to solicit business from the company'.

Stipulate means to specify, require or demand. Hence stipulation. For example, 'the contract stipulates that all payments be made in US dollars'.

Stipulation means an essential term or condition of an agreement. For example, 'the contract contains a stipulation that all payments be made in US dollars'.

Successor means a person or corporation that inherits something (e.g. the benefit of a contract) from another person or corporation. For example, 'Statchem is the successor of Alftech and accordingly now has the benefit of Alftech's contracts with third parties'.

Sundry means of various kinds. For example, 'telephones, televisions and sundry other appliances'.

Supersede means to take the place of, override. For example, 'this contract supersedes all previous agreements between the parties'.

Term means (1) A substantive part of a contract that creates a contractual obligation. For example, 'one of the terms of the contract deals with delivery of the goods'. (2) The period during which a contract is in force. For example, 'the term of this contract shall be five years from the date of execution'.

Transaction means an act or series of acts carried out in the ordinary course of business negotiations. For example, 'the company engaged in a number of transactions'.

Unenforceable means not capable of being legally enforced, not legally binding. For example, 'this contract is unenforceable'.

Uphold means to confirm (e.g. the validity of a decision). For example, 'the appeal court upheld the decision of the lower court'.

Usage means (1) The action of using something or the fact of being used. For example, 'a survey of water usage'. (2) The way in which words are used in a language. For example, 'this word is no longer in common usage'.

Vendor means seller.

Venue means the place at which something occurs or is located. For example, 'the arbitration venue shall be the International Chamber of Commerce in Geneva'.

Void means to have no legal effect. For example, 'the contract is void due to lack of consideration'.

Voidable means capable of being set aside. For example, 'the contract is voidable as a result of the other party's breach'.

Whereas means while. This word is often used in recitals in contracts. For example, 'Whereas the Company is the owner of certain intellectual property rights…'.

OBSCURE PHRASES USED IN BUSINESS CONTRACTS

Here are some examples of standard phrases that are commonly encountered in business contracts based on British or American drafting standards.

Accord and satisfaction. The substitution and performance of a new set of obligations under a contract, by means of which the parties to the contract are released from their original obligations.

Actions, costs, claims and demands. A catch-all definition including court cases, costs, formal demands for payment etc.

Act of God. An accident or event that arises independently of human intervention and that is entirely due to natural causes (e.g. an earthquake).

Aggregate amount. An amount calculated by combining different items.

Aggrieved party. A term used to describe a party to the contract in a situation in which that party has the right to bring a claim in respect of breach of contract by the other party to the contract. See also **innocent party**.

An adverse effect. A harmful or prejudicial effect.

Annexed hereto. Attached to this document.

Arising out of. Resulting from.

As contemplated by this agreement. As intended by this agreement.

As hereinafter defined. As defined later in the contract. These words alert the reader to the likelihood that the contract contains a definitions section in which the words 'the Territory' will be given a defined meaning for the purposes of the contract.

As per. In accordance with.

At any time after the signature of this Agreement. Ever. The obligation is not time limited.

Bear the costs of. Be responsible for paying the costs of.

By reason of. Because of.

Capacity to enter into and perform. Legal right to sign a contract so that it becomes legally enforceable and carry out the obligations it contains.

Circumstances beyond reasonable control. Circumstances that the party could not be expected to have any control over.

Collectively referred to herein. Referred to as a group of things in this contract.

Completion date. The date on which the main terms of the contract are carried out and ownership of goods is transferred from one party to another.

Construed in accordance with. Interpreted according to.

Defaulting party. A party to a contract who has defaulted on his or her obligations. See also **non-defaulting party**.

Defective part. A broken or faulty component.

Deliver up. Deliver, provide.

Discharge of contract/liability/obligation. The termination of a contract/ liability or obligation usually by performance.

Disclosure letter. A document in which the sellers of a company set out all the facts already revealed to the buyer that breach the warranties contained in the contract. It is usual practice for the buyer then to agree that it cannot sue for breach of warranty caused by this disclosure.

Due and owing. Owed; of money that must be paid by one party to another.

Due notice. Proper notice; notice in accordance with the requirements of the contract and/or the law.

Duly authorised representative. Someone who has been given authority by one of the relevant parties to do certain things, which are usually things that will legally bind that party.

Duly organised and validly existing. (of a company) Organised according to the applicable company regulations, having proper legal status and not being bankrupt.

Duplicate contract. An exact copy of the original contract.

During the currency of this Agreement. During the period of this contract.

Engaged in the business of. Involved in the business of.

Enters into this agreement. Accepts, signs this contract.

Except as expressly provided in this Agreement. Unless there is a clear statement to the contrary in some part of the contract.

Execution date. The date on which a contract is signed.

Execution of documents. The signature of documents so that they become legally enforceable.

Exhibits attached/annexed hereto. Particular relevant documents attached to the contract as 'exhibits'.

Expiration of a time period/limitation. When a time period/limitation has come to an end or run out.

Failure to perform. Failure to do something that was agreed to be done in the contract.

Finally settled by arbitration. Resolved by arbitration with no possibility of taking the dispute further in the event that one of the parties does not like the outcome.

From the date hereof. From the date this contract is signed.

Give and execute all necessary consents. Provide all agreements that are required and sign and do all things necessary to ensure that they are legally enforceable.

Going concern. A viable, ongoing business that may, for example, be sold as such (therefore the sale price takes into account the value of the goodwill of the business) rather than as a sale of individual assets.

Hold harmless. Indemnify.

In any manner that the parties may determine. In any manner that the parties may decide.

In consideration of. As a contractually binding promise made in return for the promise made by the other party.

Incorporated herein. Contained in this contract or to be treated by the parties as contained in the contract.

Incur expenses/fees. To run up or make oneself liable to pay expenses or fees.

In lieu of. Instead of.

Innocent party. A party to a contract who has not defaulted on his or her contractual obligations in circumstances where the other party has defaulted.

In respect of/in respect thereof. Concerning.

In satisfaction of debts. In payment of debts.

Instrument in writing. A formal written legal document.

In witness whereof. 'To confirm my agreement to the terms of this contract'.

It is contemplated that. It is intended, but there is no legally binding obligation yet.

Legally binding. Legally enforceable.

Liable to the other. Responsible in law to the other.

Make good. Repair, replace or renew something.

Material breach. A serious breach of a major term of the contract.

Material term. A significant or important term of the contract.

Matters of a product liability nature. Matters relating to manufacturing defects in the products.

Mutual consent. Both parties agree (to a certain proposition).

Mutual covenants and agreements. Things both parties have agreed in the contract.

Negotiation, drafting and execution. All the stages of drawing up the agreement including negotiating it, writing it and signing it so that it becomes legally enforceable.

Non-defaulting party. A party to a contract who has not defaulted on his or her contractual obligations. Also known as the **innocent party** in circumstances where the other party has defaulted on his or her contractual obligations.

Notice of Default. A formal document advising a party to a contract that he or she has failed to do something required to be done under the contract.

Notice shall be deemed served. Notice shall be treated or regarded for the purposes of this contract as having been served.

Notified from time to time hereunder. Advised to the other party when necessary under the terms of this contract.

Of even date herewith/hereof. Made on the same date as this agreement.

On a without prejudice basis. An offer made in legal proceedings that is not to be referred to in the final hearing of the claim.

On behalf of. As a representative of.

Other documents and papers whatsoever. Any other documents and papers.

Payment falling due on. Payment becoming due to be made on a specified date.

Principal office. Main office or headquarters.

Prior written consent. Written agreement obtained beforehand.

Provided always that. So long as, if.

Public domain. Accessible to the public, forming part of public knowledge.

Purchased hereunder. Purchased in accordance with this contract.

Purported assignment. An invalid assignment claimed falsely to be a valid one.

Pursuant to. In accordance with.

Reasonable/best endeavours. Appropriate efforts or attempts.

Release all the claims. Abandon all the claims.

Renewed for further successive periods of two years. The contract will continue indefinitely in two-year periods following the end of the first two-year period.

Save as to. Except for.

Schedule one hereto. Schedule one of this contract.

Sell or otherwise dispose of. To sell or transfer [property] in some other way.

Set aside. Treat as no longer valid.

Set forth herein. Contained in this contract or document.

Settled amicably. (of a claim or dispute) Resolved without the need for court proceedings.

Shall be held by the parties. Shall be regarded by the parties as being 'such and such'.

Shall procure that. Shall ensure that a specified action is done.

So served. Served in such a way.

Subject to the following terms. Dependent on or on the basis of the following terms.

Succeeding period. A period of time following one previously defined.

Take effect. Become legally enforceable.

Take or institute proceedings. To make a claim to a civil court.

That law or statute as from time to time amended. The law or statute and any amendments that are made to it while the contract is still valid.

The Company desires to appoint. The Company wishes to appoint.

The Company hereby acknowledges. The Company accepts as a result of this clause.

The parties acknowledge that. The parties accept (that something is the case).

The parties hereto. The parties to this contract.

The premises. (1) The building and land occupied by a business or (2) the theoretical bases of an argument.

The prevailing party. The party that wins in a court case or arbitration.

The provisions for termination hereinafter appearing. The clauses governing termination of the contract appearing later in this contract.

The requisite skills. The skills necessary for performing a particular role or task.

The same/the said/the aforesaid. The thing previously referred to.

The Seller and Buyer affirm. The parties declare.

The Territory. The specified geographical area within which a party is authorised to act on behalf of the other party to the contract.

The time of dispatch. The time of sending.

Undertakes to supply. Agrees to supply.

Which consent may not be withheld arbitrarily. Agreement must be given unless there is good reason not to.

With immediate effect. Something that is going to happen with immediate effect (e.g. the termination of a contract) will happen now, without any notice being given.

Without prejudice to the generality of the foregoing. Having no effect on the general meaning of the previous clauses in the contract.

Written mutual consent. The written agreement of both parties to the contract.

FOREIGN TERMS USED IN LAW

A large number of foreign words and phrases are used in legal and academic texts. These are frequently derived from Latin or French. A number of terms that are frequently encountered in legal texts are set out below. Examples of usage are given in respect of the terms that remain in daily use in legal English. The list is not exhaustive.

Ab initio (Latin): from the beginning. For example, 'this agreement is void *ab initio*'.

Ad hoc (Latin): made or done for a particular purpose. For example, 'an ad hoc tribunal was set up to deal with the claims'.

Ad hominem (Latin): to an individual's interests or passions; used of an argument that takes advantage of the character of the person on the other side. For example, 'that is an *ad hominem* argument that takes no account of the actual facts of the case'.

Ad infinitum (Latin): endlessly; forever. For example, 'this case seems to have dragged on *ad infinitum*'.

Ad referendum (Latin): to be further considered. This often refers to a contract that has been signed although minor points remain to be decided.

Ad valorem (Latin): according to value (as opposed to volume).

A fortiori (Latin): more conclusively. An *a fortiori* argument is one in which proof that a given fact is true can be used to prove that a second related and included fact must also be true. For example, 'all English food is revolting, and *a fortiori* fish and chips'.

Annus et dies (Latin): a year and a day.

Ante-meridiem (a.m. or am) (Latin): before noon.

A priori (Latin): based on deduction rather than experience. For example, 'these *a priori* assumptions are interesting, but need to be tested against the facts'.

Bona fide (Latin): genuine, real. For example, 'a *bona fide* purchaser is interested in buying the company'.

Bona vacantia (Latin): property not distributed by a deceased's will and to which no relative is entitled on intestacy. For example, 'certain assets were found to be bona vacantia and passed to the Crown'.

Caveat emptor (Latin): the buyer is responsible for checking the quality of goods before purchasing them (literally, 'let the buyer beware').

Ceteris paribus (Latin): all other things being equal. For example, 'reducing operating costs without loss of capacity will, *ceteris paribus*, improve the company's profitability'.

Circa (Latin): around or about. This is used for dates and large quantities; can be abbreviated to *c* or *ca*.

Cognoscenti (Italian): people who are well informed about something. For example, 'the *cognoscenti* agree that this decision is unprecedented'.

Contra legem (Latin): against the law. This term is used to describe a court decision that is contrary to the law governing the matter at hand. For example, 'the attorney argued that the decision was *contra legem*'.

Contra proferentem (Latin): against the offeror. See 10.2.2.2 for a discussion of the application of the *contra proferentum* rule in contract-drafting.

De facto (Latin): in fact, whether by right or not. For example, 'she has acquired de facto control of the company'.

De jure (Latin): rightful, by right. For example, 'Ruritania has a *de jure* claim to that territory'.

De minimis (Latin): too trivial or minor to merit consideration. For example, 'the defendant's contributions to the purchase price were held to be *de minimis*'.

Deus ex machina (Latin): an unexpected event that saves an apparently hopeless situation.

Doli capax (Latin): to be old enough and having the mental capacity to be legally responsible for committing a crime. For example, 'a child over the age of 14 is regarded as being *doli capax*'.

Doli incapax (Latin): not old enough or having the mental capacity to be legally responsible for committing a crime. For example, 'the *doli incapax* rule applies to a child under 14'.

Ejusdem generis (Latin): of the same kind. See 10.2.2.4 for a discussion of the application of the *ejusdem generis* rule in contract-drafting.

Éminence grise (French): a person who has power or influence without holding an official position. For example, 'François Leclerc du Tremblay (Père Joseph) is often regarded as the original *éminence grise*'.

Erga omnes (Latin): towards all. This is a commonly used concept in international law and is used to refer to obligations owed towards everyone. For example, 'the right of peoples to self-determination is regarded as an obligation *erga omnes*'.

Et alii (et al.) (Latin): see table of standard bibliographical abbreviations at 5.3.5.

Et cetera (etc.) (Latin): and other things.

Et sequens (et seq.) (Latin): see table of standard bibliographical abbreviations at 5.3.5.

Ex aequo et bono (Latin): as a result of fair dealing and good conscience.

Exempli gratia (e.g.) (Latin): for the sake of example.

Ex gratia (Latin): a payment given as a favour rather than because of any legal obligation. For example, 'the executor made an *ex gratia* payment to one of the beneficiaries of the estate'.

Ex officio (Latin): by virtue of one's status or position.

Ex parte (Latin): on the part of one side only. For example, 'the lawyer made an *ex parte* application to the court to obtain an emergency injunction'.

Ex post facto (Latin): by a subsequent act. It describes any legal act, such as a statute, that has retrospective effect.

Expressio unius est exclusio alterius (Latin): the inclusion of one is the exclusion of another. See 10.2.2.5 for a discussion of the application of the *expressio unius* rule in contract-drafting.

Flagrante delicto (Latin): in the commission of an offence. For example, 'the accused was caught *flagrante delicto*. He can have no possible defence'.

Force majeure (French): irresistible compulsion or coercion. Often used in commercial contracts to describe events that may affect the contract but are completely outside the parties' control. For example, 'the contract contains the usual provision regarding situations considered by the parties to constitute force majeure'.

Habeas corpus (Latin): that you have the body. This term refers to a procedural remedy whereby the lawfulness of a person's detention or imprisonment can be challenged. It is addressed to the custodian of the detained person and requires them to produce that person before the court and prove that they have the legal right to detain them. If they fail to satisfy the court, the detained person must be released.

Ibidem (ibid.) (Latin): see table of standard bibliographical abbreviations at 5.3.5.

Id est (i.e.) (Latin): that is. This term is usually used in its abbreviated form to restate something in simpler, or at least different, terms.

In absentia (Latin): while not present. For example, 'as the defendant was abroad at the date of the hearing, the case continued *in absentia*'.

In camera (Latin): in private. For example, 'due to the sensitivity of the case, the proceedings took place *in camera*'.

In curia (Latin): in open court. The opposite of **in camera**.

In extremis (Latin): in an extremely difficult situation; at the point of death. For example, 'the will was clearly made out *in extremis*'.

In lieu (Old French): in place of, instead of. For example, 'an employee may receive extra holiday in lieu of payment'.

In loco parentis (Latin): in the place of a parent. For example, 'since the child's parents are deceased, his uncle is acting *in loco parentis*'.

In re (Latin): in the matter of.

In situ (Latin): in the original or appropriate position. For example, 'the wreckage was examined in situ'.

Inter alia (Latin): among other things. For example, 'the contract provides, inter alia, that the company will be sold for the sum of…'.

Inter partes (Latin): between the parties. For example, 'the proceedings were held *inter partes* before the court'.

Inter se (Latin): between or among themselves. For example, 'the shareholders' agreement constitutes a contract between the shareholders *inter se*'.

Intra (Latin): within. Hence 'intranet'.

Ipso facto (Latin): by that very fact or act. For example, 'he was caught *in flagrante delicto*. *Ipso facto*, he is guilty of the crime'.

Jus (Latin): a law or right.

Jus cogens (Latin): compelling law. Certain internationally agreed laws, such as the prohibition of genocide, are described as *jus cogens* because they cannot be deviated from or excused and do not require the conclusion of a treaty in order to be in force.

Lacunae (Latin): void, gap. This term is used to refer to a situation that is not covered by any law. For instance, 'the company constantly sought to exploit *lacunae* in international tax treaties'.

Lex specialis derogat legi generali (Latin): a specific law that takes away from the general law. Where several laws apply to a given situation, the more specific one (*lex specialis*) overrides the general ones.

Locus standi (Latin): the legal right to bring an action or challenge some decision. For example, 'the court rejected her application. It ruled that she had no *locus standi* to make an application in these proceedings'.

Male fide (Latin): in bad faith. The condition of being fraudulent or deceptive in act or belief. The opposite of *bona fide*.

Mea culpa (Latin): my fault. For example, 'the newspaper issued a *mea culpa*'.

Modus operandi (Latin): a way of doing something. For example, 'his *modus operandi* was fascinating to watch'.

Mutatis mutandis (Latin): 'that having been changed which had to be changed' or 'with the necessary changes'. The phrase is used in contracts to indicate that a stipulation contained in one clause should also be applied in another part of the contract once the necessary changes have been made.

Non bis in idem (Latin): not twice in the same. This term is sometimes used to express the principle of double jeopardy under which a legal action cannot be brought more than once for the same offence or act.

Noscitur a sociis (Latin): 'it is known by its neighbours'. See discussion at 10.2.2.3 regarding the application of the *noscitur a sociis* rule in contract-drafting.

Nota bene (NB): note well.

Novus actus interveniens (Latin): an event that breaks the chain of legal causation and may result in the defendant not being blamed for the consequences of their original action. For example, 'the defendant successfully invoked the principle of *novus actus interveniens* in arguing that while he had injured the victim the true cause of the victim's death was an overdose of drugs accidentally administered to him in the hospital where he was being treated for his injuries'.

Obiter dictum (Latin): a remark made in passing. Something said by a judge while giving judgment that was not essential to the decision in the case but which may be of persuasive authority in future cases. For example, 'the judge said *obiter* that there did appear to be some authority for the argument the defendant had made'.

Pace (Latin): despite.

Pacta sunt servanda (Latin): agreements must be kept. This is a basic principle of civil and international law. It relates to the general principle that correct behaviour, including good faith, is a requirement for the efficacy of the whole system. In international law, it means that every treaty in force is binding upon the parties to it and must be performed by them in good faith.

Pari passu (Latin): in equal step. This term is often seen in venture capital term sheets, and indicates that one series of equity will have the same rights and privileges as another. For example, 'these shares rank *pari passu*'.

Per annum (p.a.) (Latin): for each year. For example, 'the director earned £550,000 *per annum* before tax'.

Per capita (Latin): for each person.

Per curiam (Latin): through the court. A decision delivered by a panel on which a number of judges are sitting is regarded as being delivered by the court itself as opposed to situations where the individual judges are named.

Per diem (Latin): for each day. For example, 'the employee received a *per diem* allowance for travel'.

Per se (Latin): by or in itself. For example, 'the government is not opposed to further European integration per se, but it does have certain concerns about the manner in which it is done'.

Persona non grata (Latin): a person who is not welcome somewhere. For example, 'following his disastrous handling of the case, he became *persona non grata* at the firm'.

Per stirpes (Latin): among families. Used by lawyers in connection with the distribution of inheritance.

Post eventum (Latin): after the event.

Post meridiem (p.m. or pm) (Latin): afternoon.

Post mortem (Latin): after death. Generally used as a noun to describe the clinical investigation of a dead body.

Prima facie (Latin): on the face of things; accepted as so until proved otherwise. For example, 'prima facie you appear to have an arguable claim, although I will need further information before giving an informed opinion on its merits'.

Pro bono (Latin): for good. This refers to professional work done for free. For example, 'many lawyers do pro bono work on occasion'.

Procès-verbal (French): an informal record or memorandum of international understandings resulting from negotiation.

Pro rata (Latin): proportional; proportionally. For example, 'our fees will rise pro rata with operating costs'.

Pro tanto (Latin): only to that extent. For example, 'the judge made an order that payments should be made for a period of one year, *pro tanto*'.

Quantum meruit (Latin): as much as deserved. In contract law it means something like the reasonable value of services and is imposed to avoid the unjust enrichment of one party at the expense of another. It applies (1) where a person employs another to do work without agreement as to the compensation to be paid, the law implies a promise that payment will be made for the services provided in the amount that they merit; and (2) where there is a contract for a set amount, and this is not paid, the claimant may repudiate the contract and seek payment on a *quantum meruit* basis.

Quid pro quo (Latin): a favour or advantage given in return for something.

Quod erat demonstrandum (QED) (Latin): thus I prove.

Ratio decidendi (Latin): the reason for deciding; the principles of law on which the court reaches its decision.

Re (Latin): with regard to, in the matter of.

Res ipsa loquitur (Latin): the thing speaks for itself. A principle often applied in the tort of negligence that states that if an accident happens that is of a kind that usually only happens as a result of negligence, and the circumstances that gave rise to the accident were under the control of the defendant, it may be assumed, unless there is evidence to the contrary, that the accident was caused by the defendant's negligence.

Res judicata (Latin): a matter judged. This refers to a matter that has been finally adjudicated upon so that no further appeal or action is possible. For example, 'this matter is now *res judicata*'.

Restitutio in integrum (Latin): restoration to the original position that existed before the events that triggered legal proceedings (re. damages).

Sic (Latin): thus; used in brackets in quotes to show that the writer has made a mistake. For example, 'Vladimir Puuttin [*sic.*] opposed the plan'.

Sine die (Latin): (of proceedings) adjourned indefinitely. For example, 'the case was adjourned *sine die*'.

Sine qua non (Latin): without which, not. Used to refer to anything indispensable, and without which another cannot exist.

Stare decisis (Latin): to stand by [things] decided. This refers to a judge's obligation to adhere to a previous precedent, as is the case in common law jurisdictions.

Stet (Latin): let it stand or do not delete; cancels an alteration in proof-reading; dots are placed under what is to remain.

Sub judice (Latin): being considered by a court of law and therefore not to be publicly discussed elsewhere. For example, 'I cannot discuss this matter with you as it is currently *sub judice*'.

Subpoena (Latin): under penalty. This is a form of court order by which a witness may be compelled to attend court or to produce evidence to the court and will be penalised for failure to do so.

Sub rosa (Latin): literally 'under the rose': used to describe something that is occurring but not on an official basis. For example, 'it was discovered that additional payments were being made *sub rosa*'.

Sui generis (Latin): unique, of its own kind. For example, 'the European Union is often described as being *sui generis* in its functioning'.

Travaux préparatoires (French): preparatory works that provide a background to the enactment of legislation.

Ultra vires (Latin): beyond the powers. This describes an act by a public authority, company or other body that goes beyond the limits of the powers that it has. For example, 'the court ruled that the authority had acted *ultra vires* in approving the plans without first carrying out public consultation'.

Vice versa (Latin): the other way around. This refers to something that is the same either way. For example, 'accountants often need to take professional advice from lawyers, and vice versa'.

Videlicit (viz.): contraction of 'videre licit', which means 'it is permitted to see', but which in practice is used to mean 'namely' or 'that is'. For example, 'the largest country by land area, viz. Russia'.

Vis-à-vis (French): in relation to; as compared with. For example, 'the company's position vis-à-vis its shareholders is precarious'.

Volenti non fit injuria (Latin): a defence in a legal dispute that means that if a person voluntarily accepted a risk then their claim should not succeed. For example, 'the boxer's claim was dismissed by the court on the basis of volenti non fit injuria as it was ruled that he had consented to being hit by the defendant'.

LEGAL TERMINOLOGY

The following is a non-exhaustive list of specific legal terminology and terms of art often found in commercial as well as certain other branches of law.

Abandonment. The act of giving up the ownership of something covered by an insurance policy and treating it as if it has been completely lost or destroyed.

Abatement. The proportionate reduction in the payment of debts that takes place if a person's assets are insufficient to settle with his or her creditors in full.

Absolute title. Ownership of a legal estate in registered land with a guarantee by the state that no one has a better right to that estate.

Acceptance. Consent, assent or approval. The acceptance of an offer to create a contract must be unqualified and may be either by word of mouth or by conduct.

Account of profits. A remedy that a litigant can claim as an alternative to damages in certain circumstances, e.g. in an action for breach of copyright. A successful claimant is entitled to a sum of money equal to the profit the defendant has made through wronging the claimant (e.g. by infringing the claimant's copyright).

Accumulation. The continual addition of the income of a fund so that the fund grows indefinitely.

Accused (the). A person who has been formally accused of a crime in a criminal court.

Action. A case brought before a civil court. Also known as legal proceedings.

Affidavit. A sworn written statement generally used to support certain applications, and also sometimes used as evidence in court proceedings. Also known by the term **sworn statement**.

Agency. The relationship of principal and agent where the principal is bound by contracts entered into by the agent with third parties.

Agent. A person who is employed to act on behalf of another person who is known as the principal. The work of an agent is to conclude contracts with third parties on behalf of the principal.

Allotment. A method of acquiring previously unissued shares in a limited company in exchange for a capital contribution.

Annually. Every year.

Annul. To declare a contract to be no longer valid.

Appellant. A person who makes a legal appeal against a decision of a court. See also **respondent**.

Arbitration clause. A clause in a contract in which the parties agree to submit to arbitration if disputes arise between them.

Arbitrator. An independent person who is appointed by agreement between parties to a contract or by a court to hear and decide a dispute. The process is known as arbitration.

Arrears. The accumulation of financial liabilities that have not been settled by their due dates. For example, rent arrears occur when rent has not been paid as it falls due.

Articles of association. Regulations for the management of registered companies. They form, together with the provisions of the memorandum of association, the company's constitution.

Asset. Property; anything that can be turned into cash.

Assignment. The transfer of a legal right by one legal or natural person to another.

Audit. A detailed inspection of a company's accounts by outside accountants usually in connection with the preparation of the annual accounts of the company at the end of the year. Hence **auditor**: a person who carries out such an inspection.

Authorised capital (nominal capital). The total value of the shares that a registered company is authorised to issue in order to raise capital.

Bailment. The transfer of the possession of goods by the owner (the **bailor**) to another (the **bailee**) for a particular purpose, e.g. the hiring or loan of goods.

Balance of probabilities. A legal standard by the court in civil cases in many jurisdictions that requires that the dispute be decided in favour of the party whose claims are more likely to be true. This can be contrasted with the higher standard of proof required in criminal cases, in which the defendant must be shown 'beyond reasonable doubt' to be guilty of the crime of which he or she is accused.

Balance sheet. A document presenting in summary form a true and fair view of a company's financial position at a particular time.

Bankruptcy petition. An application to the court for a bankruptcy order to be made against an insolvent debtor.

Bearer. A person in possession of a bill of exchange or promissory note that is payable to the bearer.

Beneficial interest. The right to benefit from a trust, contract or other form of agreement. In respect of land law, the term implies that a party has an interest in a property on the basis of equity although they have no legal title to it.

Best endeavours. Best efforts. An **undertaking** to use best endeavours to do something means that the person giving the undertaking must try to do what he or she has undertaken to do, but is not absolutely obliged to achieve it.

Bill of exchange. An unconditional order in writing, addressed by one person (the **drawer**) to another (the **drawee**) and signed by the person giving it, requiring the drawee to pay on demand a specified sum of money to a specified person (the **payee**) or to the bearer.

Bill of lading. A document acknowledging the shipment of a consignor's goods for carriage by sea.

Binding. Having legal force. A contract that is binding is a valid contract the obligations of which may be enforced against the parties to it.

Bond. (1) A document issued by a government, local authority or other public body undertaking to repay long-term debt with interest, or (2) a deed by which one person (the obligor) commits himself or herself to do something or refrain from doing something.

Bonus issue (capitalisation issue). A method of increasing a company's issued capital by issuing further shares to existing company members.

Breach. The infringing or violation of a right, duty or law. For example, 'Statchem have breached paragraph 14 of the contract by their actions'.

Burden of proof. The duty of a party to litigation to prove a fact in issue. Generally, the burden of proof falls on the party who relies on the truth of a particular fact to support their argument.

Capacity. The legal competence to enter into and be bound by the terms of a contract.

Capital (share capital). A fund that represents the nominal value of shares issued by a company.

Capital allowance. A tax allowance for businesses on capital expenditure on particular items (e.g. plants and equipment).

Cargo. Goods other than the personal luggage of passengers carried by a ship or aircraft.

Cartel. A national or international association of independent enterprises formed to create a monopoly in a given industry.

Charge. (1) An interest in land securing the payment of money (see also **mortgage**) or (2) an interest in company property created in favour of a creditor to secure the amount owing.

Charterparty. A written contract in which a person (the **charterer**) hires from a shipowner, in return for the payment of freight, the use of a ship or part of it for the transportation of goods by sea.

Chattel. Any property other than real estate (e.g. goods).

Chose in action. A right (e.g. to recover a debt) that can be enforced by legal action.

Claimant. A party who brings a claim before a court in civil proceedings. Also known as a **plaintiff**.

Class rights. Any rights attached to a class of shares; e.g. preference shares. Such rights relate to dividend, return of capital and voting rights.

Clause. A sentence or paragraph in a contract.

Clearance. Either (1) a certificate acknowledging a ship's compliance with customs requirements or (2) an indication from a taxing authority that a certain proviso does not apply to a particular transaction.

Collateral. Security that is additional to the main security for a debt. For example, a lender may require as collateral the assignment of an insurance policy in addition to the principal security of a mortgage on the borrower's home.

Collateral contract. A subsidiary contract that induces a person to enter into a main contract.

Collusion. An improper agreement or bargain between parties.

Commission. A sum payable to an agent in return for the performance of a particular service.

Compulsory purchase. The enforced purchase of land for public purposes by a statutory authority.

Condition. A major term of a contract, which is regarded as being of the essence of the contract. Breach of a condition is a fundamental breach of contract that entitles the injured party to treat the contract as discharged. Contrast with **warranty**.

Confidentiality. Refers to information – generally important commercial secrets – that is given in confidence and may not be disclosed to specified classes of people, generally persons outside the firm. Hence **confidentiality agreement**. See also **non-disclosure agreement**.

Consent. Agreement or compliance with a course of action or proposal. For example, 'no assignment shall be valid unless both parties have given their consent in writing prior to the proposed assignment being made'.

Consideration. An act, forbearance or promise by one party to a contract that constitutes the price for which the promise of the other party is bought. Consideration is essential to the validity of any contract other than one made by deed.

Contentious. Relating to litigation. Contentious business means the work of a solicitor where there is a contest between the parties involved.

Contraband. Goods the import or export of which is forbidden.

Conveyance. A legal instrument used to transfer the ownership of land from one party to another.

Convict (verb). To find guilty of a criminal offence in a court of law (e.g. 'the accused was convicted of robbery').

Conviction. (1) Being found guilty of a criminal offence by a court. For example, 'John has three convictions for theft'. (2) A firmly held belief or opinion. For example, 'John has a strong conviction that other people's property should belong to him'.

Copyright. The exclusive right to reproduce or authorise others to reproduce original literary, dramatic, musical and artistic works, whether published or unpublished. It is held by authors of such works and within the EU endures for the author's lifetime plus 70 years.

Costs. Sums payable for legal services. In civil litigation, the court generally orders the losing party to pay the costs of the winning party.

Court bailiff. An officer of the court whose role is to serve court documents and to enforce court orders.

Creditor. One to whom a debt is owed. See also **debtor**.

Damages. A sum of money awarded by a court as compensation for a tort or a breach of contract. Damages should be distinguished from **damage** (which means loss or harm, but not compensation for such loss or harm).

Debenture. A document that states the terms of a loan, usually to a company, including the date of repayment and the rate of interest.

Debtor. One who owes a debt.

Deed. A written document that must make it clear on its face that it is intended to be a deed and must be validly executed as a deed. It takes effect on delivery. Deeds are often used to transfer land and are enforceable even in the absence of **consideration**.

Deemed. Treated in law as being something. Many documents rely on this concept, e.g. by stating that a certain thing is to be deemed to fall within a certain expression or description used in them.

Default. Failure to fulfil an obligation. For example, 'the company has defaulted on its repayment schedule'.

Defendant. A person against whom court proceedings are brought. See also **prospective defendant**.

Defined territory. A geographical territory defined in an agreement.

Delegation. The grant of authority to a person to act on behalf of one or more others for agreed purposes.

Delivery. The transfer of possession of property from one legal person to another.

Demotion. The opposite of **promotion**. In employment situations, demotion occurs when a person is appointed to a position lower than the one he or she previously held.

Deposit. (1) A sum paid by one party to a contract to the other party as a guarantee that the first party will carry out the terms of the contract. (2) The placing of title deeds with a mortgagee of land as security for the debt.

Derogation. In EU law, a derogation is an exemption clause that permits a member state of the EU to avoid a certain directive or regulation.

Designate. (1) To officially name or give a status to. For example, 'the discussion took place in the designated meeting room'. (2) To appoint to a particular job or role. For example, 'Ms Hardcastle is the company's designated safety officer'.

Detriment. Harm or damage. For example, 'the company has acted to its detriment in agreeing to a variation of the original contract'.

Dilapidation. A state of disrepair. The term is usually used in relation to repairs required at the end of a lease or tenancy.

Discharge. To release from an obligation. For example, 'the parties shall be discharged from all liability once all the terms of the contract have been performed in full'.

Disclose. Make known, reveal. For example, 'the company disclosed certain information to the distributor'. Hence **disclosure**.

Dispose. To sell or transfer [property]. For example, 'the company had to dispose of some of its assets in order to pay its debts'.

Disposition. The transfer of property by its owner.

Distress. The seizure of goods as security for the performance of an obligation. This occurs (1) between a landlord and tenant when the rent is in arrears or (2) when goods are unlawfully on an occupier's land and are causing or have caused damage. In the second case the occupier may hold onto the goods until compensation is paid for the damage.

Distribution agreement. An agreement whereby a distributor is granted the right to offer a company's goods for sale to customers within a **defined territory**.

Dividend. The payment made by a company to its shareholders out of its distributable profits.

Domicile. The country that a person treats as his or her permanent home and to which that person has the closest legal attachment.

Draft. A preliminary version of a legal document; e.g. a draft order or a draft contract.

Duress. Pressure, particularly actual or threatened violence put on a person in order to make them act in a particular way. Acts carried out under duress usually have no legal validity.

Emoluments. A person's earnings, including salaries, fees, wages, profits and benefits in kind (e.g. company cars).

Encumbrance. A right or interest in property owned by someone other than the owner of the land itself (e.g. leases and mortgages).

Enforce. To compel, impose or put into effect. Hence **enforceable** (capable of being enforced) and **enforcement** (the process of enforcing). When a court order is enforced, this means that steps are taken by the court to force the defendant to comply with its terms.

Estoppel. A common law rule that states that when person A, by act or words, gives person B reason to believe a certain set of facts upon which person B takes action, person A cannot later, to his or her benefit, deny those facts or say that his or her earlier act was improper.

Exclusive agreement. An agreement made between specified parties on terms that neither may conclude agreements for the same purposes on similar terms with other parties. For example, an exclusive distribution agreement arises where a company grants the distributor the right to distribute goods or services in a **defined territory** on terms that no other distributor will be granted similar rights in the same territory by the same company.

Execution. (1) The carrying out or performance of something (e.g. the terms of a contract) or (2) the signature of a contract or other legal document. For example, 'the parties executed the contract'.

Expropriation. The taking by the state of private property for public purposes, normally without compensation.

Extradite. Extradition is the surrender by one state to another of a person accused or convicted of committing an offence in the jurisdiction of the state that requests extradition (in order to try and punish the person whose extradition is requested).

Fiduciary duty. An individual in whom another has placed the utmost trust and confidence to manage and protect property or money is referred to as a fiduciary and is therefore subject to certain duties. A fiduciary is obliged to act for the other person's benefit and avoid conflicts of interest in fulfilling their duties and must not make a secret profit as a result of their position. Typical fiduciary relationships include those between trustees and beneficiaries, directors of a company and its shareholders and lawyers and their clients.

Flotation. A process by which a public company can, by issuing securities (shares or debentures), raise capital from the public, e.g. by way of a **prospectus issue** in which the company itself issues a prospectus inviting the public to acquire securities.

f.o.b. (free on board) contract. A type of contract for the international sale of goods in which the seller's duty is fulfilled by placing the goods on board a ship.

Frustration. The termination of a contract caused by an unforeseen event that makes performance of the contract impossible or illegal. It is also referred to as **force majeure**. Frustration brings the contract to an end and automatically discharges the parties from any further obligations in relation to it.

Gaming contract. A contract involving the playing of a game of chance by any number of people for money or money's worth. Gaming contracts are generally void and no action can be brought to enforce them.

Garnishee. A person who has been warned by a court to pay a debt to a third party rather than to his or her creditor.

General damages. (1) Damages given for losses that the law presumes are the natural and probable consequences of a wrong (e.g. libel is presumed to have damaged someone's reputation without proof that that person's reputation has actually suffered). (2) Damages given for a loss that cannot be precisely estimated (e.g. for pain and suffering). See also **special damages**.

Good faith. Honesty. An act carried out 'in good faith' is one carried out with honest intentions.

Goodwill. The advantage arising from the reputation and trade connections of a business.

Guarantee. A secondary agreement in which a person (the **guarantor**) is liable for the debt or default of another (the **principal debtor**).

Harassment. Behaviour deliberately intended to torment, bully or interfere with another person.

Incapacity. (1) Lack of legal competence. (2) Lack of ability to do something.

Indemnity. An agreement by one person (X) to pay to another person (Y) sums that are owed, or may become owed, by a third person (Z).

Infringe. To violate or interfere with the rights of another person. For example, 'the company infringed upon another company's intellectual property rights'. The noun form is 'infringement'.

Injunction. An order of the court directing a person to do or refrain from doing a particular thing.

Instrument. A legal document, usually one which directs that certain actions be taken (e.g. a contract).

Intangible asset. An asset (i.e. property) that has no physical existence, e.g. a **chose in action**.

Intention. The state of mind of one who aims to bring about a particular consequence.

Invitation to treat. An invitation to others to make offers, for example by displaying goods in a shop window. An invitation to treat should be differentiated from an offer.

Issue. (1) To print, publish or distribute. For example, 'the company issued shares'. (2) A person's descendants. (3) To commence civil court proceedings = to issue proceedings.

Joint and several liability. If two or more people enter into an obligation that is said to be joint and several, this means that liability for a breach can be enforced against all of them together in a joint action or against any one of them by an individual action.

Jurisdiction. The power of a court to hear and decide on a case before it.

Jury. A panel of 12 persons randomly selected from the general public at large who have to attend a criminal trial and give a verdict (of guilty or not guilty) based on the evidence produced at trial.

Know-how. (1) Practical knowledge or skill. (2) Technical information amounting to a form of intellectual property (often used in connection with a patent).

Landlord. A person who grants a lease or tenancy. See also **tenant**.

Layperson. A person without professional or expert knowledge: in the context of law, a non-lawyer.

Lease. A contract that creates an estate in land for a period of time, involving the right to occupy the land.

Legal person. A natural person or a juristic person. A juristic person is an entity such as a corporation that is recognised as having legal personality, i.e. it is capable of having legal rights and duties. Since a corporation is a legal person, it has the right to sue and be sued in a court of law.

Legal proceedings. Action taken in a court of law to settle a dispute or prosecute a person suspected of a crime.

Legislation. The whole or any part of a country's written law. In common law countries, a distinction is made between Acts of Parliament (which are legislation) and case law (which is distinct from legislation).

Letter of credit. A document whereby a bank, at the request of a customer, undertakes to pay money to a third party (the beneficiary) on presentation of documents specified in the letter.

Levy. (1) The imposition of a tax, fee, fine etc.; and (2) the sum of money raised by a levy (e.g. 'to levy taxes').

Liability. (1) An obligation or duty imposed by law, or an amount of money owed to another person. For example, 'the company is liable to pay damages to the employee'. (2) A sum of money owed – a debt. For example, 'the assets and liabilities of the company'.

Licence. (1) Formal authority to do something that would otherwise be unlawful (e.g. driving licence). (2) In land law, a permission to occupy a person's land for a particular purpose.

Lien. The right of one person to retain possession of goods owned by another until the possessor's claims against the owner have been satisfied.

Liquidation. A procedure by which a company can be dissolved. It may be instigated by members or creditors of the company (voluntary liquidation) or by order of the court (compulsory liquidation) and involves the distribution of a company's assets among its creditors and members prior to dissolution. It means the same as **winding-up**.

Litigation. (1) The taking of legal proceedings by a litigant or claimant. (2) The field of law concerned with all contentious matters.

Material. Relevant, important, essential. For example, 'breach of a material term of the contract can give the innocent party the right to rescind the contract'.

Maturity. The time at which a bill of exchange becomes due for payment.

Minutes. Records of company business transacted at general meetings, board meetings and meetings of managers.

Misrepresentation. An untrue statement of fact made by one party to the other in the course of negotiating a contract that induces the other party to enter into the contract.

Mistake. A misunderstanding or incorrect belief about a matter of fact or matter of law. Mistakes of fact may render a contract void or voidable.

Monopoly. A market in which there is only one seller.

Mortgage. An interest in property created as a form of security for a loan or payment of a debt and terminated on payment of the loan or debt.

Mutual. (1) Experienced or done by two or more people equally; (2) (of two or more people) having the same specified relationship to each other; (3) shared by two or more people; (4) joint. For example, 'no assignment may take place without the parties' mutual agreement in writing'.

Negligence. Carelessness amounting to the culpable breach of a duty: failure to do something that a reasonable person would do or doing something that a reasonable person would not do.

Non-disclosure agreement (NDA). An agreement between two or more parties that specifies confidential information that may be shared between the parties for certain purposes and the basis on which this may be done and restricts access to it by third parties. Also referred to as a confidentiality agreement.

Notice. Information or warning addressed to a party that something is going to happen or has happened; a notification. See also **due notice**. For example, 'any notice required to be served under this contract must be served in accordance with paragraph 18'.

Notice of severance. The formal notification that a joint tenancy is to be severed, creating a tenancy in common.

Notice to quit. The formal notification from a landlord to a tenant (or vice versa) terminating the tenancy on a specified date.

Null. Invalid, having no legal force. For example, 'the contract is null [and void]'.

Offer. An indication of willingness to do or refrain from doing something that is capable of being converted by acceptance into a legally binding contract.

Omission. A failure to act. It is not usually a crime or tort to fail to act in a particular situation but may be in certain cases. For instance, if one has a duty to take care of someone (e.g. a child) and fails to do so, this may be a crime. Similarly, in certain civil law situations, the law imposes a duty to take action to prevent harm to others. For example, occupiers of premises are under a duty to ensure that their visitors are reasonably safe from danger or harm.

Onerous. Involving much effort and difficulty. For example, 'the duties laid upon the company are onerous'.

Option. A right to do or not to do something, usually within a specified time. For example, an option to purchase land generally gives the right for a person to have first refusal on the purchase of a piece of land within a specified time period.

Ordinary shares. These shares make up the risk capital as they carry no prior rights in relation to dividends or return of nominal capital.

Overriding public interest. This term is frequently used in European public law, but it is not very clear what it precisely means. It is often used in situations where a certain plan or project is considered to be indispensable in respect of citizens' lives (considered in terms of health, safety and the environment), in respect of fundamental state policy and in terms of carrying out activities of an economic or social nature that fulfil specific obligations of public service. For instance, Article 6(4) of Directive 92/43/EEC of 21 May 1992 on the conservation of natural habitats and of wild fauna and flora states as follows:

If, in spite of a negative assessment of the implications for the site and in the absence of alternative solutions, a plan or project must nevertheless be carried out for imperative reasons of overriding public interest, including those of a social or economic nature, the Member State shall take all compensatory measures necessary to ensure that the overall coherence of Natura 2000 is protected. It shall inform the Commission of the compensatory measures adopted.

Passing off. Conducting business in such a way as to mislead the public into thinking that one's goods and services are those of another business. It is not necessary to prove intention – innocent passing off is actionable.

Patent. The grant of an exclusive right to exploit an invention. To qualify for the grant of a patent in the UK, the applicant must show that the invention is new, is not obvious and is capable of industrial application. A patent remains valid (on payment of the relevant fee) for a period of 20 years from the date of application.

Patentee. A person or company that owns patent rights in respect of an invention.

Patent agent. An expert who prepares applications for patent.

Petitioner. A person who presents a petition to the court (e.g. a divorce petition or a petition for bankruptcy). See also **respondent**.

Piracy. (1) Any illegal act of violence, imprisonment or robbery committed on a private ship for personal gain or revenge, against another ship, people or property on the high seas. (2) (in marine insurance) One of the risks covered by a marine insurance policy, which extends beyond the criminal offence to include a revolt by the crew or passengers and plundering generally. (3) Infringement of copyright.

Plaintiff. See **claimant**.

Pre-emption. The right of first refusal to purchase an asset (e.g. land) in the event that the grantor of the right should decide to sell.

Preference. (1) Where an insolvent debtor favours one particular creditor (for example by paying one creditor in full when there is no possibility of paying the others); (2) a floating charge created for the benefit of an existing creditor within one year before the commencement of winding-up.

Preference share. These shares carry a right to a fixed-percentage dividend (e.g. 10% of the nominal value) before ordinary shareholders receive anything.

Preference shareholders also have the right to the return of the nominal value of their shares before ordinary shareholders (but after creditors).

Preliminary ruling. A decision made by the European Court of Justice (ECJ) on the interpretation of European Union law, made at the request of a court of an EU Member State. The Member State remains responsible for resolving the specific dispute before it, but stays (i.e. temporarily halts) its own proceedings until its questions about the interpretation or validity of EU law have been answered. The ECJ's competence to give preliminary rulings derives from Article 267 of the Treaty on the Functioning of the European Union (TFEU).

Premium. (1) The sum payable, usually annually, by an insured person to the insurer under a contract of insurance. (2) A lump sum that is sometimes paid by a tenant at the time of the grant, assignment or renewal of the lease or tenancy.

Presumption. A supposition that the law allows or requires to be made. For instance, in criminal law, there is a presumption that the accused is not guilty until proven guilty. In civil law, there is a presumption that a person who signs a contract is sane and therefore able to form a valid contract. Most legal presumptions are rebuttable presumptions, which means that they can be reversed if there is evidence to support such reversal. For example, the presumption that a person accused of a crime is not guilty can be reversed on production of evidence that proves that person's guilt.

Principal. The person on whose behalf an agent acts.

Privity of contract. The relationship that exists between the parties to a contract. In common law, only the parties to a contract can sue or be sued on the contract: the contract cannot confer rights or impose liabilities on others.

Promotion. (1) The opposite of **demotion**. In employment situations, promotion occurs when a person is appointed to a position higher than the one he or she previously held. (2) The activity of publicising a product, service or person in connection with sales.

Proprietor. A person who owns property or a business.

Prospective defendant. A person against whom a civil claim (e.g. for damages) is contemplated, and who may therefore become the defendant in future proceedings.

Prospectus. A document inviting the public to invest in shares or debentures issued by a public company.

Provision. A term or clause of a contract. For example, 'the contract contains provisions dealing with termination'.

Proviso. A clause in a statute, deed or other legal document introducing a qualification or condition to some other provision, frequently the one immediately before the proviso.

Proxy. A person (not necessarily a company member) appointed by a company member to attend and vote in his or her place at a company meeting.

Quorum. From Latin, meaning 'of whom', used to indicate the minimum number of persons required to be present to constitute a formal meeting.

Quotation. (1) A listing of a share price on a stock exchange. (2) A passage or remark repeated by someone other than the person who originally said or wrote it (e.g. 'a quotation from the works of Shakespeare'). (3) A formal statement of the estimated cost of work (e.g. 'I have received a quotation from the plumber').

Reasonable. (1) Fair and sensible. (2) Appropriate in a particular situation. (3) Fairly good. (4) Not too expensive. For example, 'the company is entitled to alter the price of the goods on giving reasonable notice'.

Rebuttable presumption. A presumption that can be reversed if evidence to the contrary is produced.

Receiver. (1) A person appointed by the court to preserve and protect property that is at risk. (2) A person appointed under the terms of a debenture or by the court to liquidate charged assets and distribute the proceeds to those entitled.

Recklessness. Being aware of the risk of a particular consequence resulting from your actions but deciding to continue with those actions and take the risk.

Redeemable share. A share issued subject to the condition that it may be bought back by the company.

Redundancy. The loss of a job by an employee not through his or her own fault, but because the job has ceased to exist or because there is no longer work available (e.g. for economic reasons). In this situation, the employee receives compensation for loss of the job (known as a 'redundancy payment').

Reinsurance. Where an insurer that has underwritten liability in an earlier contract insures itself with another insurer against liability for that risk.

Remedy. Any method available in law to enforce, protect or recover rights, usually available by seeking a court order. For example, 'the primary remedy is to claim damages'.

Remuneration. A sum of money paid for work performed, usually in an employment context.

Repeal. To officially cancel or revoke. This term is only used in the context of laws.

Repudiation. An anticipatory breach of contract; i.e. where a contracting party's words or actions make it clear that they do not intend to perform the contract in the future.

Rescission. The setting aside of a voidable contract, which is then treated as if it had never existed.

Resolution. A decision reached by a majority of the members at a company meeting.

Resolved amicably. This is a well-known lawyers' euphemism that in practice means no more than 'resolved out of court'.

Respondent. (1) A person named as the defendant in a petition. (2) A person who defends an appeal from a lower court to a higher court made by an **appellant**.

Restitution. The return of property to the owner or person entitled to possession.

Restraint of trade. A contractual term that limits a person's right to exercise his or her trade or carry on his or her business.

Restrictive covenant. (1) A clause in a contract that restricts a person's right to carry on his or her trade or profession. For example, a contract covering the sale of a business might include a clause seeking to restrict the seller's freedom to set up in competition against the buyer. (2) An obligation created by deed in relation to land that restricts the rights of the owner of the land in some way.

Retention of title. A stipulation on a contract of sale that ownership of the goods shall not pass to the buyer until the buyer has paid the seller in full or has discharged all liabilities owing to the seller.

Return. A formal document, such as an annual return or the document giving particulars of shares allotted and to whom.

Revenue. Any form of income.

Revoke (revocation). To cancel, annul or withdraw. For example, 'we revoked the order we had placed'.

Rights issue. A method of raising share capital for a company from existing members rather than from the general public. Members are given a right to acquire further shares, usually in proportion to their existing holdings and at a price below the market value of existing shares.

Rights of audience. The right to appear as an advocate representing a client before a court.

Royalty. A sum payable for the right to use someone else's property for the purpose of gain. For example, 'J.K. Rowling has received substantial royalties from the sale of her books'.

Salvage. The service rendered by a person who saves or helps to save maritime property.

Sealed copies. In court proceedings, 'sealed copies' means official legal documents sealed with the official seal of the court. The imprint of the seal indicates that the documents have been authenticated as genuine court documents.

Search. The examination of the register of an official authority, e.g. the Land Registry. Hence **search fee** – the fee payable for carrying out such an examination.

Secured creditor. A person who holds some security, such as a mortgage, for money he or she has lent.

Securities. These include stocks, shares, debentures, bonds or any other rights to receive dividends or interest.

Service. The delivery of a document relating to court proceedings or to a contract in a manner specified by the court or in the contract.

Share certificate. A document issued by a company that shows that a named person is a company member and stating the number of shares registered in that person's name and the extent to which they are paid up.

Share premium. The amount the price at which a share was issued exceeds its nominal value.

Share transfer. A document transferring registered shares, i.e. shares for which a share certificate has been issued.

Soft law. An international law term that refers to guidelines of behaviour that have no legally binding force but are more than mere statements of political aspiration. Examples include treaties not yet in force, UN resolutions or international conferences.

Sole practitioner. A person who runs an unincorporated professional practice on his or her own.

Sole trader. An individual who runs an unincorporated business on his or her own.

Special damages. (1) Damages given for losses that are not presumed but have been specifically proved. (2) Damages given for losses that can be quantified (e.g. loss of earnings).

Special resolution. A decision reached by a majority of not less than 75% of company members voting in person or by proxy at a general meeting.

Specific performance. A court order to a person to fulfil their obligations under a contract. The remedy is only available in certain cases, generally those in which the payment of damages would not be a sufficient remedy.

Stakeholder. One who holds money as an impartial observer. He or she will part with it only if both parties agree or if ordered by the court.

Statement of claim. A document filed with the court and served upon the defendant in a court action that sets out the material facts and argument on which a claim is based.

Statutory instrument. Subordinate legislation made under the authority of a statute.

Statutory rights. Rights provided by a statute; i.e. by an Act of Parliament.

Strict liability. (1) In criminal law, liability for a crime imposed without the need for proving that the accused intended to cause the harm done by the crime (applicable in product liability and road traffic offences). (2) In tort law, liability for a wrong that is imposed without the claimant having to prove that the defendant was at fault (applicable in product liability and defamation claims).

Subsidiary. A subsidiary company is one that is controlled by a holding company.

Subsidy. A payment by a government to producers of certain goods to enable them to sell the goods to the public at a low price, to compete with foreign competition, to avoid making redundancies and creating unemployment etc.

Suspended order. An order that does not take effect immediately. In civil claims, a suspended order is generally made on certain terms that the defendant must fulfil. If the defendant fulfils these terms, the order will eventually be dismissed.

Tenant. A person or company to whom a lease or tenancy is granted. See also **landlord**.

Tender. An offer to supply goods or services. Normally a tender must be accepted to create a contract.

Term. (1) A substantive part of a contract that creates a contractual obligation. For example, 'one of the terms of the contract deals with delivery of the goods'. (2) The period during which a contract is in force. For example, 'the term of this contract shall be five years from the date of execution'.

Termination clause. A clause in a contract that specifies the manner in which the contract will or may be terminated.

Testator. A person who makes a will.

Title. A person's right of ownership of property.

Title deeds. The documents that prove a person's ownership of land.

Trademark. A distinctive symbol that identifies particular products of a trader to the general public, and which may consist of a device, words or a combination of these. In the UK, trademarks may be registered and such registration confers exclusive rights to use the trademark in connection with the goods for which it was registered.

Transaction. This either refers to a specific instance of buying or selling, or to the action of conducting business.

Trustee. A person having a nominal title to property that he holds for the benefit of one or more others, the **beneficiaries**.

Undertaking. (1) A promise to do or not to do a specified act. In the English legal system, an undertaking given by a solicitor to the court or to another solicitor is binding, and failure to fulfil it may result in professional disciplinary action being taken. (2) A business.

Undue influence. A doctrine that states that if a person enters into an agreement in circumstances that suggest that he or she has not been allowed to exercise free and deliberate judgment on the matter, the court will set aside the agreement.

Void. Having no legal effect. For example, 'the contract is void due to lack of consideration'.

Waiver. The act of abandoning or refraining from asserting a legal right; e.g. by agreeing to a variation of the original terms of a contract.

Warranty. (1) (in contract law) A term or promise in a contract, breach of which will entitle the innocent party to damages but not to treat the contract as discharged by breach. (2) (in insurance law) A promise by the insured, breach of which will entitle the insurer to treat the contract as discharged by breach.

Winding-up. A procedure by which a company can be dissolved. It may be instigated by members or creditors of the company (voluntary winding-up) or by order of the court (compulsory winding-up) and involves the distribution of a company's assets among its creditors and members prior to dissolution. It means the same as **liquidation**.

Without prejudice. A phrase used to enable parties to negotiate settlement without implying any admission of liability. Letters and other documents headed 'without prejudice' may not be produced as evidence in any court proceedings without the consent of both parties.

Witness statement. A statement made by a witness for the purpose of court proceedings that sets out the evidence to which the witness will testify.

Written resolution. A resolution signed by all company members and treated as effective even though it is not passed at a properly convened company meeting.

Chapter answer key

15.1 COMPETITION LAW: THE CONCORDIA BUS CASE

Exercise 1: terminology

1 progressively

2 tender notice

3 awarded

4 fleet

5 discriminatory

6 took the view

7 entity

8 quashed

9 stay

10 expressly

A

Exercise 2: comprehension

Suggested answer

Memorandum: the Concordia Bus Case

TO: Whom it may concern
FROM: Rupert Haigh
DATE: 16 February 2018

SUBJECT: The Concordia Bus case

The purpose of this memorandum is to give an analysis of the Concordia Bus case by reference to the questions enumerated in italics below.

1   What criteria did Helsinki City Council lay down regarding the bus network tender?

Helsinki City Council would award the contract to the undertaking whose offer was economically most advantageous to the city. This would be judged by reference to three categories of criteria: the overall price asked for operation, the quality of the bus fleet and the operator's quality and environment programme.

2   What were the factual grounds of Concordia's complaint about discrimination?

Concordia complained that points were awarded for using a type of bus that only HKL-Bussiliikenne was able to provide.

3   What reasoning was adopted by the Competition Council?

The Competition Council said that the contracting entity could define what type of bus fleet it wanted, and that all the competitors had the possibility to acquire buses powered by natural gas. Therefore, it had not been proved that the criterion discriminated against Concordia.

4   What was the key question the Supreme Administrative Court wanted guidance about from the Court of Justice?

The key question was whether Community legislation (as it was then called) allowed a municipality that organises a tender procedure for the operation of an urban bus service to include operators' ecological and quality management as criteria to be used in the comparison of tenders.

5   What did the Court of Justice say?

The Court of Justice ruled that these criteria could be taken into account, provided that they were connected with the subject-matter of the contract, did not give the contracting authority unrestricted freedom of choice, were mentioned in the contract documents or the tender notice, and complied with all the fundamental principles of Community law, in particular the principle of non-discrimination.

The Court of Justice also said that the principle of equal treatment does not prevent the taking into consideration of criteria of protection of the environment merely because the transport operator to whom the contract is awarded is one of the few undertakings able to offer a bus fleet that meets those criteria.

15.2 LEGISLATIVE EXCERPT: THE ENTERPRISE ACT 2002

Exercise 1: terminology choice

1   provisional

2   prescribed

3   disproportionate

4   disapplied

5   ground

6   property

7   debentures

8   aggregate

9   annulment

10   transitional

Exercise 2: multiple-choice comprehension

1   (c)

2   (a)

3   (d)

4 (c)

5 (b)

Exercise 3: drafting exercises

Suggested answers:

1 *What does this section cover?*
The section relates to floating charges over property owned by companies subject to liquidation, administration or receivership, and deals with the circumstances in which such property can be distributed to unsecured creditors.

2 *What provision does the liquidator need to make for the settlement of unsecured debts?*
The liquidator must reserve part of the company's net property for the settlement of unsecured debts and may not distribute this reserved part to the owner of a floating charge unless there is surplus available, given the amount needed to satisfy the unsecured debts. There are certain exceptions to this rule, as noted below.

3 *In what situations is the liquidator not required to make the provision for the settlement of unsecured debts the Act prescribes?*
There are a number of exceptions to the rule requiring the liquidator to reserve part of the company's net property for the settlement of unsecured debts, including: (1) where the net property falls below the prescribed minimum and the liquidator believes that the cost of making a distribution would outweigh the benefit of doing so; (2) where a voluntary arrangement is in place in respect of the company; (3) where a compromise has been reached between creditors and members under section 425 of the Companies Act; and (4) where a court order has been made ruling that subsection two does not apply.

4 *What does 'net property' constitute?*
For the purposes of subsections (2) and (3) 'net property' means the value of property that would be available to satisfy claims made by holders of debentures secured by floating charges or holders of floating charges created by the company but for the provisions of this section of the Act.

15.3 INDEPENDENT CONTRACTOR AGREEMENT

Exercise 1: terminology

1 engages

2 render

3 withholding

4 eligible

5 exclusive

6 business areas

7 verbal

8 designated

9 execution

10 mutual

11 pursuant to

12 itemised

13 disbursements

14 foregoing

15 proprietary

Exercise 2: true or false

1 true

2 false

3 false

4 true

5 false

Exercise 3: email drafting

Suggested answer:

Dear Stephen,

Thank you for your email.

I agree that the contract basically looks fine, but please find below answers to the specific points you raise.

1 What is the point of the first para. of the contract? It looks like a load of waffle.

Essentially the point of the first clause is to set out the legal basis on which you will provide your services to Pan-Oceanic Shrimp Ltd. It makes it clear that you are a contractor, not an employee. You are therefore responsible for paying your own taxes and will not receive paid holiday, health insurance and other benefits from the company. While this may all seem obvious enough, this is a fairly standard clause in this type of contract, as companies are keen to ensure that the courts don't interpret sub-contracting arrangements as employment in the event that the litigation takes place.

2 What expenses can I have reimbursed, and how does it work?

Clause seven of the contract does not contain any specific guidance as to which expenses are reimbursable. It simply states that you have to obtain the company's prior approval before incurring any particular expense, and that in order to obtain reimbursement you need to present receipts for the expenses. The contract also notes that you cannot obtain reimbursement for the cost of travelling to and from the company's premises.

3 About the confidentiality clause – I get the general point that I have to keep the company's confidential information confidential, but what other information is covered by this rule?

Clause nine also covers information related to the company's clients and 'affiliates'. The use of this word 'affiliate' means that confidentiality extends to any other company or person controlled by Pan-Oceanic Shrimp Ltd. The confidentiality obligation applies whether or not the information is provided in a written form and is permanent in duration.

4 Innovations made during the contract – it looks like if I come up with some new innovation, the company owns it. Are there any exceptions to this?

Yes, clause ten states that in the event that you produce an innovation or invention while working for the company, it becomes the company's exclusive property. The clause also refers to innovations or inventions you might have developed before you started working for the company but which you use during the course of working for the company. In that case, the company has a 'licence' (i.e. permission to use, but not ownership) in respect of it, which it can also pass to one of its 100%-owned subsidiaries.

I hope the notes above are helpful, but please let me know if you require any further assistance or advice on this matter.

Best regards

X

15.4 CORRESPONDENCE

First letter: exercise

Suggested answers:

1   The solicitor has carried out a search at Companies House, which reveals that Greenscape is not registered and can therefore be used as the company's name.

2   The solicitor has drafted the memorandum and articles of association.

3   Initially 100 £1 shares will be issued: 51 to Joanne Goodman and 49 to Amanda Shorter.

4   The shareholders will be Joanne Goodman and Amanda Shorter.

5   A shareholders' agreement is desirable because it can be used to protect the individual interests of the shareholders in a way that cannot be achieved under the articles of association.

Second letter: exercise

Rangle & Co
10 Ark Street
London

Benjamin Ward
127 Dranglet Drive
Reading

Dear Mr Ward,

Your business plan

Thank you for coming in to see me on Tuesday when we discussed your business plan. As advised, a private limited company is the most appropriate format given the nature of the business you outlined.

While writing, I acknowledge receipt of the sum of £1000 paid on account, and would confirm that all information provided to us in relation to your case will be held in strict confidence by this firm.

The procedure for formation of a limited company is fairly straightforward, and you instructed me to carry out the necessary steps. I have already searched the company register and established that the name 'Esoteric Guitar Widgets for Droning Shoegaze Bands' remains available for use.

You advised as follows:

1   The object of the company will be the sale of guitar accessories to consumers either over the counter or by mail order.

2   The company's share capital will be divided into 100 £1 shares, of which 49 will be held by Bill Ardley and 51 by you. This value given to each share is par value rather than market value – the purpose of this is to provide a means of calculating the relative size of the shareholdings.

3   Both you and Bill Ardley will be appointed directors of the company.

4   The company's registered address will be your home address at 127 Dranglet Drive. Incidentally, you should ascertain whether there is anything in your tenancy agreement that prevents you from using the premises for business activities.

Please confirm that the details set out above are correct.

I will now draft the necessary documents, including the memorandum and articles of association and register the company.

We also discussed the question of the shareholders' agreement. Briefly, this is an agreement between the shareholders (in this case, you and Bill Ardley) about how the company should be run. It is worth having mainly because it can be used to protect your individual interests in the company in ways that cannot be achieved through the articles of association, and deals with issues including what would happen if one of you wishes to sell his shares or dies and how to deal with disputes between you. We should consider this issue in more detail once the company is registered.

I will be in touch again as soon as registration is completed. In the meantime, please do not hesitate to contact me if you have any questions or require any further information.

Yours sincerely,

X

Index

Locators in **bold** refer to tables.